IMAGES
of America

NODAWAY COUNTY

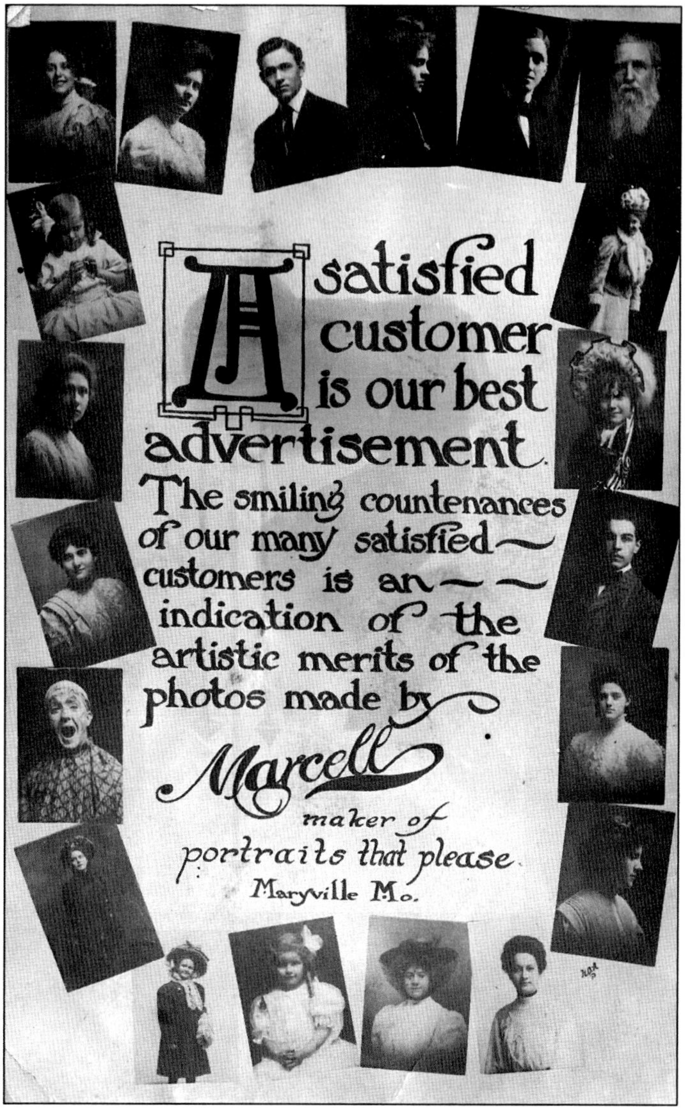

A considerable debt is owed to the many professional photographers who have recorded history on film. While photographers like Ralph Marcell typically paid their bills taking portraits in the studio like those in his advertisement above, they also spent countless hours making artistic images of people in the spaces in which they conducted their lives. These images have enlivened a connection to the past immeasurably.

On the cover: Part of Nodaway County's rich agricultural diversity was the production of poultry. From the pioneering period of the Civil War era to the commercial boom of the dawn of the 19th century, poultry went from being supplementary to the farmstead to a major industry. By 1910, the county was exporting two and a half million pounds of poultry annually along with two million dozen eggs. Like the careful breeding of horses, cattle, and hogs in Nodaway County, hatcheries like the one seen here in Maryville in the early 1920s developed highly efficient fowl that produced more eggs and gained more weight. The commercial poultry industry peaked in 1925, however, and the value it enjoyed early in the county's history diminished considerably. (Courtesy of the Nodaway County Historical Society.)

IMAGES
of America

NODAWAY COUNTY

Michael J. Steiner

ARCADIA
PUBLISHING

ISBN 978-0-7385-5221-7

Published by Arcadia Publishing
Charleston, South Carolina

Printed in the United States of America

Library of Congress Catalog Card Number: 2007909424

For all general information contact Arcadia Publishing at:
Telephone 843-853-2070
Fax 843-853-0044
E-mail sales@arcadiapublishing.com
For customer service and orders:
Toll-Free 1-888-313-2665

Visit us on the Internet at www.arcadiapublishing.com

For Lori, Danny, and David

CONTENTS

ACKNOWLEDGMENTS

Many people have helped in the production of this book, some by their direct assistance in finding images and information and others through their years of collecting the history of Nodaway County. Many of the county's communities are blessed with enthusiastic residents who maintain, formally or otherwise, collections of artifacts, images, and stories that illustrate tremendous pride in our shared heritage.

The Nodaway County Historical Society has provided most of the images and information for this book and to its board, volunteers, and supporters, I offer my gratitude. Margaret Kelley in particular was of considerable help in identifying images worth sharing through this book. Melissa Middleswart also offered direct assistance for which I am grateful. All images, if not otherwise indicated, are from the collection of the Nodaway County Historical Society or the author.

The Barnard Community Historical Society maintains an excellent collection, and I thank Janet Hawley for her generous assistance in procuring images and continuing to scour Grant and Washington Townships for more. The Skidmore community has tremendous pride for its heritage, and I am grateful for access to their museum's collection. In particular I thank Anna Roberts for her help in Skidmore and C. E. Linville for the use of his family's photographs. The Hopkins Historical Society offered generous access to its collection of images and wonderful assistance from its volunteers. Coby Lamb's great collection of Maryville postcards was extremely beneficial, and I sincerely thank him for his contributions. Additional assistance came from Thomas Sullivan, OSB, of Conception Abbey, Emily McLain and her evident pride in Parnell and Ravenwood, and Raymond "Tillie" Porterfield.

At Northwest Missouri State University, I would like to thank the following: Cathy Palmer in the university archives; the Center for Information Technology in Education (CITE) office staff, who offered technical support, including Kris Bakko, Jolaine Zweifel, Darla Runyon, and Roger Von Holzen; the Department of History, Humanities, Philosophy, and Political Science; and the College of Arts and Sciences.

I cannot express enough my gratitude to Tom Carneal, who has been my mentor and friend for many years. His enthusiasm for local history, his love of Nodaway County and its heritage, his considerable reserve of information, and his words of encouragement and friendship have made my involvement in local history and this book possible.

However, for any errors of commission or omission in this book, I take responsibility and apologize.

— Michael J. Steiner

INTRODUCTION

During the 1820s and 1830s, the settlement that had allowed for the contentious statehood of Missouri swelled, as ambitious explorers, farmers, merchants, craftsmen, and pioneering combinations of all these pushed along the Missouri River into the western part of the state and up capillaries of settlement to real estate ripe with resources and opportunity. The flow of settlement was such that agreements with the native people were quickly made and more quickly violated, and the boundaries of the state were expanded in the far northwestern corner along the Missouri River with the Platte Purchase. Like most unsettled lands, particularly in regions more treeless than the East and South, the viability of intensive agriculture seemed at first improbable. Continued exploration and experimentation, however, convinced early settlers that they had found an extraordinarily good place. Three rivers coursed through the area that became Nodaway County (most likely named from a Native American word meaning "placid"), separating wide-open prairies punctuated by substantial stands of good trees. Numerous springs produced fresh water, and rainfall was substantial enough that the wilderness could be made a garden. Settlers followed old Native American trading trails into the region, including Isaac Hogan and a company of men who in 1839 set up camp a mile south of what is now the town of Graham. A year later, Hiram Hall claimed a handsome track along the One Hundred and Two River, which he quickly parlayed into cash by selling to Col. Isaac Prather of Kentucky, who brought wealth adequate to accumulate 3,000 acres, slaves to labor over his crops, and a love of fine horses.

In 1845, the state legislature formally created Nodaway County, and during that decade and the next, small communities emerged as settlement accelerated. Maryville, at the center of the county along the One Hundred and Two River, became the county seat, and the map of Nodaway County began to emerge. Still, in 1869 when the railroads (and the first cameras) arrived the region was only beginning to shed its frontier character and experience a complex pattern of modern economic and social development.

Towns and farms both were marked by substantial transformation after the arrival of the railroads. The first farmers certainly hoped to produce surplus on their farms, but they also had to respond to the reality of needing to clear land, turn soil, and build the infrastructure necessary to produce surplus and get it to markets. The first settlers, primarily from Kentucky and Tennessee, were inclined by their experience to hold close to the forested areas along the rivers and creeks where enormous energy went into felling trees, hewing logs, and damming waterways for mills. They experimented with the land, planting hemp, tobacco, buckwheat, and other crops as well as introducing livestock. The first generation made a place in which the next generation of Midwestern farmers could produce the desired surplus, and produce they did. By the 1880s the farmstead was transformed not only by access to markets through the railroads but also by technology that increased production and efficiency just like the urban factories for which they held an ironic disdain. But technology alone did not change the rural residents; they also adopted new organizational models that reshaped the way they viewed production, their interaction with market centers, and their collaboration with one another. The result for most farmers in Nodaway County was the satisfaction of possessing land, producing substantial crops, and breeding fine animals. This was tempered by the reality that they still failed to experience the capital accumulation that drew money first into the small towns, then the large towns, and ultimately the urban market centers.

From their initial settlement, the makers of towns envisioned growth as essential to the stability of the web of local market economies and essential to acquire the services and civility that were increasingly available in American life. The arrival of the railroad to some of the hamlets of Nodaway County in the 1870s launched growth that put on the map a dozen robust towns, leaving, too, at least as many ghost towns. For those that got a rail stop, including two each in Maryville, Burlington Junction, and Conception, the next three decades became a golden age of rapid construction, diverse economic development, and solidifying of all the necessary institutions of modern civility.

Today one sees community pride that continues the heritage of a century ago, but it is hard to imagine the enthusiastic boosterism that accompanied this strong sense of local sovereignty. Certainly there were difficulties, and numerous historians lately have demonstrated the myriad ways in which the good old days were not so good. The rain that blessed farmers also occasionally swelled rivers and flooded towns without insurance. The open plains that gave the cattlemen room to build empires also gave free reign to tornados. Sickness, poverty, and racial hostility created difficulties that dulled the luster of modern life at the dawn of the 20th century. Many of the new inventions, like automobiles, canned meat, and combine harvesters seemed to make life easier, but by the 1920s they were bringing to a close much of the robustness of rural communities. Yet the famers and townsfolk of Nodaway County enjoyed lives filled with family gatherings, parades, festivals, cornet bands, and social affairs centered in schools, churches, and towns. In doing so they reinforced a passionate commitment to one another through the community that was, and is, Nodaway County.

One

MAKING SOMEPLACE

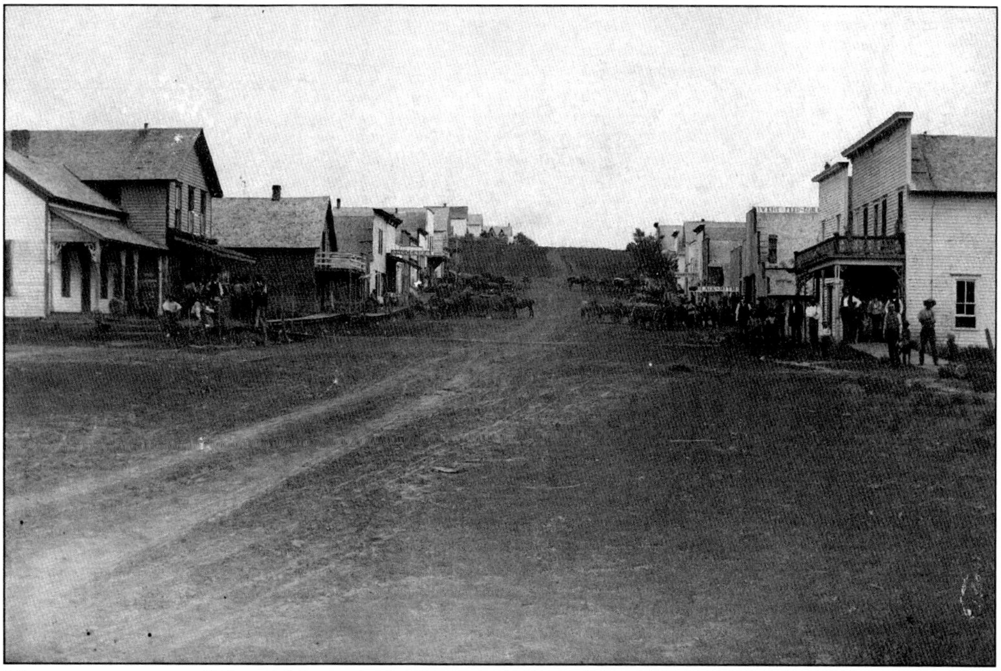

The prairie town of Elmo, first named Ebbony, then St. Elmo, is seen here in perhaps its earliest photograph. It had not yet gained the permanence of a brick business district. The Wabash Railroad and the Western Improvement Company planted the town in 1879 and in 1882 shipped 100,000 bushels of grain from surrounding Lincoln Township. Two grain offices were the second and third buildings in town. The fourth was J. Lamme's saloon followed by Ecker's hotel. By the end of its second year this main street on the prairie had 25 businesses.

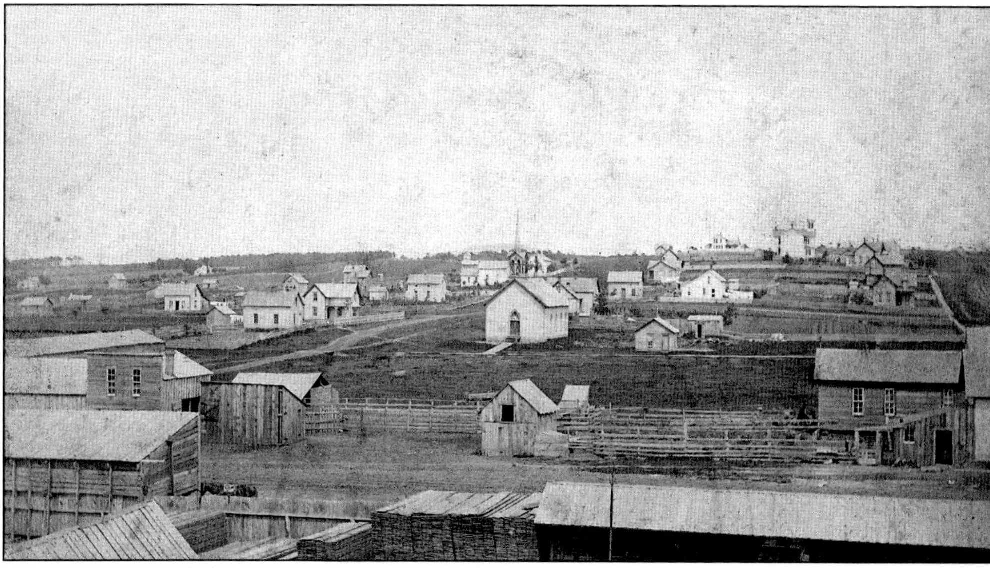

This 1878 view of the east side of Hopkins shows the town in its early stages of construction. Prominent in the view is the Hopkins School building at the top of the hill, completed in 1877. Hopkins saw its first brick building in 1877 with a second following the year after. The Presbyterians completed the church in the center of the image in 1876, and the lumberyard in the foreground stocked itself amply for a town that had grown rapidly once the Kansas City, St. Joseph, and Council Bluffs Railroad established a terminus at the site in the spring of 1871. (Courtesy of the Hopkins Historical Society.)

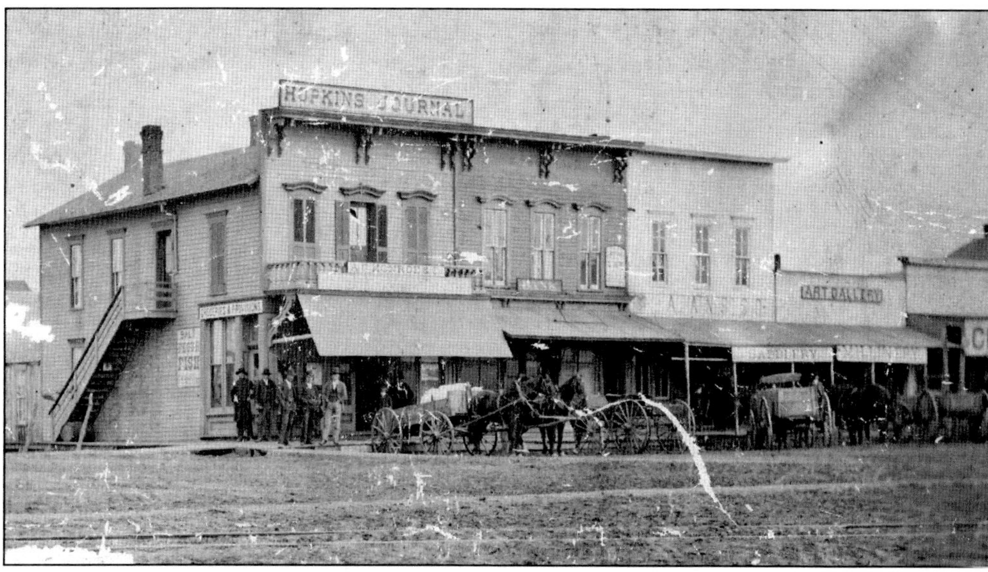

The southeast corner of Barnard and Third Streets in Hopkins was the location of Cam Monroe's Corner Grocery in 1878 with the *Hopkins Journal* above it on the second floor. Next door the Goodsill and Dunning Bank shares space with R. H. Wilfrey's law office above. A saddlery, a millinery, and a photographer's gallery join them on the block. Constructed in the early 1870s, the frontier appearance of the Hopkins business district began giving way to the brick commercial blocks that signified progress by 1885. (Courtesy of the Hopkins Historical Society.)

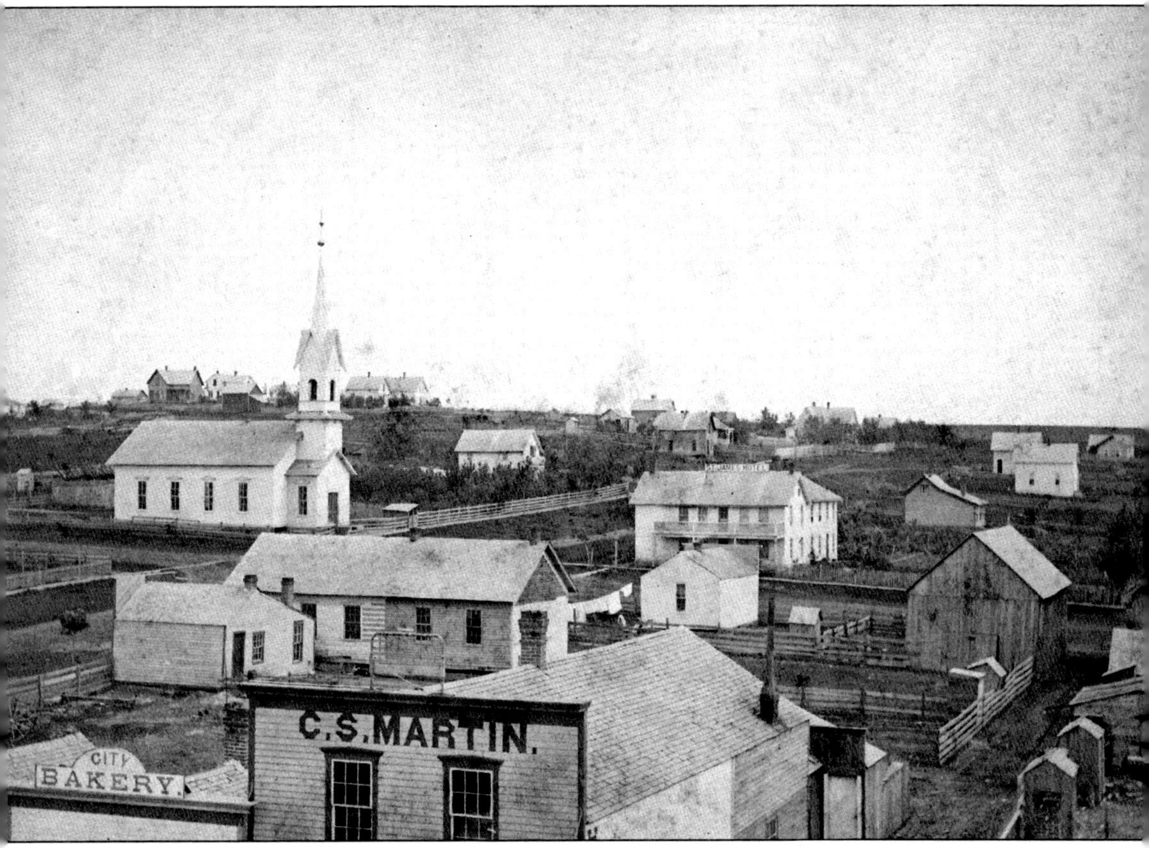

The arrival of the Kansas City, St. Joseph, and Council Bluffs Railroad line in December 1870 set off a boomtown in Hopkins, whose remarkably rapid growth was rivaled only by Burlington Junction and Maryville. This view of Hopkins in the 1870s, looking south from the depot, features the first Methodist church building, constructed the summer after the railroad arrived. Across Fourth Street from the church at the corner of Roseberry Street stood the Johnston House Hotel. Pioneering construction east of the rail yard also included Randolph and Goodsell's hardware, Wolfers' dry goods, Riggs' grocery, C. Martin's hardware, and the City Bakery. First utilizing the wooden, balloon frame, false front architecture common to frontier boomtowns, by the early 1880s investors added permanency to the town's more than 80 business with brick structures. (Courtesy of the Hopkins Historical Society.)

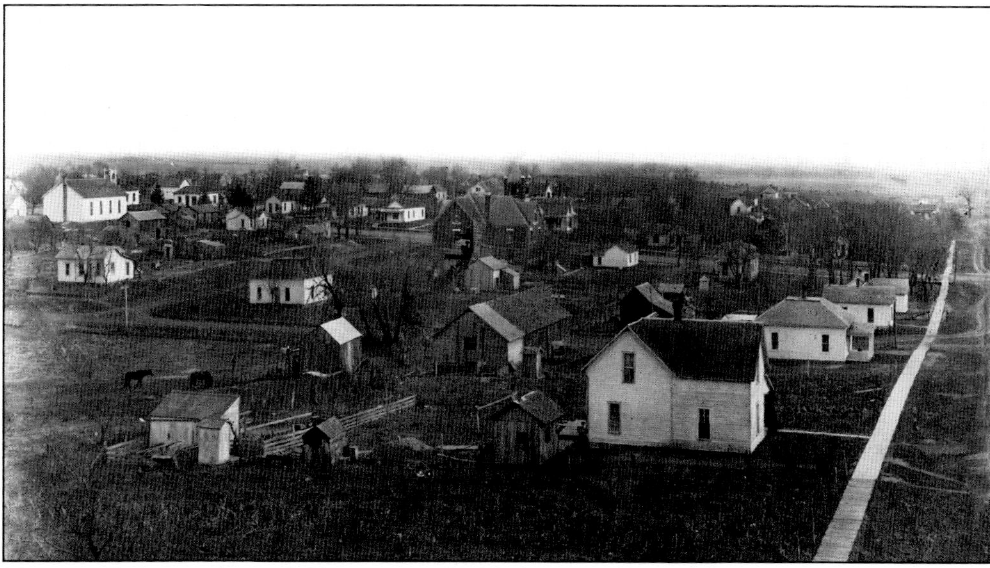

Marteny Skidmore donated 20 acres to the Nodaway Valley Railroad Company to locate a railroad station nearby on a site already serving as a trade center for farmers and mills operating along the Nodaway River. With the line nearing completion in the summer of 1880, Skidmore platted out the town site that would bear his name. H. H. Joy started the commercial center the same year with a dry goods store, and by the time of this photograph in the mid-1880s, a bustling town of about 400 laid out plank sidewalks and constructed churches and a school. (Courtesy of the Skidmore Museum.)

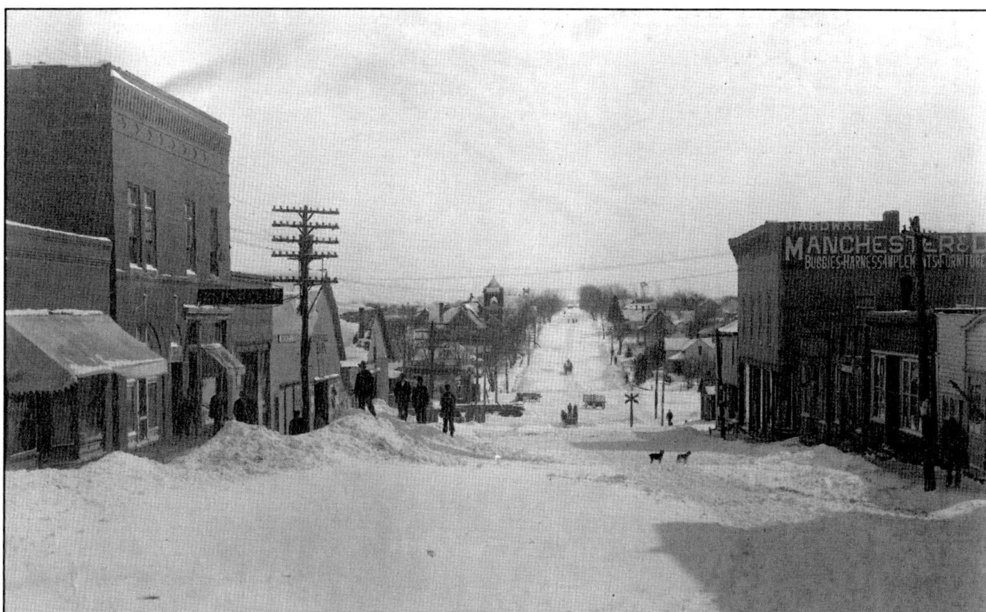

Looking east down Elm Street, now Highway 113, in Skidmore around 1900 reveals that business could be slowed on a thriving main street but horse traffic and sleighs were still undeterred, which suggests some advantage to transportation before automobiles. Numerous businesses lined Elm Street, with the rail yard crossing at the bottom of the hill and the imposing United Methodist Church visible in the distance.

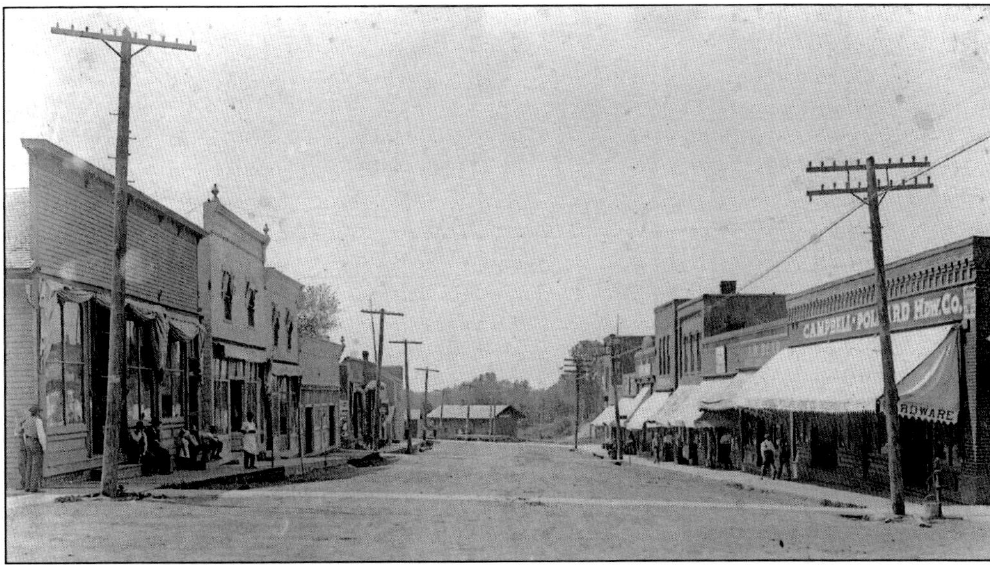

The small settlement of Prairie Park was replaced a mile north by Barnard and in 1910 had just over 400 residents, almost 100 less than 20 years earlier. The older gentlemen looking out on this quiet street may have already been pining for the old days when Barnard seemed a busier place. Main Street was still in good shape, however, with a bank, two physicians, two general stores, a hardware store, a coal dealer, a hotel, and many other businesses. The town's four fraternal lodges were surely busy as well promoting the continued success of the town as it proceeded with paving sidewalks and using its busy rail stop as a trade center. (Courtesy of the Barnard Community Historical Society.)

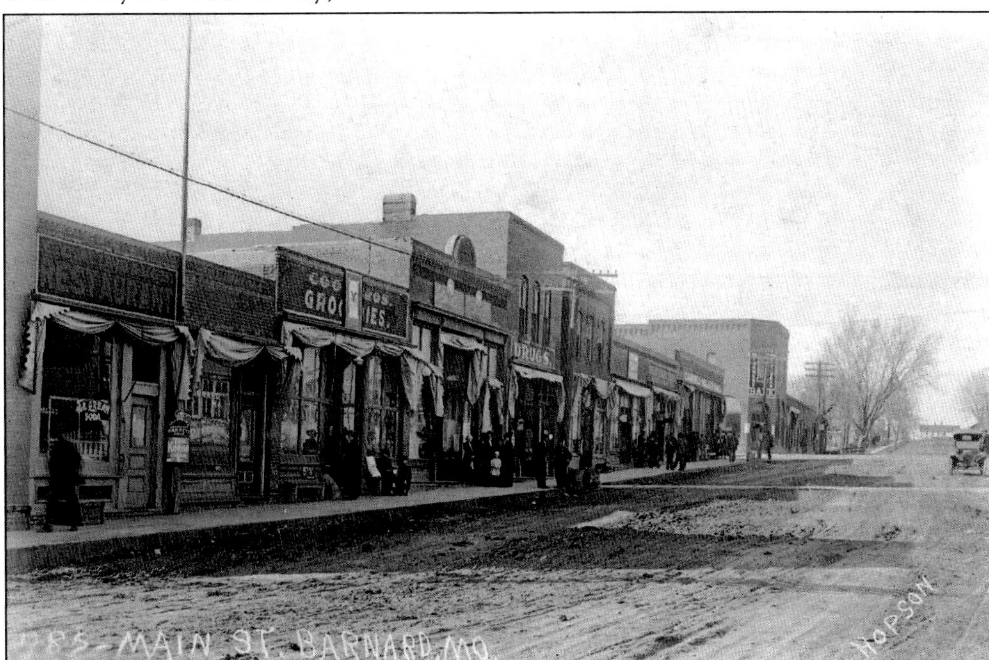

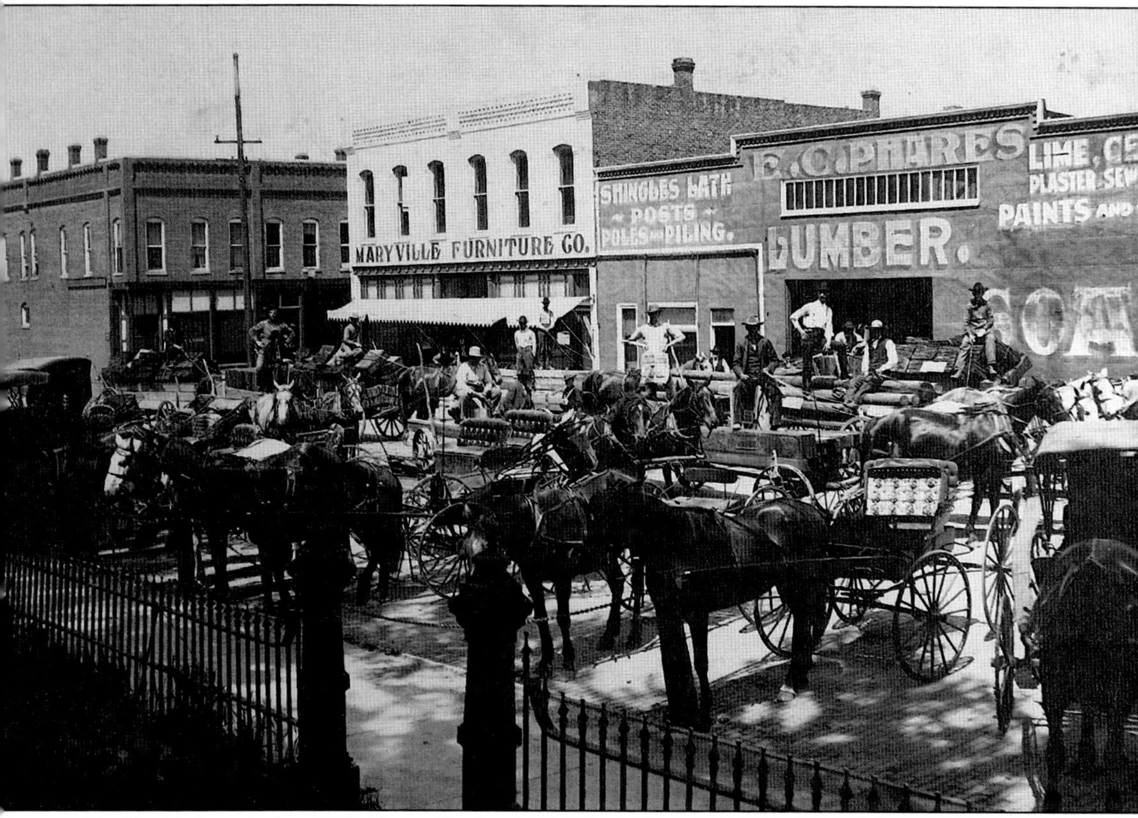

Brick paving in the 1890s kept the business district and its patrons much cleaner, signified progress, and in the next decade made the streets more manageable for the automobiles that started to appear. But customers who came into town by horse-and-buggy remained proud of their traditional rigs. Freight drays, closed-backed Stanhope buggies, two-seated double buggies, and simple, light roadsters pack the street for a photograph of horse-drawn pride. The brick paving could not absorb the considerable manure left by this kind of traffic, and during the transition years it presented an odorous problem for businesses around the square. Animal traffic persisted, however, well into the age of the automobile, and the Barmann and Wolfert Carriage and Wagon Works on North Main Street continued to build and repair buggies and wagons.

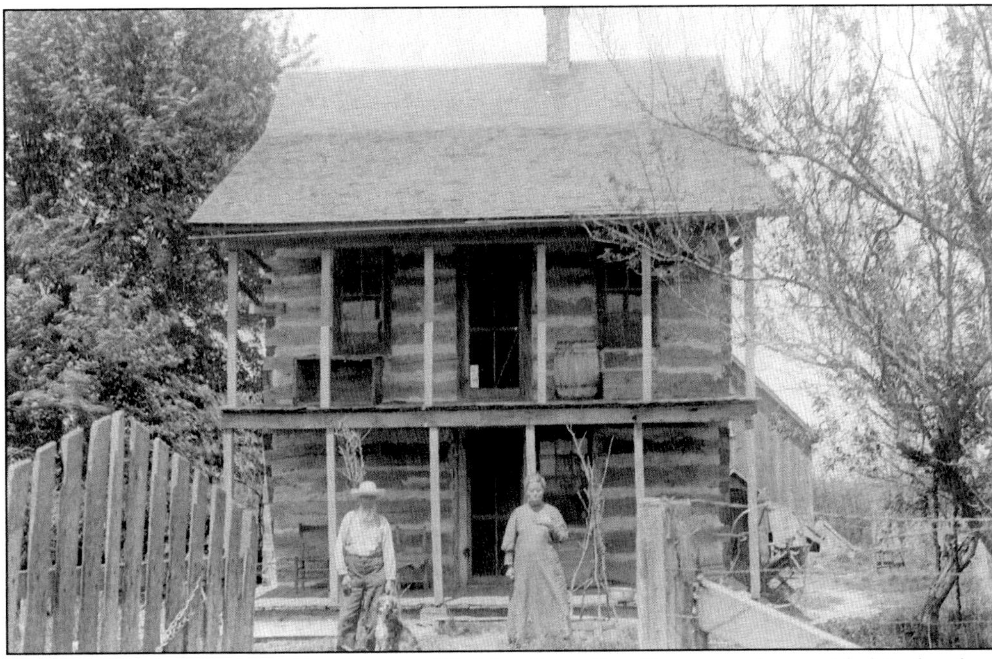

This sturdy settler's cabin was built in 1866 by Cornelius Yost, seen here with his daughter Mary. This unusually fine example of frontier construction featured a full second story, glass windowpanes, and shingled roofing. Sturdily built as well, the house was still standing and in use as late as 1938.

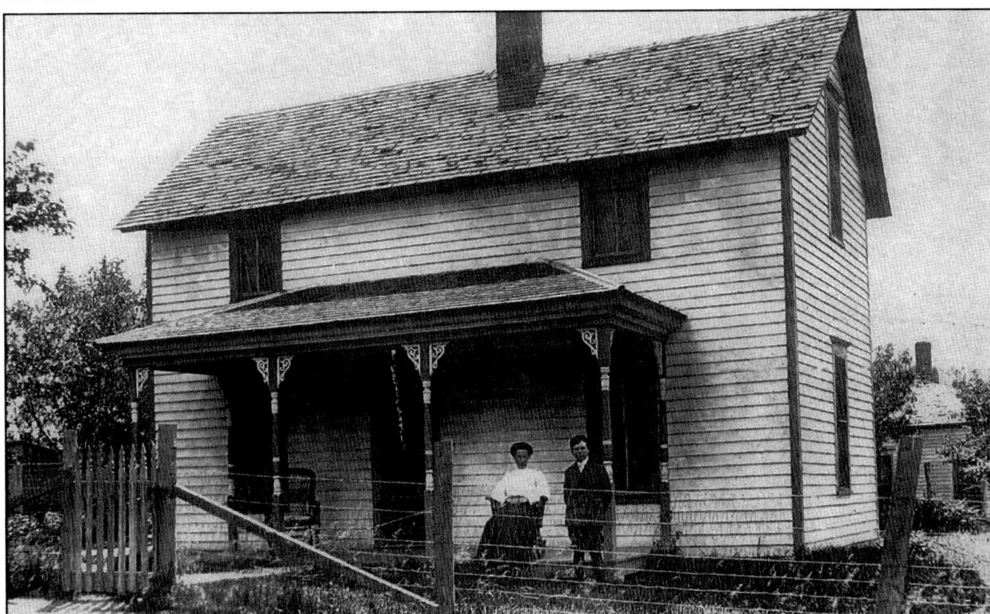

Frank Bloomfield built this house in Parnell and opened a butcher shop when the town was still in its first decade. The home was a balloon-framed I-house with a central fireplace, a vernacular form that had for a half century spread westward with settlement. Relatively inexpensive and efficient, it also presented a prosperous-looking, two-story facade to the street and a pleasant porch for Blanch and Troy Bloomfield. (Courtesy of Emily McLain.)

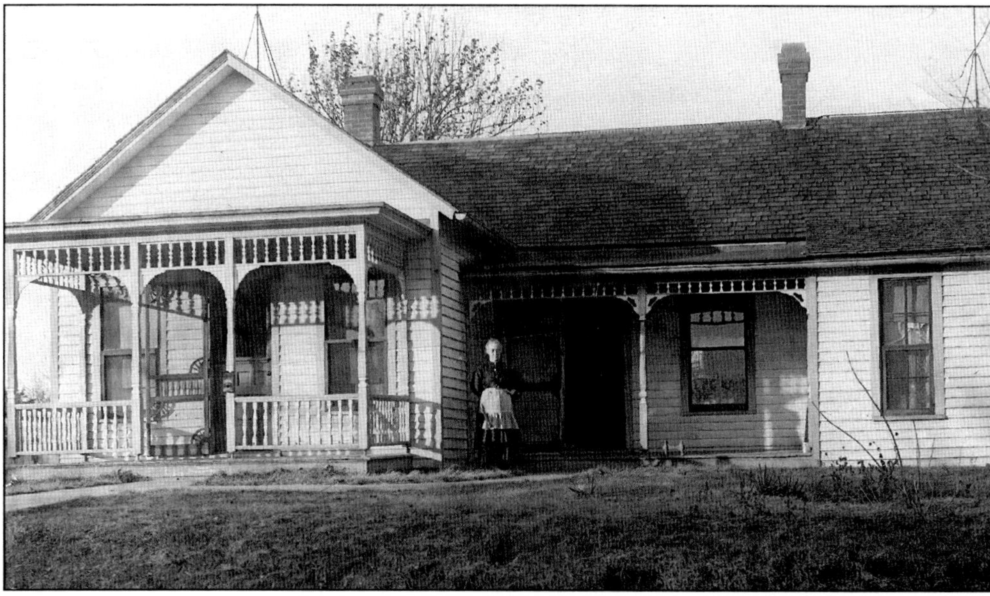

While more humble than many of the showplaces that followed, the folk Victorian homes of Nodaway County were typically designed by the carpenters who built them. Such homes were often L-shaped with porches that featured simple Queen Anne spindle work. Developing towns required homes that were affordable, comfortable, and practical. This home also took advantage of the local production of lightning rods to protect it from the region's electrical storms. (Courtesy of Coby Lamb.)

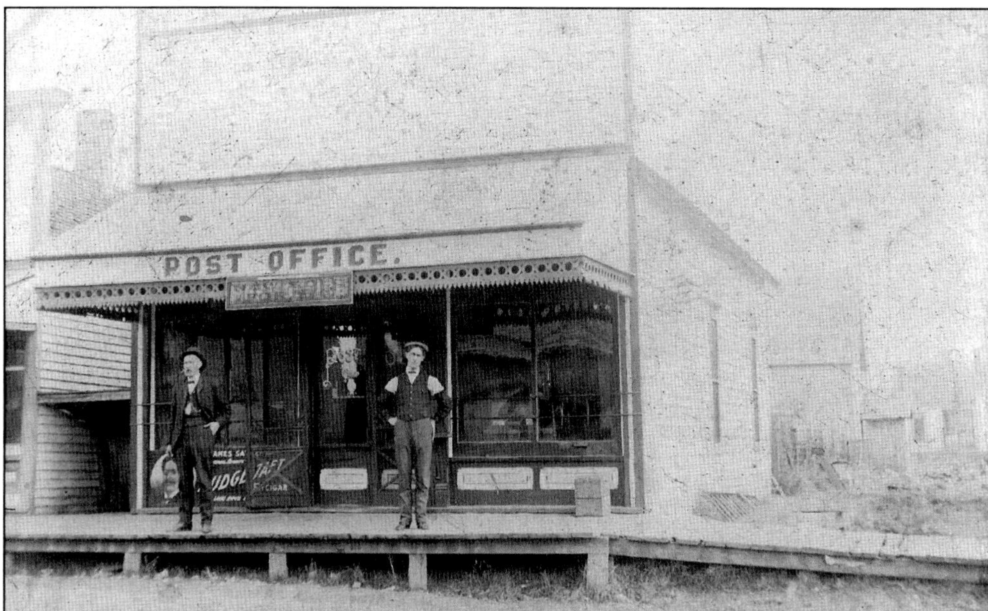

In 1903, postmaster James Sawyer (left) and Eldon W. Irvin supervise the first post office in Ravenwood, located on the east side of Main Street. The office served a thriving community that planted itself along the Chicago, St. Paul and Kansas City Railroad's Maple Leaf line in 1887. Methodist and Disciples of Christ churches were quickly erected, a bank followed in 1892, and mills on the Platte River served farmers.

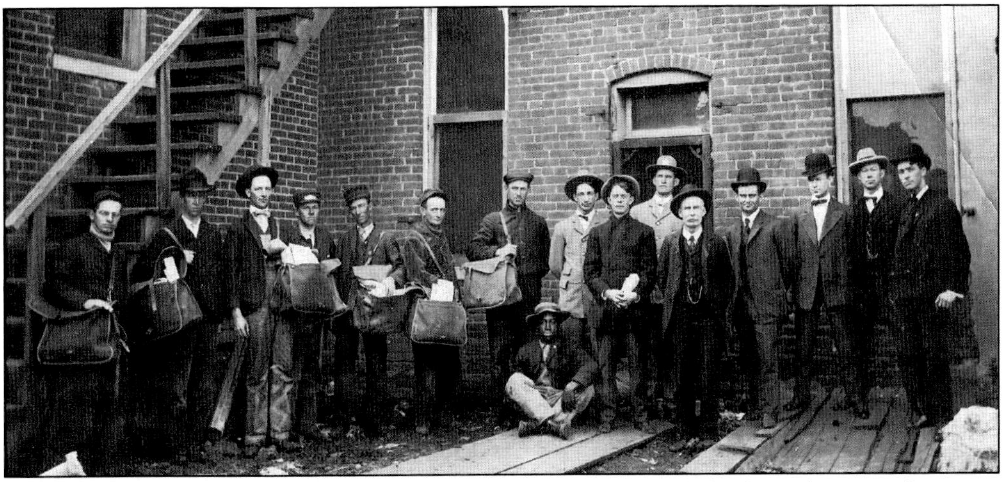

Caleb Burns and Amos Graham delivered the first mail out of the log cabin courthouse in Maryville in 1846, retrieving it first from St. Joseph on horseback. Beginning in 1869 it came by hack service from Savannah. With the growth of the town the post office was moved to a rented space on the north side of the square behind which this photograph was taken. Free delivery in town began the following year, not long before this photograph of the town's intrepid carriers and office staff was taken.

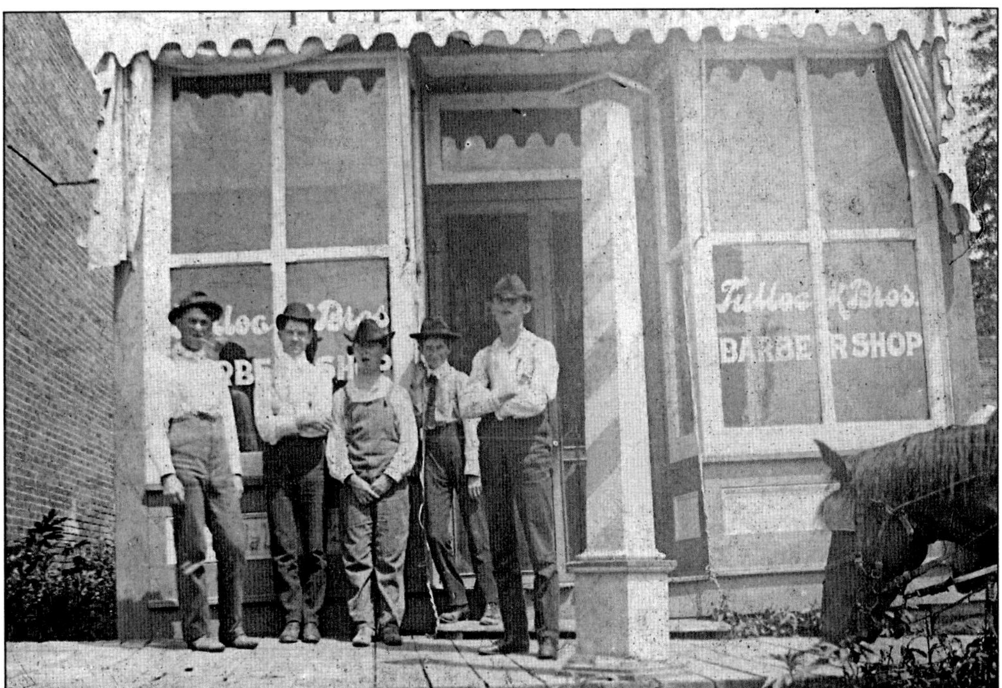

The Tulloch brothers served the barbering needs of the 1,600 citizens of Barnard and surrounding Grant Township when photographed in 1902. Rich agricultural land along the One Hundred and Two River and a station on the Burlington line made Barnard a thriving market town that provided all the necessary services expected of a respectable town looking for any opportunity to grow. (Courtesy of the Barnard Community Historical Society.)

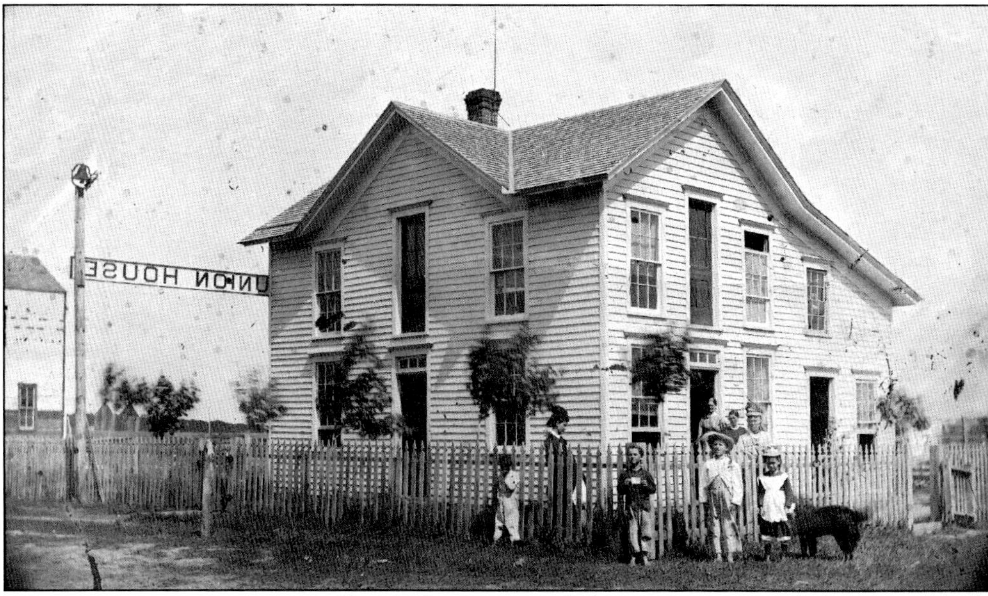

The Union House, one of Hopkins's earliest structures, was an early boardinghouse located at the northwest corner of the Union Block west of the railroad tracks. It is seen here in a tintype image from the early 1870s. Tintype photography produced an image that was the reverse of what was seen by the naked eye. The Union House soon had to compete with the larger and more luxurious Hopkins House next door, which was constructed by David Bender. (Courtesy of the Hopkins Historical Society.)

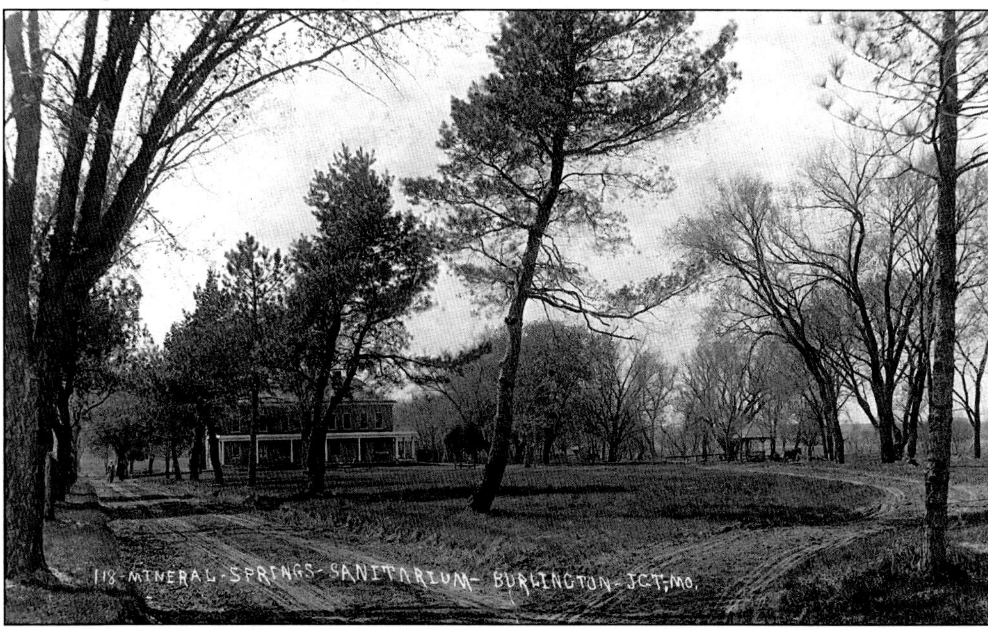

From 1888 to 1920, Burlington Junction hosted a popular mineral spring one and a half miles southwest of town. Patrons bathed in and drank the springwater, which was bottled under the label Nekroc in honor of landowner Samuel Corken. The Burlington Junction Mineral Springs Corporation built a resort on the site that could host as many as 60 patrons. A fire in 1920 destroyed the hotel and ended the town's run as a health resort destination.

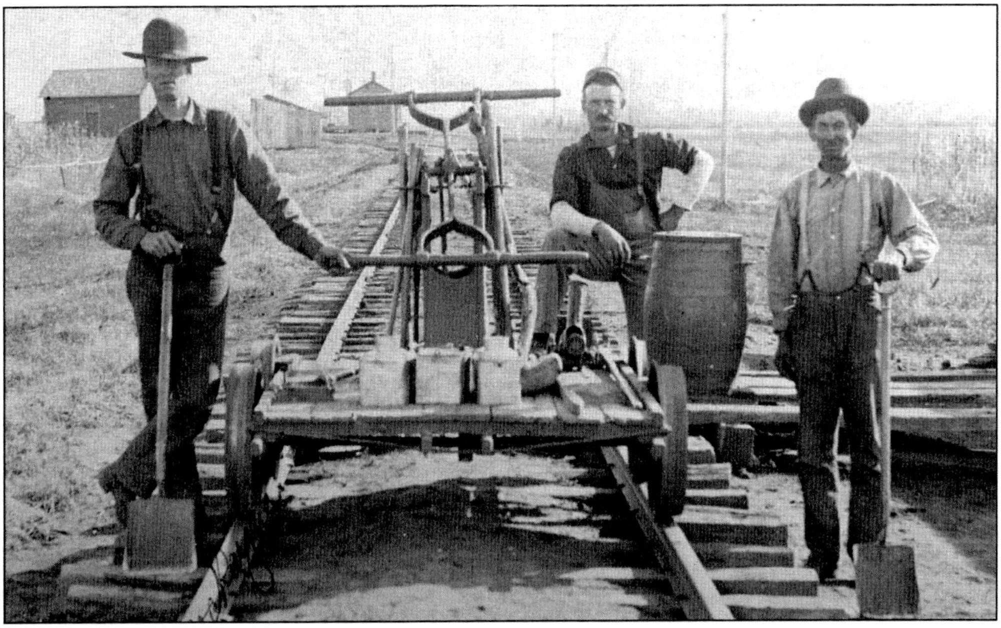

A group of linemen, including Charles Cockayne at left, work one of the rail lines in Nodaway County and pose with their handcar around 1900. Based on the velocipedes of the Victorian era that were the forerunners of the bicycle, handcars were essential tools for line inspection and maintenance particularly since they were light enough to be moved on and off the rails relatively easily.

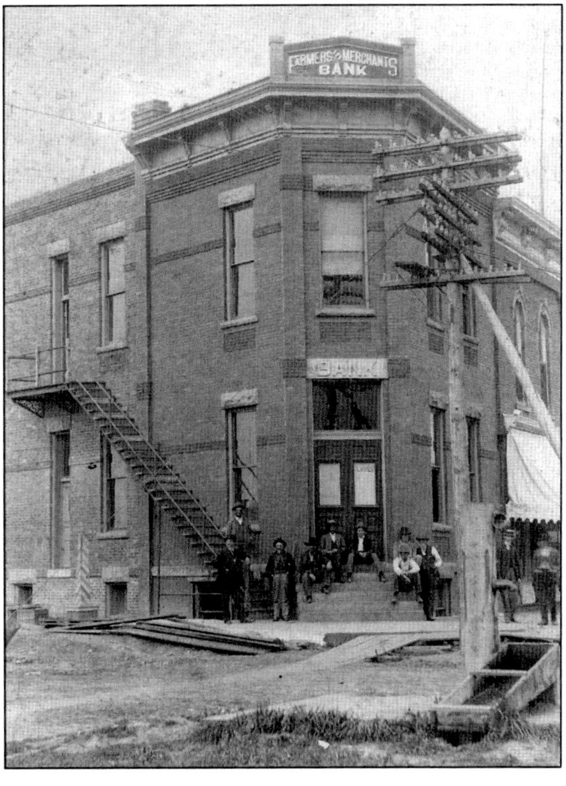

The Farmers and Merchants Bank was established in its new location in November 1900. C. S. Martine served as president, A. B. Sheley served as vice president, and J. B. Stewart was the cashier. Billie Miles located his barbershop in the basement of the new building. The Farmers and Merchants Bank served Hopkins well before succumbing to the financial disaster that collapsed over eight percent of all banks in the United States in 1931 alone. (Courtesy of the Hopkins Historical Society.)

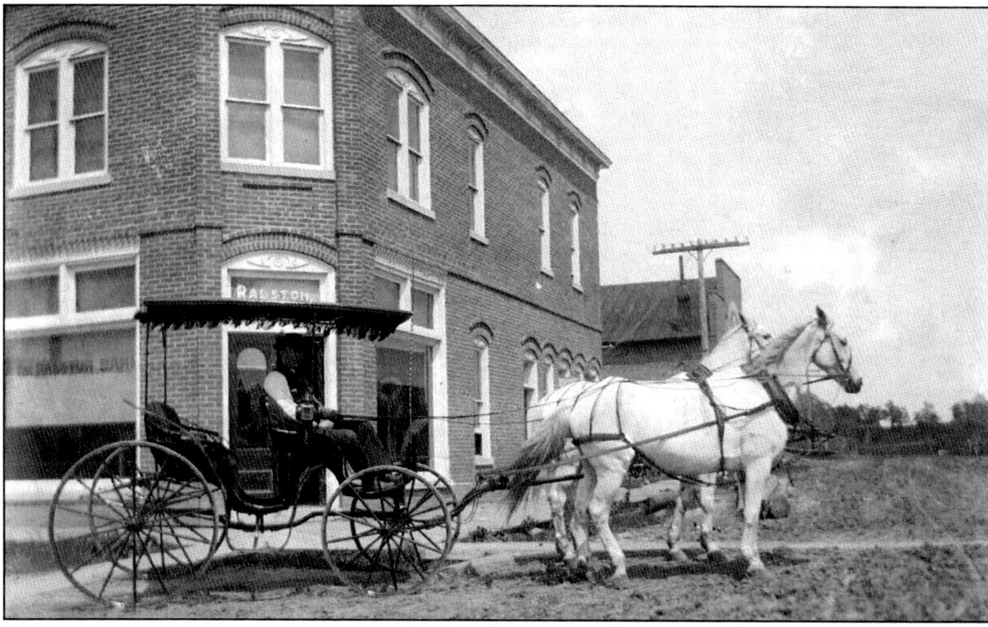

E. H. Ralston partnered with land baron John Sliker Bilby in Quitman and Elmo, and in 1905, Ralston served as president of the Farmers State Bank of Conception Junction. His banking enterprises put nearly a quarter of a million dollars in deposits under his management at the dawn of the 20th century. Joseph D. Young pauses in his fine surrey in front of the bank while driving horses Gordon and Smokey.

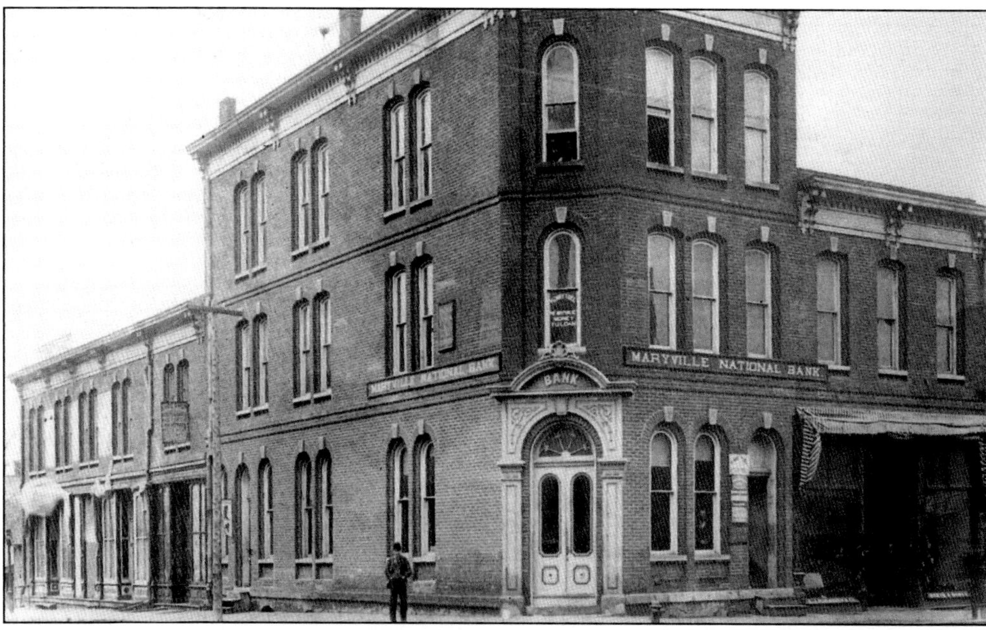

George Baker, John Saunders, and Richard Saunders founded a banking house in Maryville in 1874 that became Maryville National Bank in 1889. Seen here in 1889, its imposing three-story structure at the corner of Fourth Street and Main Street indicated the prosperity already arriving in the late 1880s. Through the first decade of the next century the bank maintained the largest deposits among the county's many banks.

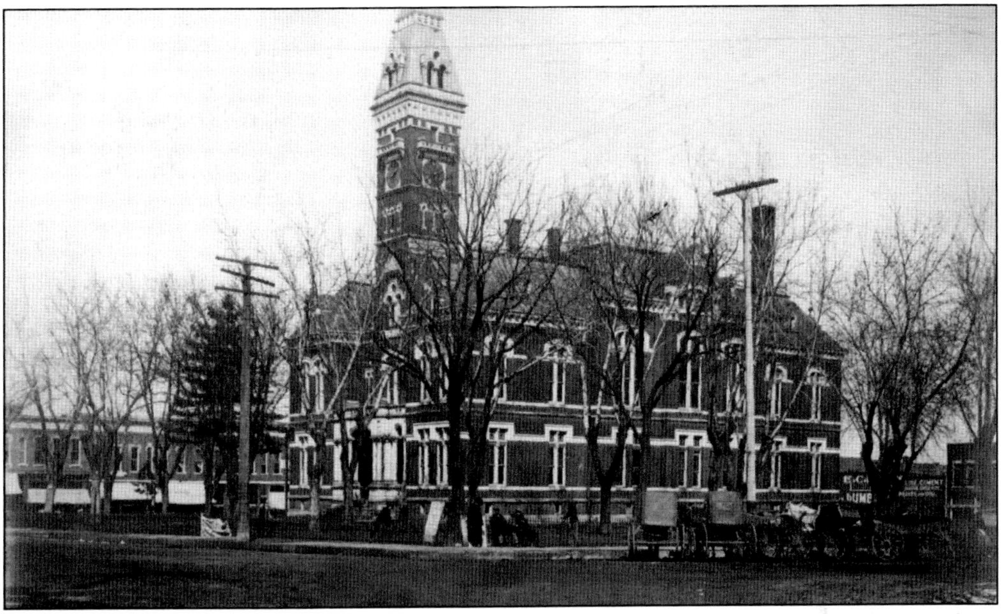

Nodaway County's first courthouse, built in 1846, was a 32-by-20-foot log cabin, and its replacement, a modest brick structure, was built in 1853. In 1881, not long before this picture was taken, citizens celebrated completion of the impressive new courthouse whose Renaissance tower still stands today at 111 feet. The steam-heated building provided water to its tenants through a force pump that drove water from a cistern in the basement.

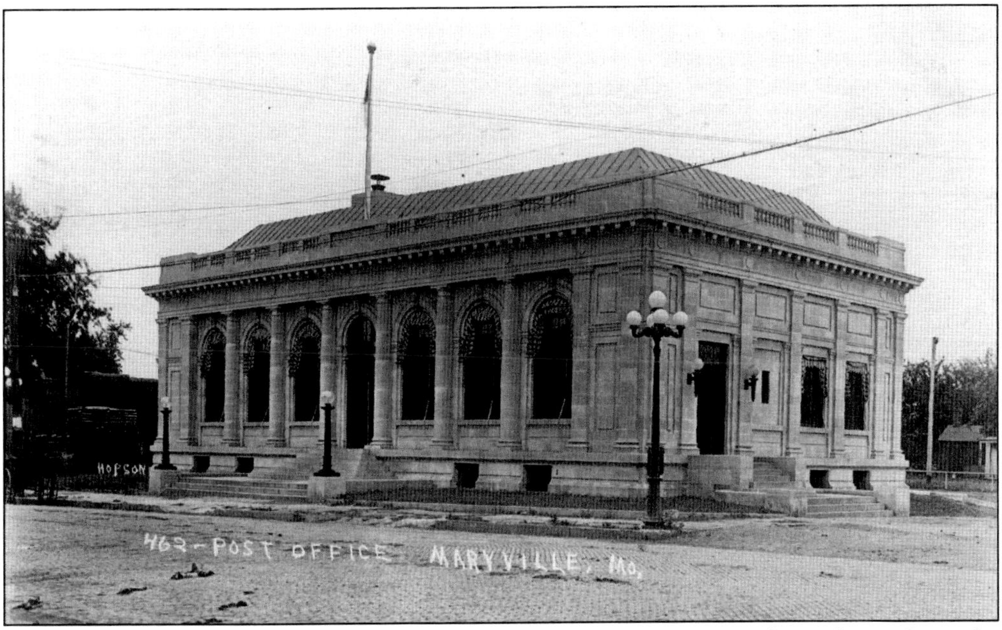

The Maryville Post Office delivered its first mail in 1845 out of the original courthouse. Later the mail was sorted and delivered out of a leased space on the north side of the town square until the federal government provided this grand neoclassical structure in 1912 on North Main Street. Since 1962 it has served as the Maryville Public Library. Rural free delivery out of Maryville began in 1899 on seven routes covering 175 miles.

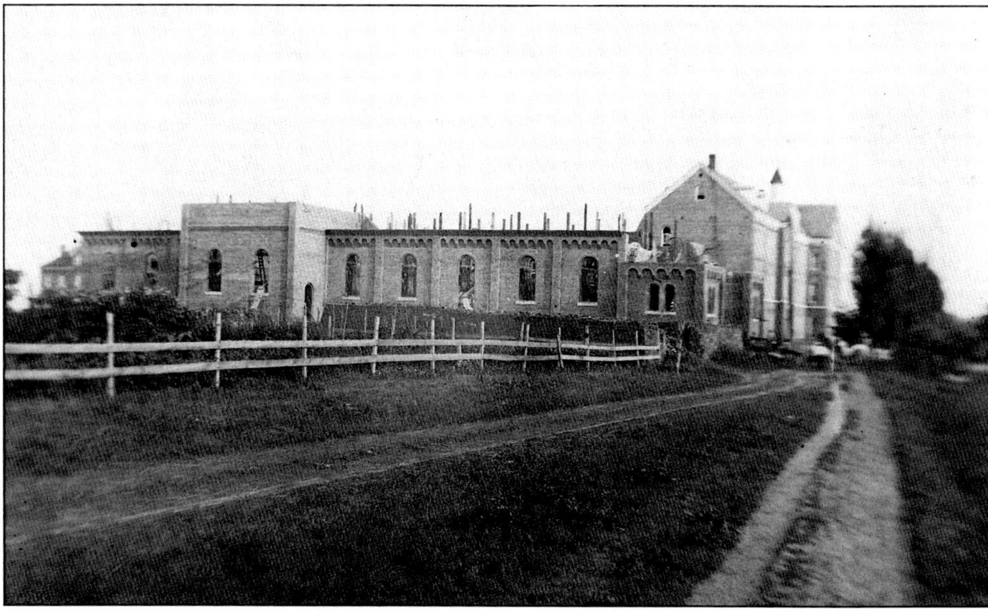

The depression of 1857 sent Irish Catholics west from Pennsylvania in search of peace and opportunity. Seventeen of those migrants settled Conception, and in 1873, Fr. Frowin Conrad arrived from Switzerland to found a novitiate built on the principles of St. Benedict in the frontier solace of Nodaway County. By 1880 a brick monastery building was in place, and by 1890 it was accompanied by an impressive church. The abbey is a 206-foot-long, three-story structure, with the church measuring a matching 206 feet in length, 56 feet in height, and 104 feet in width at the transept. Unlike most of the more decorative baroque-style Benedictine monasteries in Europe, Conrad preferred the simplicity of a Romanesque design for Conception Abbey. Nonetheless, the structure tested the skills of masonry workers brought into Conception to complete the magnificent structure in 1889. (Courtesy of Conception Abbey.)

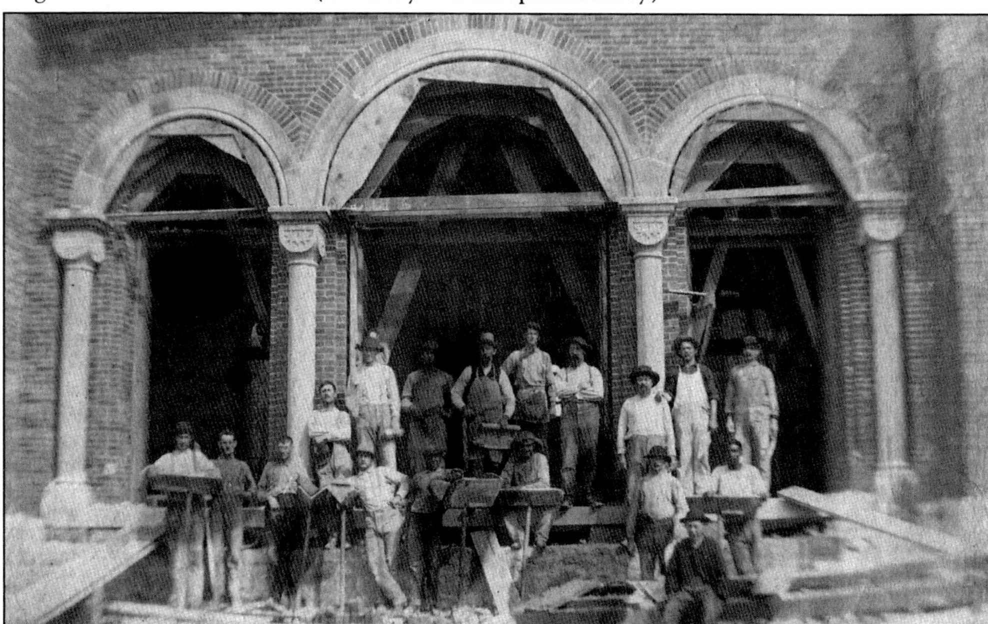

During the winter of 1892–1893 the water froze in the steel water tower, bursting the tank that had been serving the town of Maryville at the corner of Ninth and Mulberry Streets. The town replaced it with this impressive brick tower, enclosing another steel tank, which was imitative of the fashion of fine urban water towers popular in the Gilded Age after the Civil War.

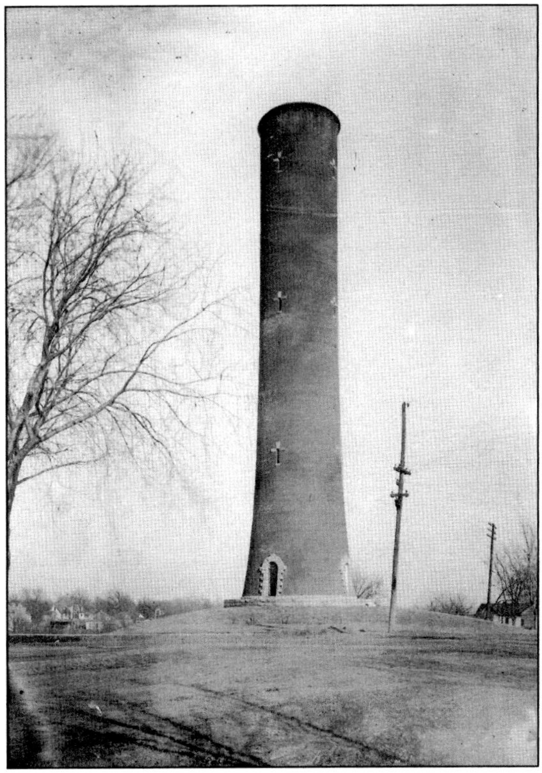

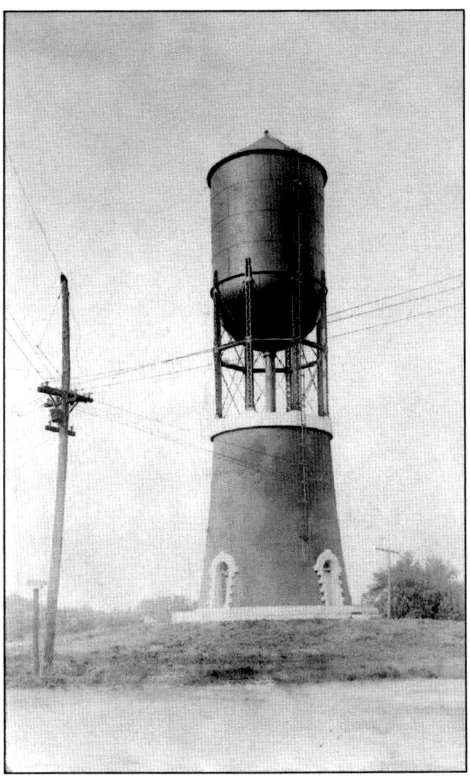

The brick tower had not been particularly well built or adequate in size. After only a decade, the upper three quarters were removed and a new steel tank was placed on the lower quarter as a foundation. Still unique in appearance, it gained some fame as the subject of noted author and playwright Homer Croy's *West of the Water Tower* (1923). Croy reminisced about a time in his youth when a slab of ice slid from the top of the tower, burst open the tank, and flooded the surrounding neighborhood. His country school took the afternoon off "so that we scholars could go too town to see the holocaust." (Courtesy of Coby Lamb.)

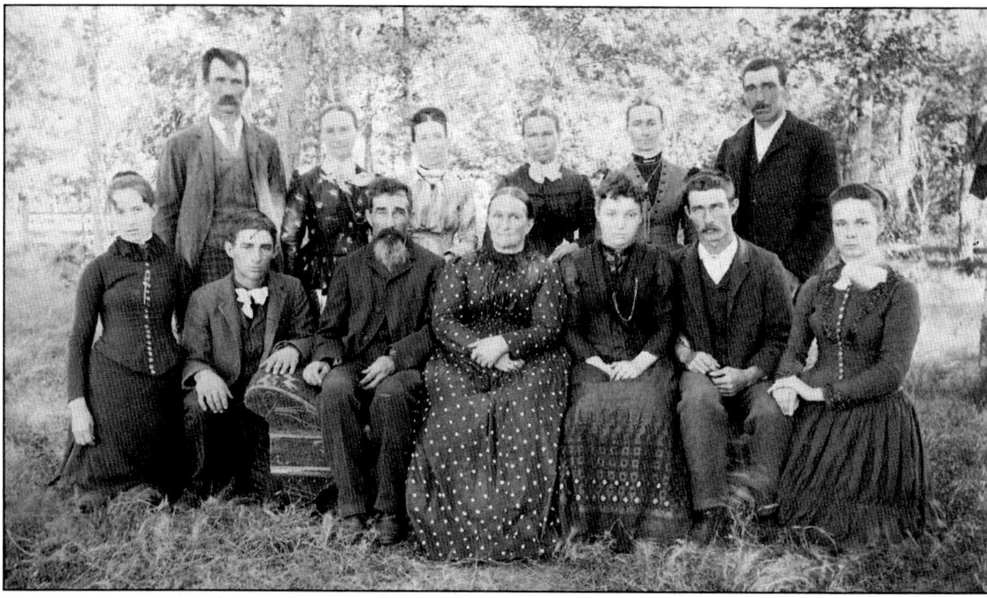

Isaac Lanning, seated third from the left in front with his family, migrated from Ohio and settled on the fertile land along the west bank of the Platte River in 1852 two miles north of present-day Ravenwood, where he farmed and built a mill. Later, under the management of Cooper Gooden, Lanning's pioneer mill was essential to area settlers for the next half century. The mill employed an unusual wheel of flint for wheat that had come through the port of New York as ballast on a ship from France. (Courtesy of Emily McLain.)

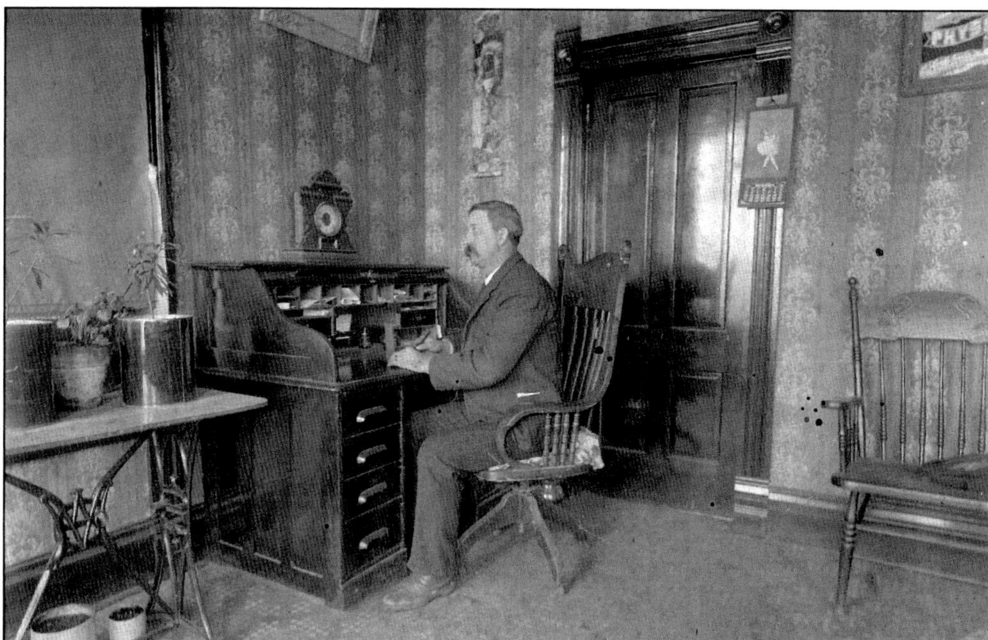

Four physicians, including Dr. S. D. Large, served the county's second-largest city in 1900. Most of these early physicians also operated drugstores and fulfilled a variety of needs in the community. Large brought Hopkins its first automobile, an Oldsmobile that helped him visit rural patients as long as the roads were dry. (Courtesy of the Hopkins Historical Society.)

Clyde "Fatty" Perkins, born near Arkoe in 1890, became a well-known and much-loved character in Nodaway County. An accountant by training, Perkins worked a wide variety of jobs around Nodaway County, played a horn in community bands, and managed a baseball team. Having gone to Jefferson City to serve a term as accountant to the Missouri House of Representatives and another as postmaster to the Missouri senate, he returned to Nodaway County to serve as county treasurer.

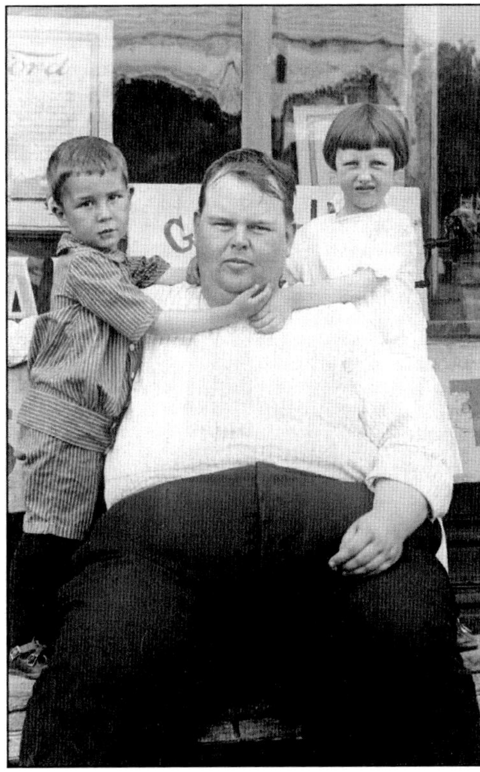

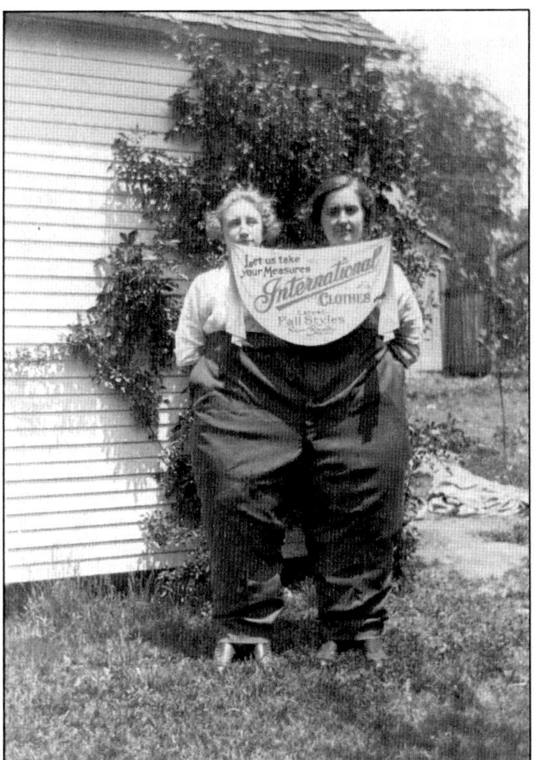

Seen here in 1917, Lavona Cook and Blanche Stalling pose together in a pair of overalls and jacket made by the International Clothing Company for Perkins, who was easily recognizable around the county at a sizeable 536 pounds. Local legend holds that he turned down offers from Hollywood movie producers, not wanting to humiliate himself as an object of comedy. Life for Perkins was not always easy, but he found numerous ways to contribute to the life of the county before dying in 1936 at age 45.

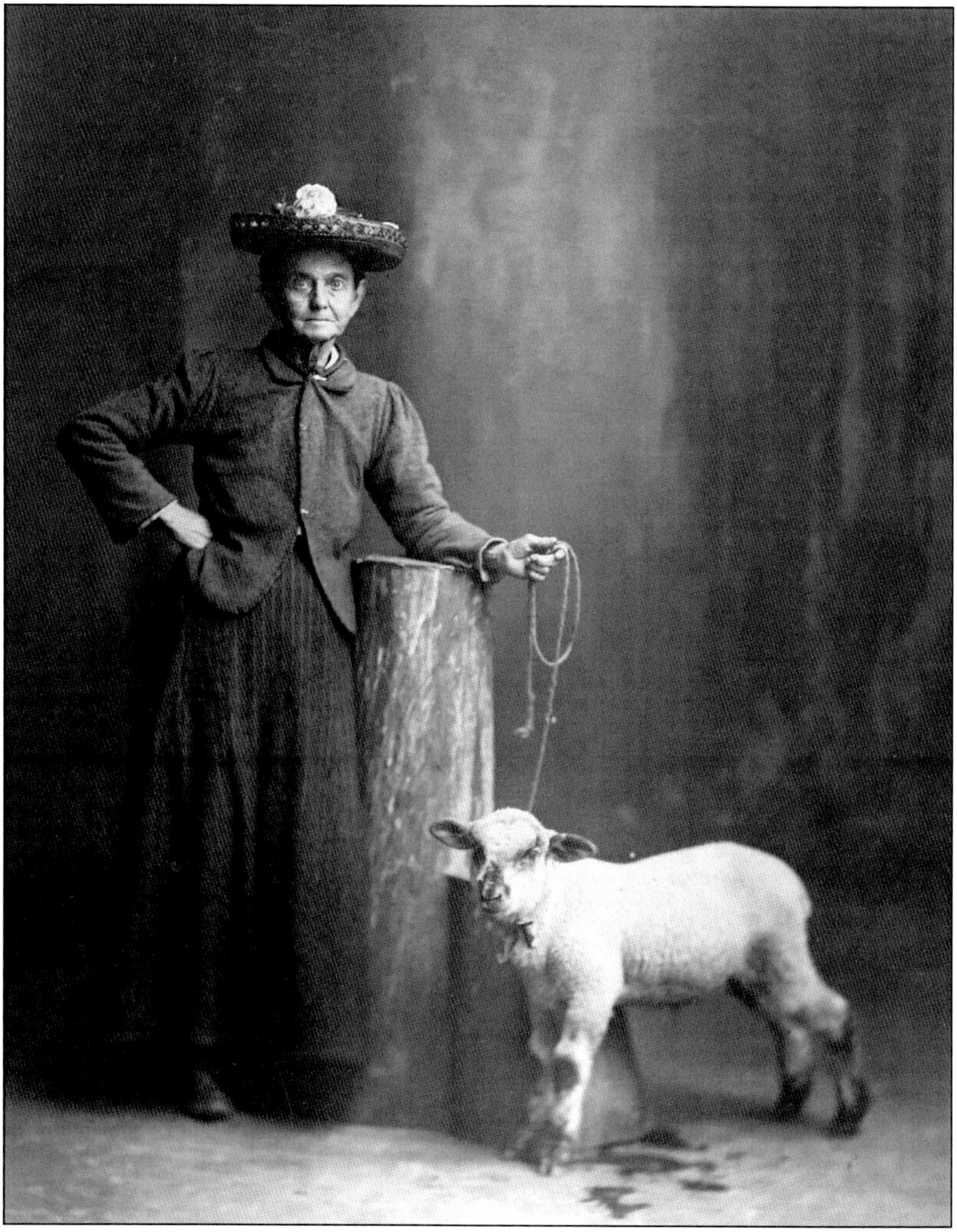

"Aunt" Betsy Robinson and her pet lamb lived in the first house west of the water tower in Maryville and served for many years in an important role as one of the town characters essential to flavoring local lore. Her greatest moment of fame came when she served as a witness in federal court in a suit against the Ringling Brothers for a tent collapse in Maryville that took the lives of two and injured many others. The *Maryville Daily Tribune* noted discreetly that she "stands out distinctly," and her testimony was "sure to teem with some unique linguistic expressions." She was an enthusiastic baseball fan and could be found sitting in the front row rooting for the home team in all kinds of weather. She cut a striking figure in her 1880s-style polonaise dress, while chewing, smoking, and swearing as needed.

Two

LAND RICH

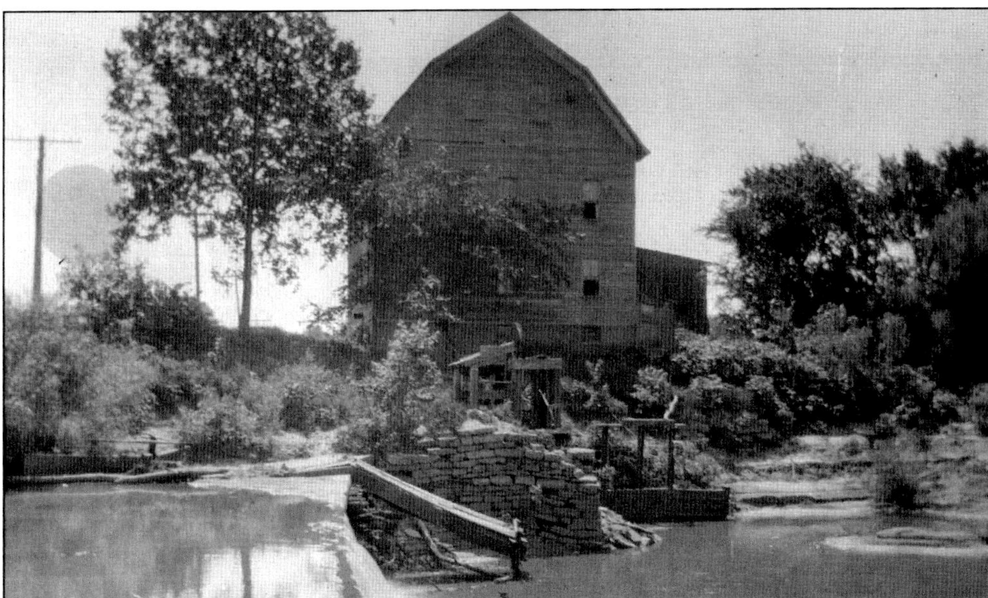

Located just outside of Nodaway County on the One Hundred and Two River, the mill at Rosendale served farmers up the river into Nodaway County. Built as a saw- and gristmill in 1845, it provided lumber and ground grain for farmers for 30 years. D. L. Max rebuilt the mill into a woolen mill in 1874, and then Watson and Agee converted it back into a roller mill in 1890, about the time it is seen here. Both times much of the original lumber was used. The waterwheel utilized an eight-foot drop in the river to generate about 50 horsepower. (Courtesy of the Barnard Community Historical Society.)

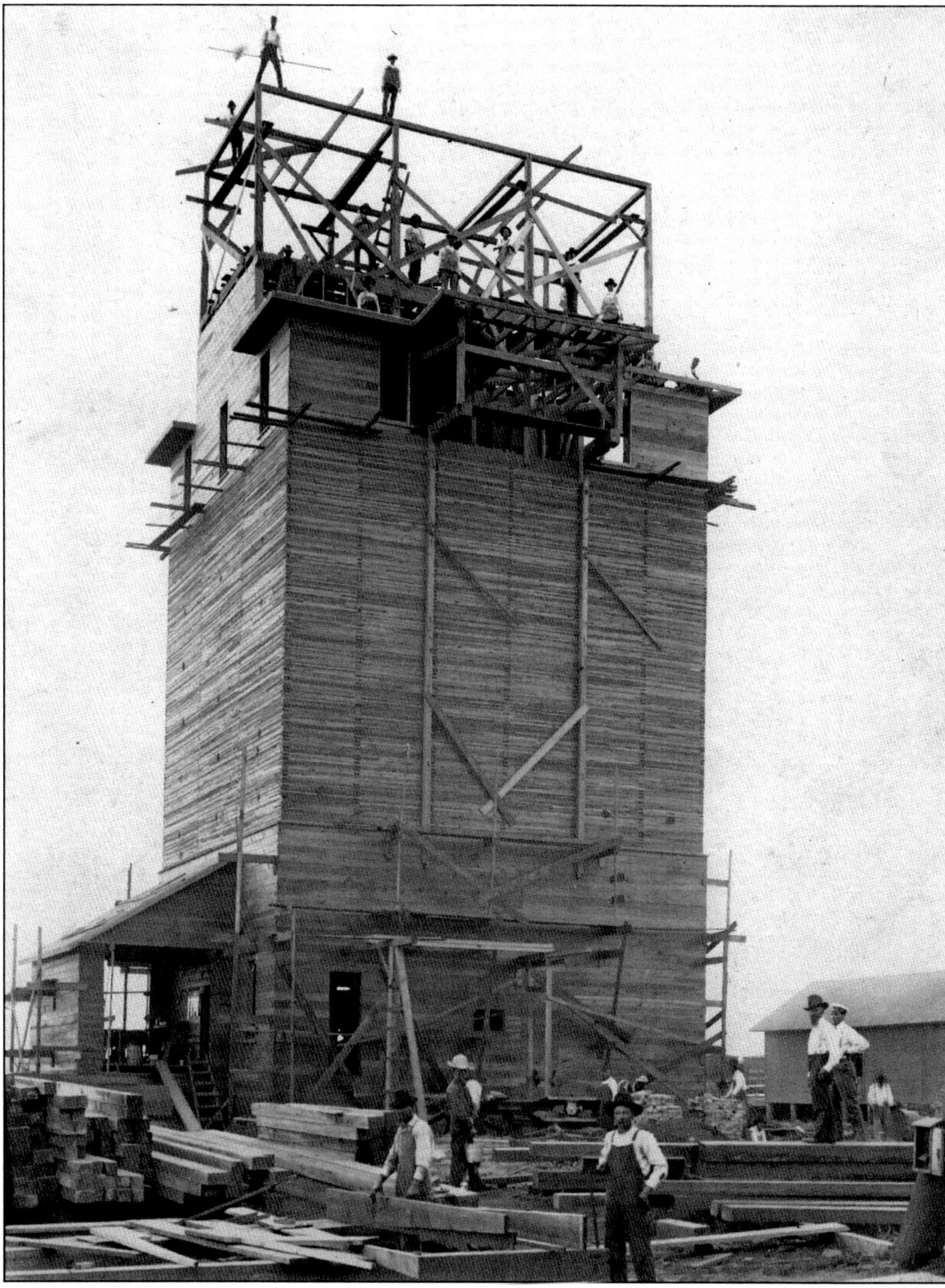

Jeremiah Gillinger came to Quitman in 1886 with his wife Elizabeth, the sister of land baron John Sliker Bilby. After trying several business enterprises Gillinger went into construction contracting with Frank Koucher Construction out of St. Joseph in 1900. As a builder, this elevator in Quitman was his crowning achievement before retiring in 1920. Like many mechanically inclined men of his time, Gillinger was an inveterate tinkerer and chugged around Quitman in the late 1880s in a horseless carriage of his own design. He also acquired a patent on a design for a power-generating river barge.

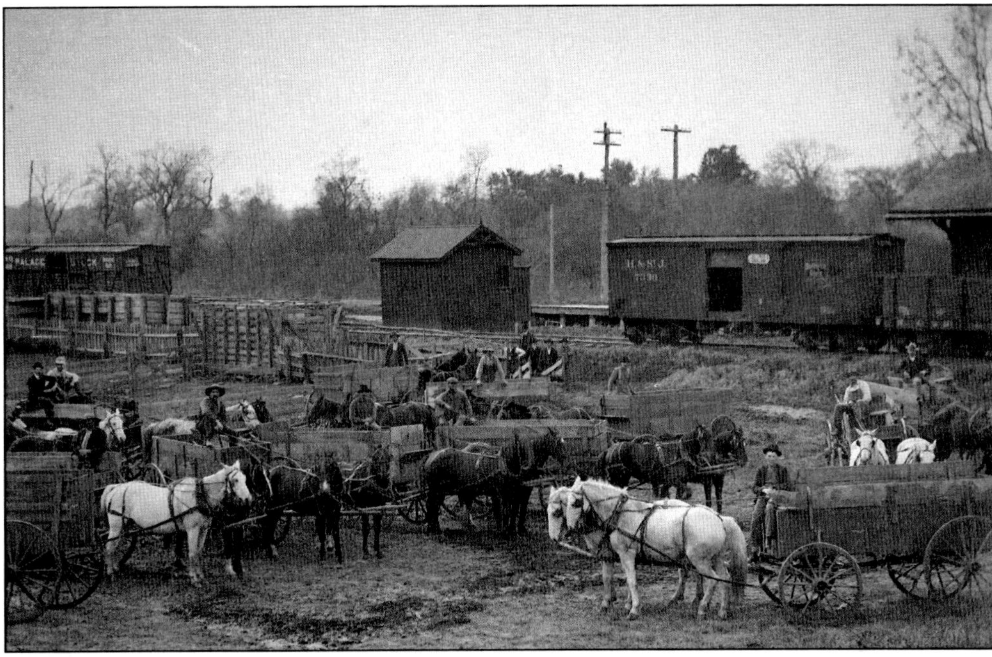

Sam Icke Sr. brings his hogs to the depot in Barnard, accompanied by sons Dave, Bert, and Sammie, along with Perry Duncan, Oren Silver, and Jim Phelps. The Kansas City, St. Joseph, and Council Bluffs Railroad came to Barnard in 1870. (Courtesy of the Barnard Community Historical Society.)

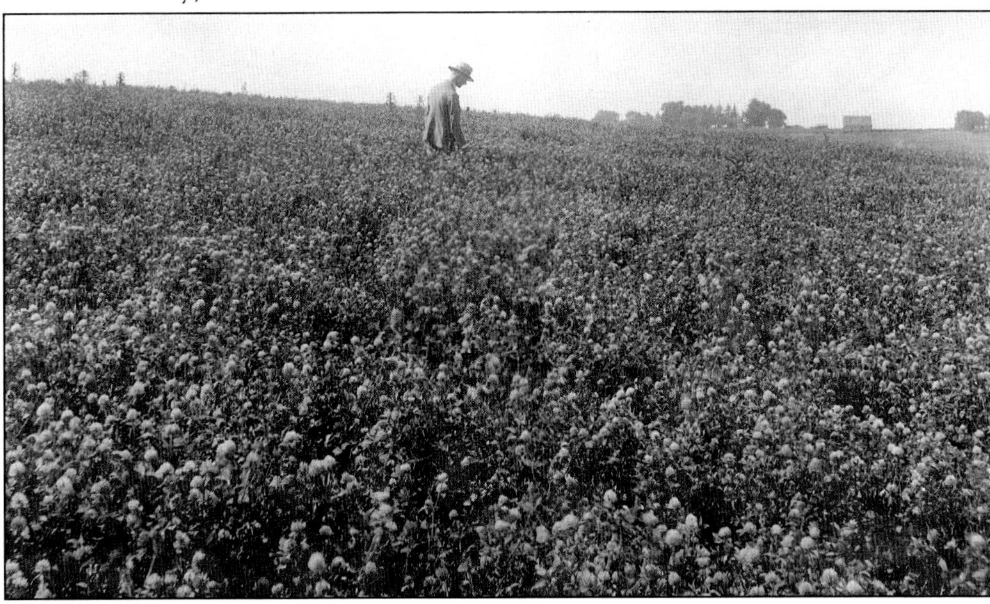

The first settlers in Nodaway County before the Civil War grazed livestock on open prairie land and brought hemp, flax, buckwheat, and some tobacco from Kentucky and Tennessee, and a few farmers used slave labor. Following the war, agriculture changed considerably as rapid settlement and rail access to markets increased cultivation of corn, wheat, and the fencing of ranchland for livestock. In the process, red clover became a ubiquitous source of hay and an effective method for replenishing soil following wheat and other grains.

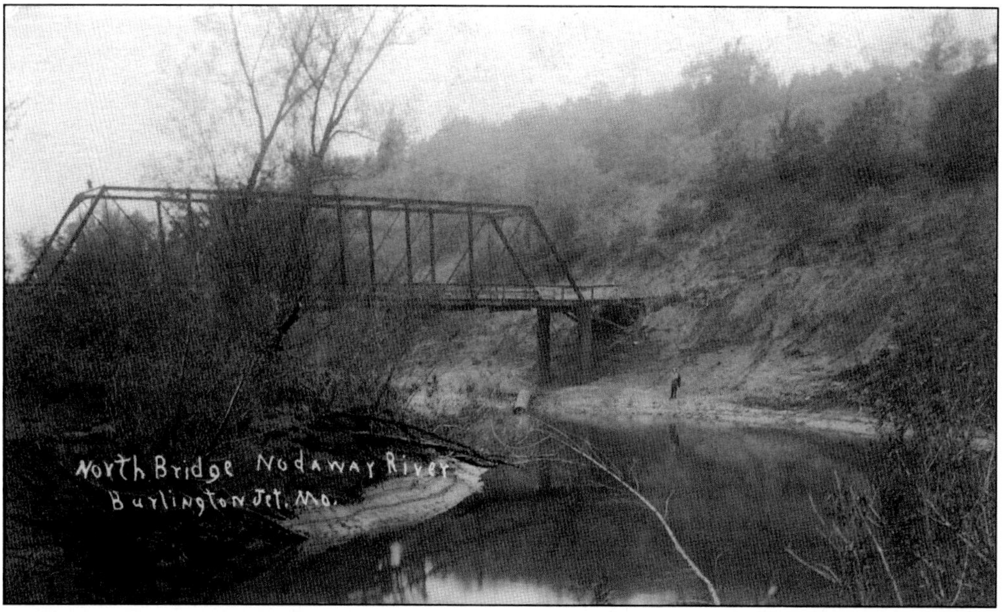

While the county's three rivers gave it great advantages, knitting the rural economy together required a significant number of bridges. By 1889 there were only four iron bridges in the county. Wooden bridges were cheaper to construct but more frequently collapsed under the weight of cattle and heavy steam and oil tractors of the 1890s. A push for construction of iron bridges around 1900 produced spans like this bridge over the Nodaway River near Burlington Junction, seen in 1910.

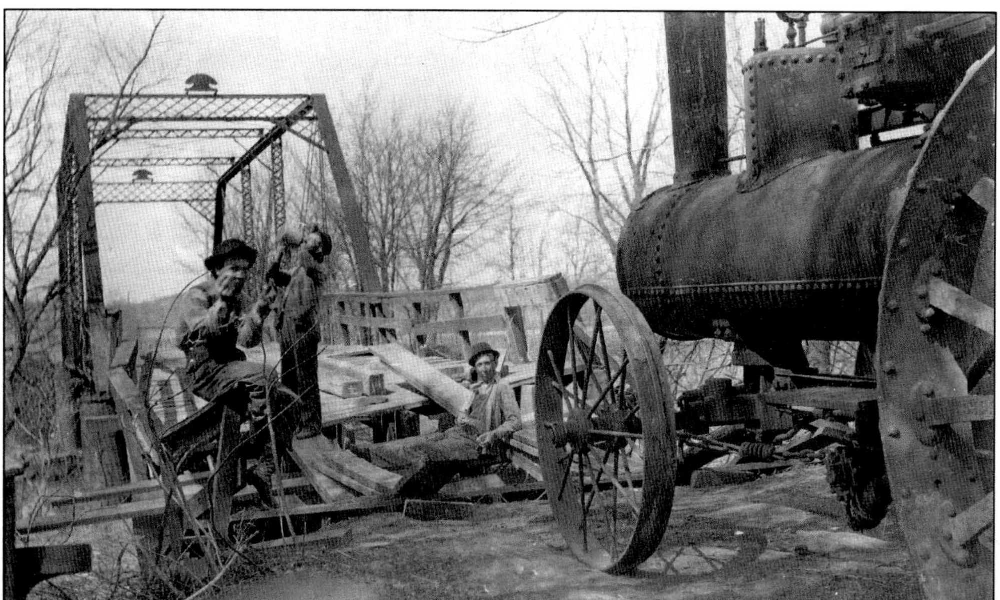

Having done serious damage to the approach to the Burch bridge on the One Hundred and Two River southwest of Hopkins, Dick and George Applegate, along with a helper, pause to take a drink and mug for the camera. Removing the heavy equipment from the wreckage had been a significant chore followed by the problem of repairing the bridge. (Courtesy of the Hopkins Historical Society.)

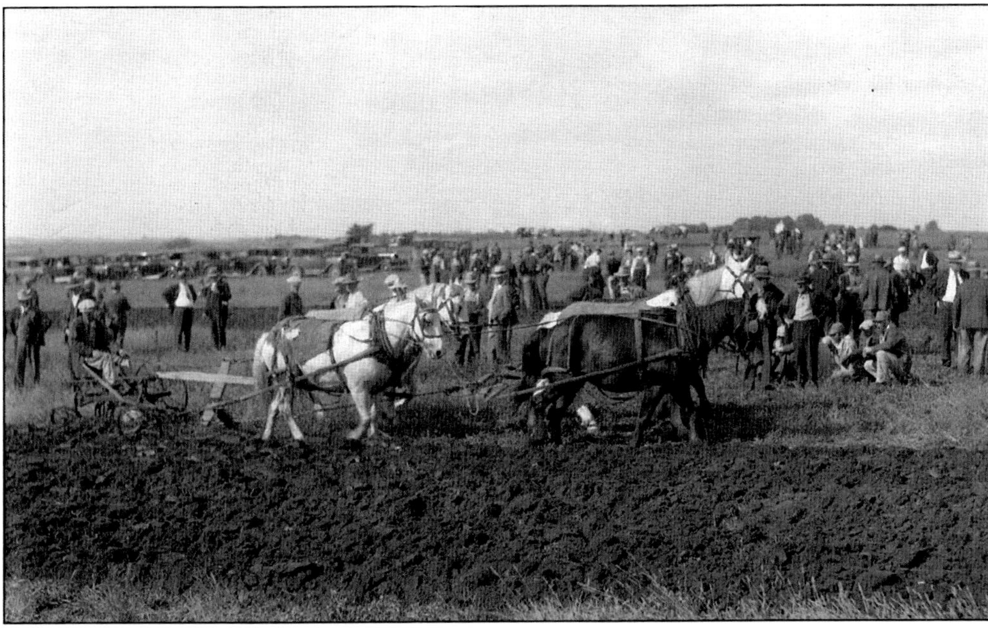

By the mid-1920s the roads of Nodaway County were seeing more cars than horse teams, and the fields were coming under the wheels of steam and gas tractors, but farmers and stockbreeders still took great pride in the quality and strength of their animals. This horse pull at Graham, like others around the county, drew strong interest among county men who now required a parking area for their automobiles.

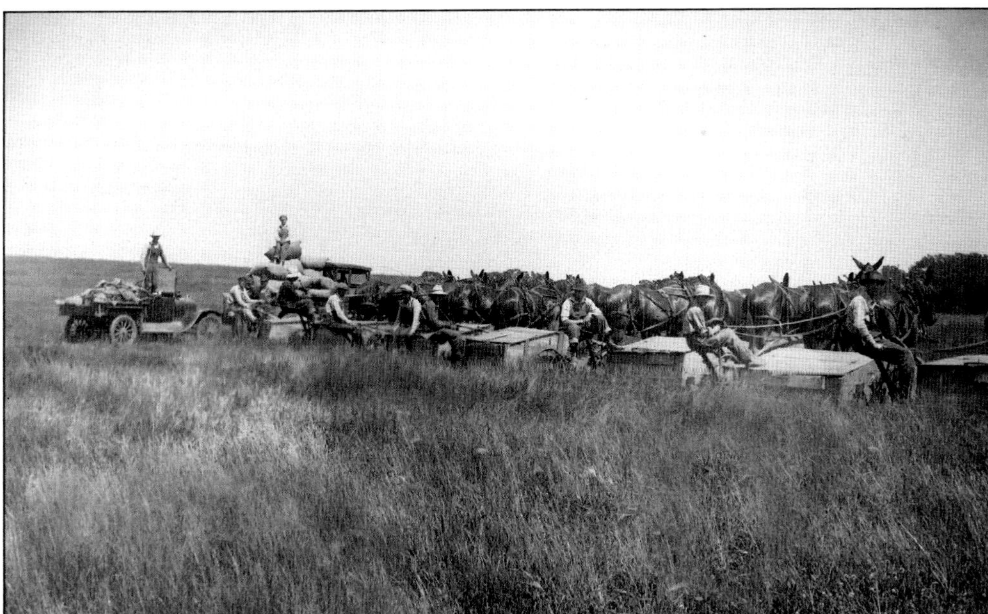

Jehu Ware introduced bluegrass cultivation to Nodaway County as early as the 1850s, and it steadily emerged among the profitable crops of early Nodaway County farmers. Local foundries manufactured bluegrass strippers that could efficiently harvest the seeds, with the grass serving the growing demand for livestock producers. Earl McCleave's bluegrass yard north of Guilford eventually became the largest in the country at 1.1 million pounds.

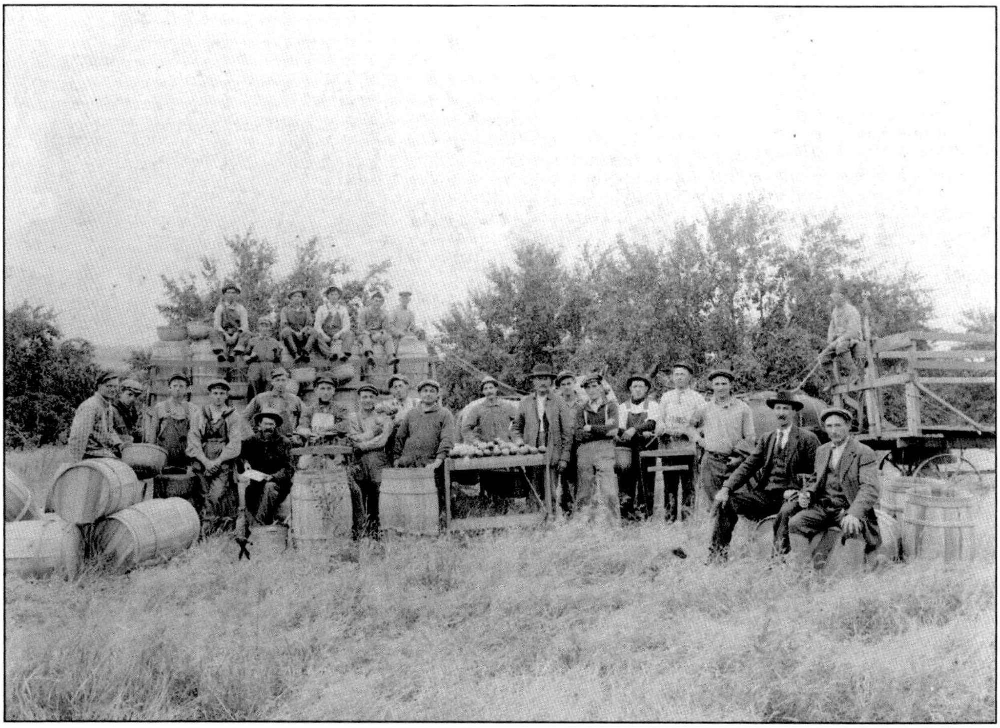

The crew of W. W. Grigsby's orchard show off a fall harvest at the dawn of the 20th century. Settlers brought fruit tree seedlings from Andrew County as early as 1852, and the Gaunt nursery established in Maryville in 1857 helped stimulate propagation. Thousands of acres in the western part of the county were planted in apple orchards. W. W. Grigsby's orchard was the largest at over 100 acres, located two miles southwest of Skidmore.

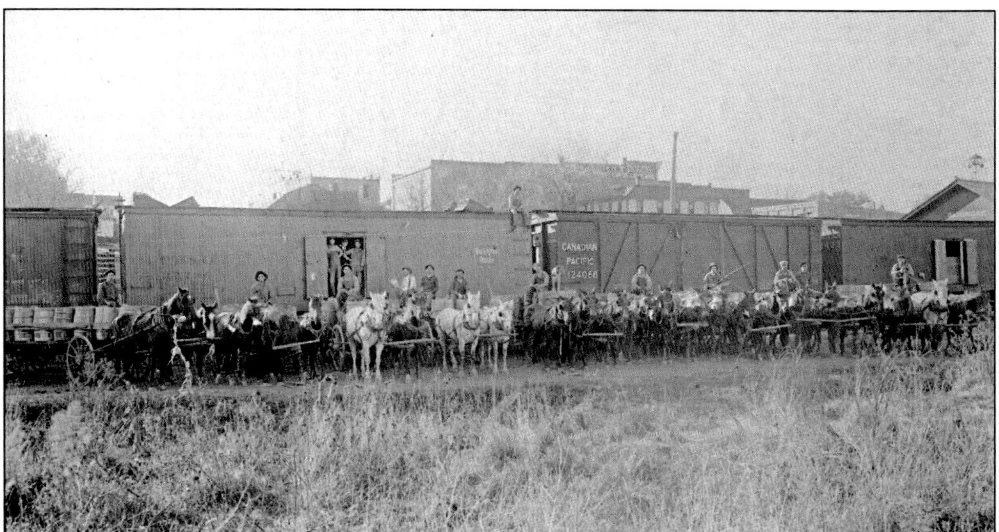

The orchards around Skidmore utilized the town as a shipping point and by 1900, 90 to 100 cars of apples were shipped out of the Burlington yard every year. (Courtesy of the Skidmore Museum.)

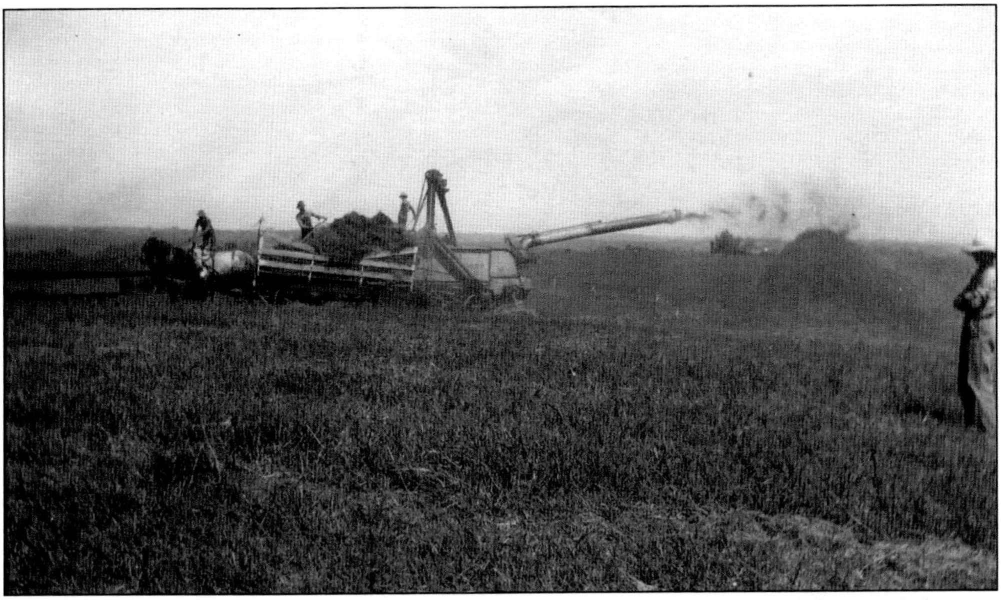

Harvesting and threshing remained sequential tasks on the western plains, including in northwestern Missouri, until well into the 20th century. While sometimes thought of as technologically conservative and reluctant to embrace new inventions, western farmers eagerly accepted and often pioneered advanced technology. The triumph in mechanical threshing by the end of the 19th century was a machine that not only separated the grain but also efficiently fanned the chaff. (Courtesy of Raymond T. Porterfield.)

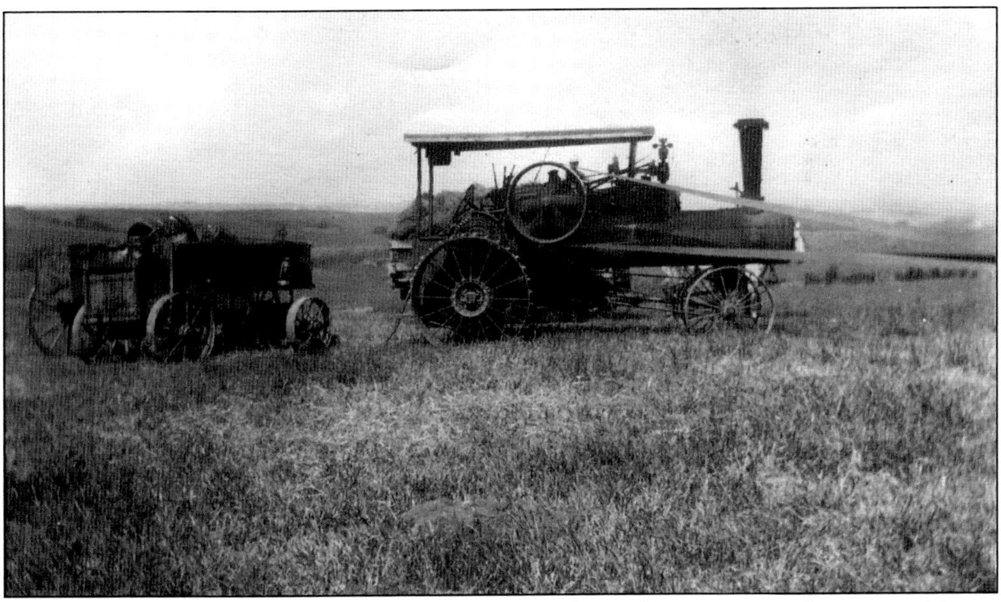

By the end of the 19th century steam power was replacing horsepower in driving machinery, using lengthy belts to transfer power from a steam tractor to the threshing machine. Farmers were at first justifiably nervous about steam engines because early boilers occasionally exploded, and sparks and straw presented a bad combination. But improved engine technology won farmers over to steam. (Courtesy of Raymond T. Porterfield.)

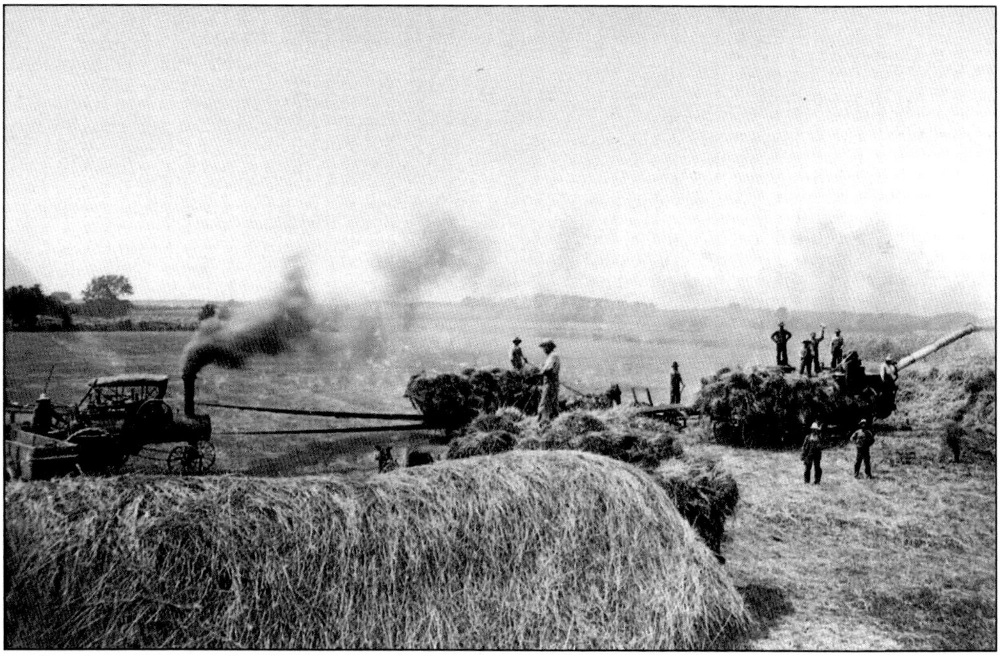

A threshing crew works the Alva Pride farm in the Union School area of Nodaway County in 1911. The significant cash required for modern steam threshing necessitated a special kind of capitalist that invested in machinery, hired engineers and other laborers, and worked the plains signing contracts with farmers for jobs.

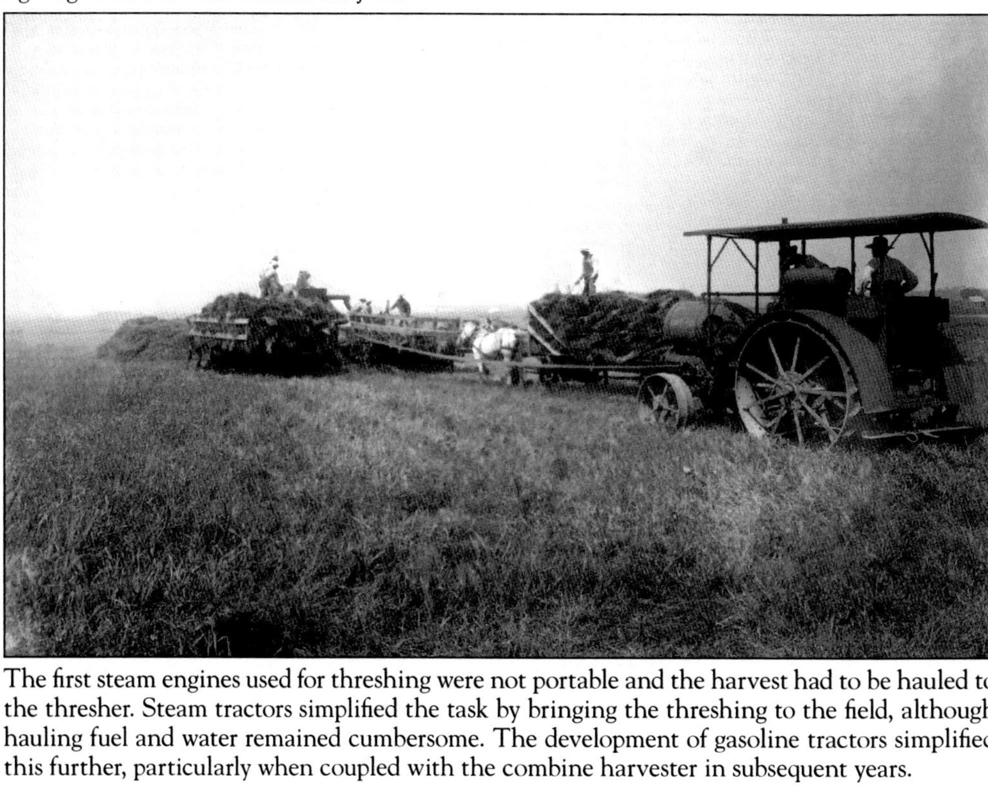

The first steam engines used for threshing were not portable and the harvest had to be hauled to the thresher. Steam tractors simplified the task by bringing the threshing to the field, although hauling fuel and water remained cumbersome. The development of gasoline tractors simplified this further, particularly when coupled with the combine harvester in subsequent years.

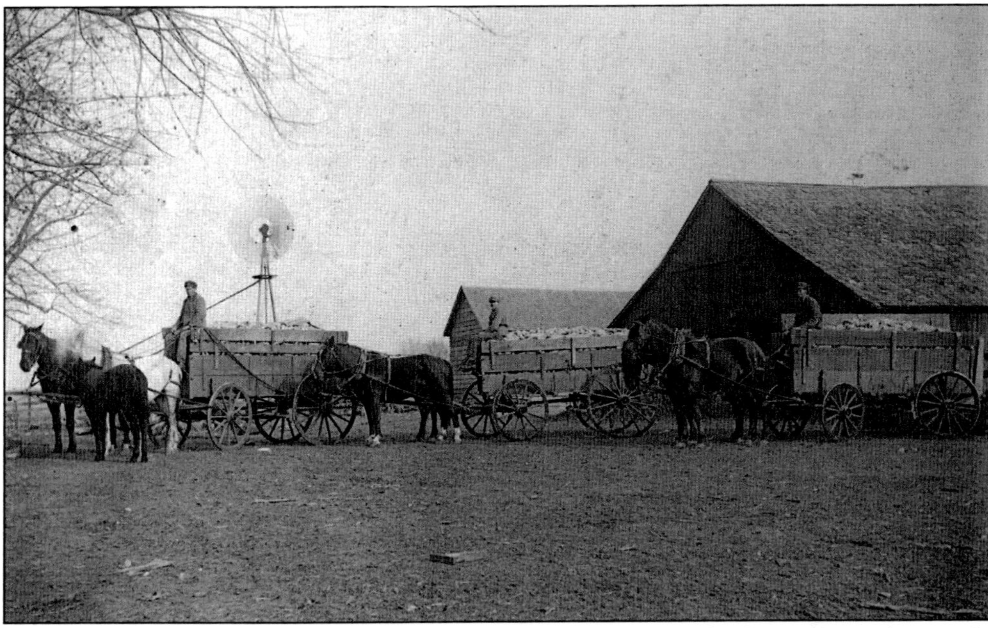

Charles, Fred, and Robert Carter (from left to right) are ready to haul corn to market on the Eastman place near Barnard. The land in Grant Township along the One Hundred and Two River proved excellent for grain production, and in 1869, James McCandliss utilized a dam in the river to operate a gristmill. The arrival of the railroad the following year opened a substantial grain business out of Barnard. (Courtesy of the Barnard Community Historical Society.)

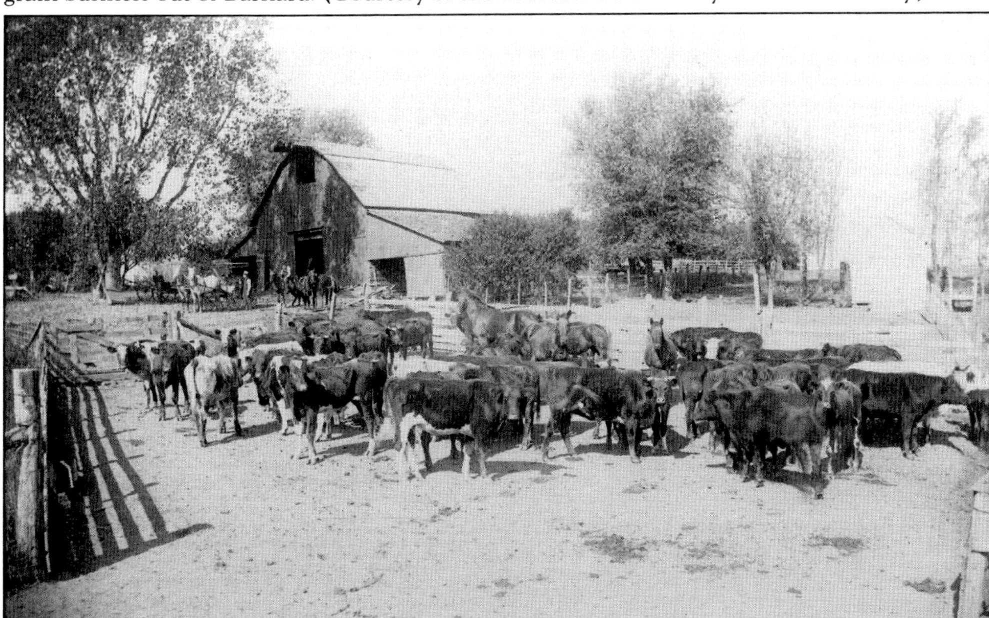

On land where buffalo roamed a century earlier, farmers and ranchers raised livestock that rapidly gained recognition for their superior quality. Small operations, like the Campbell farm five miles west of Barnard shown here in 1903, shared the county with the massive Bilby holdings along the Nodaway River near Quitman. Large or small, Nodaway County herdsmen gained national recognition for their registered livestock.

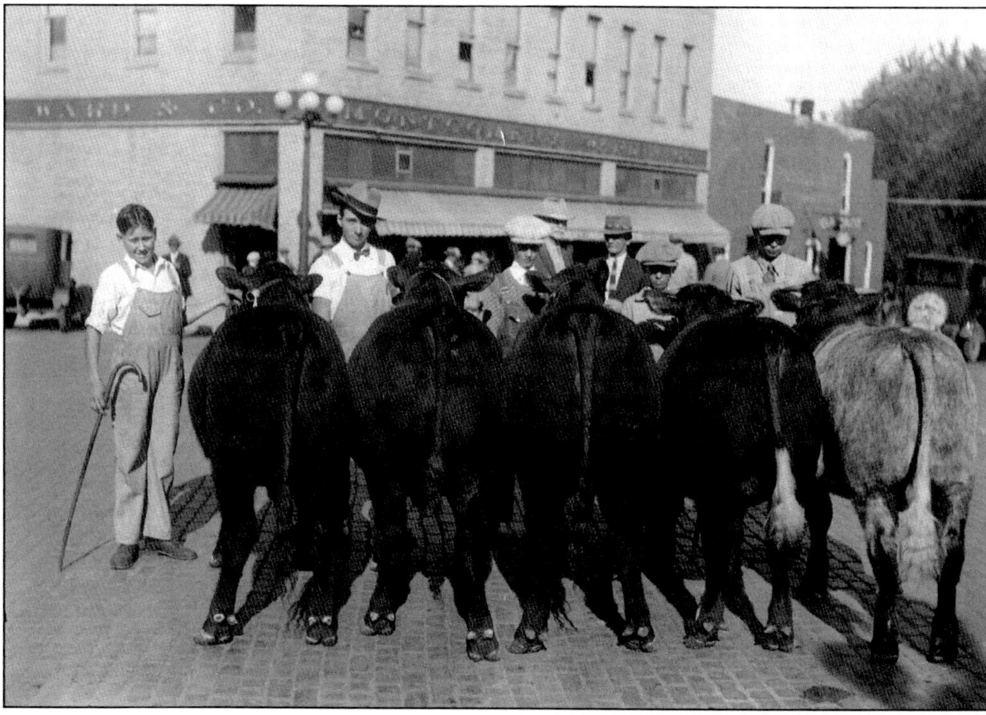

Livestock breeders proudly display their work on the square in Maryville. The occasion required young men from the country to complement their overalls with a clean shirt, tie, and smart hat. During its first century of development the rural economy of Nodaway County relied heavily on the production of livestock. Farmers and businessmen alike agreed by 1870 that the value of the industry was dependent upon careful breeding of quality stock. One measure in that direction was to institute a county stock show in 1871. Within a decade, Nodaway County breeders like Frank Bellows and M. W. B. Harmon were producing cattle that were nationally competitive.

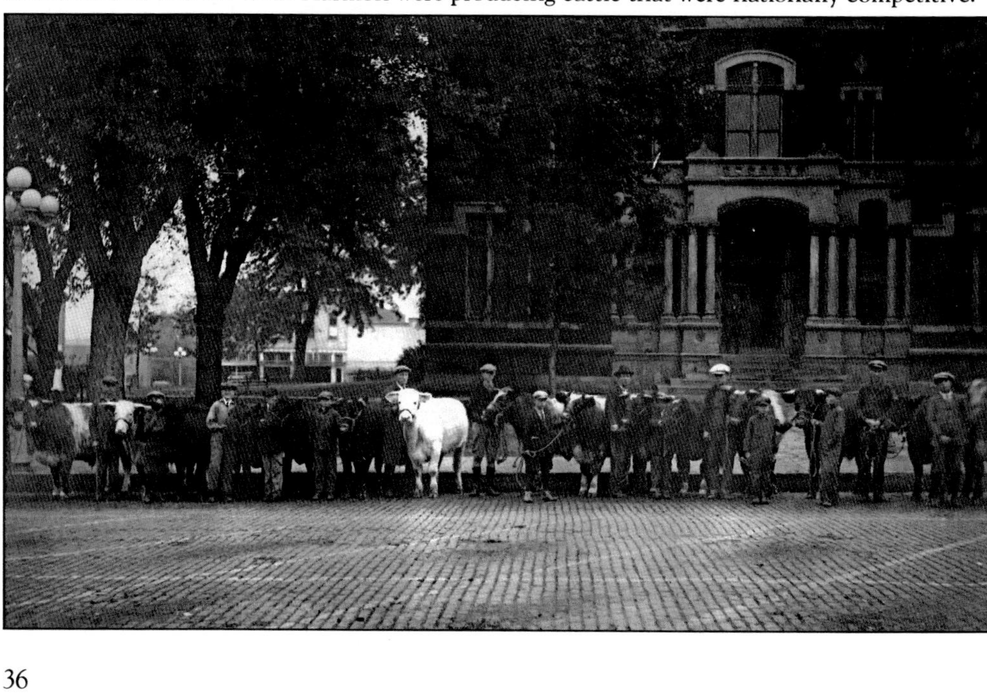

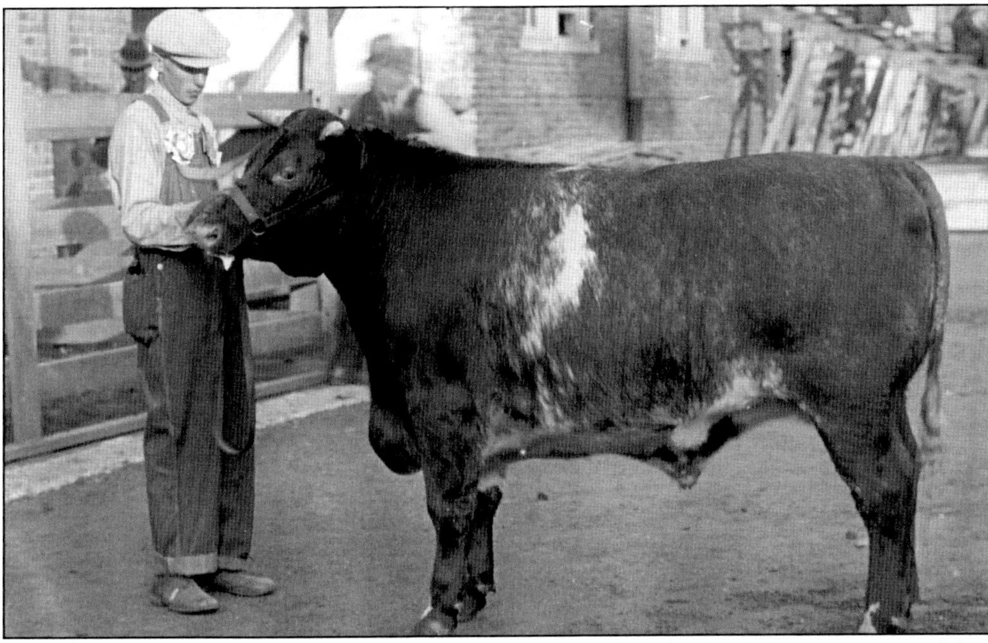

Settlers from Kentucky who arrived in Nodaway County before the Civil War spent most of their efforts cultivating hemp. Following the war, corn took over most of that land, but by the 1880s livestock production increased considerably. In 1884, the Northwest Missouri Poland-China Breeders Association instituted what became a national tracking system for pedigrees of the breed. Eugene Espey (above) displays his reserve champion. Gordon Medsker (below) bucked the local breed preference of the association with his prize-winning Saddleback barrow.

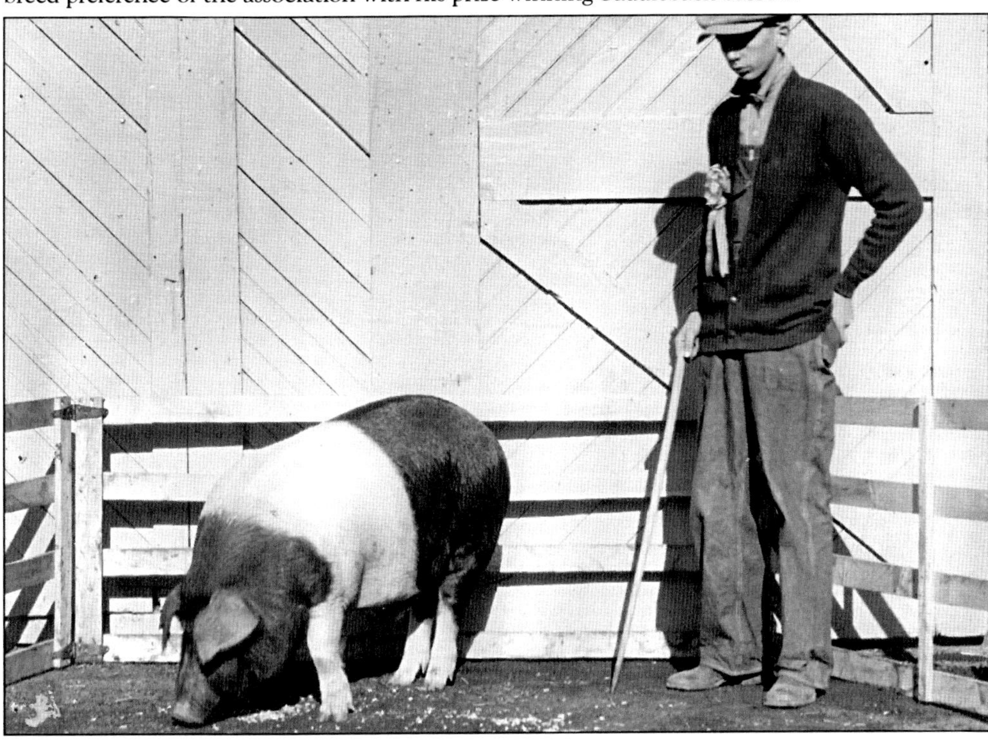

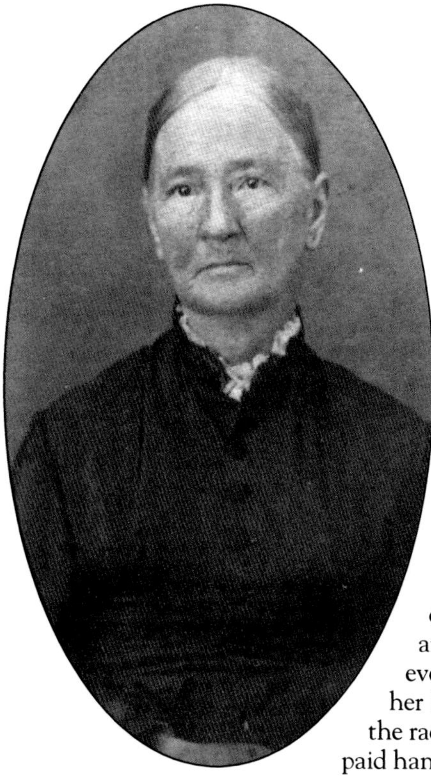

Emma Prather was the daughter-in-law of Col. Isaac Prather, a founding settler from Kentucky who brought fine horses for breeding on what became the famous Faustiana Stock Farm. When her husband James died in 1891, Emma purchased some of the horses that his will had ordered to be sold at auction and continued breeding at Faustiana. The product of her efforts was a thoroughbred named Elwood who won the Kentucky Derby in 1904. Elwood was sired by Free Knight and the mare Petticoat. Laska Durnell, who became the first female owner of a Kentucky Derby winner, purchased Elwood and took him to Louisville, Kentucky. She had not even told the horse's trainer, who also happened to be her husband Charles, that she had nominated Elwood for the race. Elwood entered the derby with the longest odds but paid handsomely with a win.

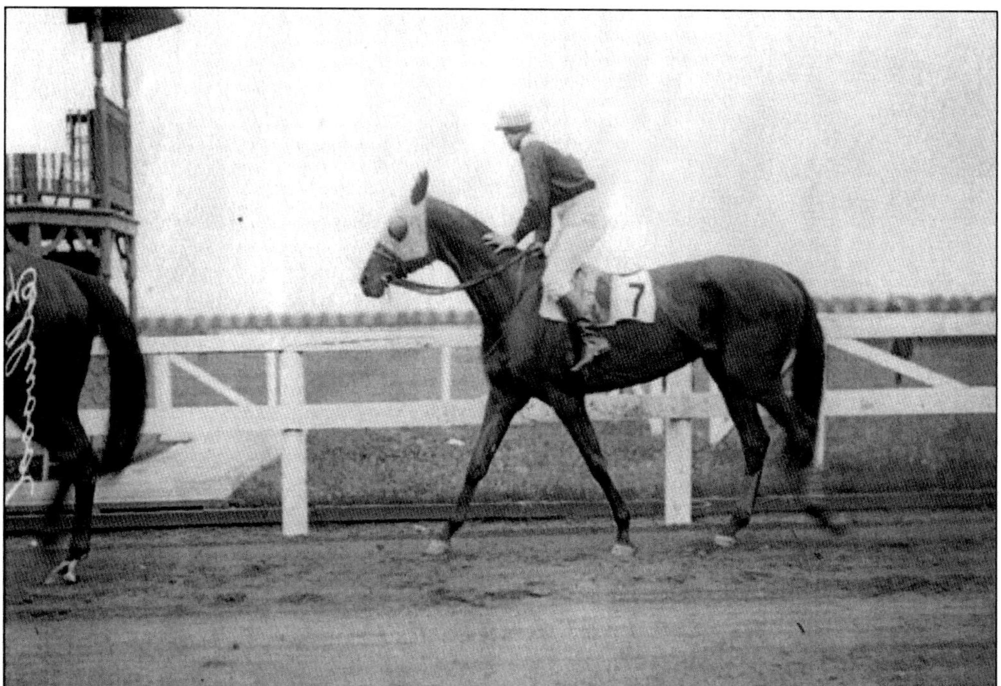

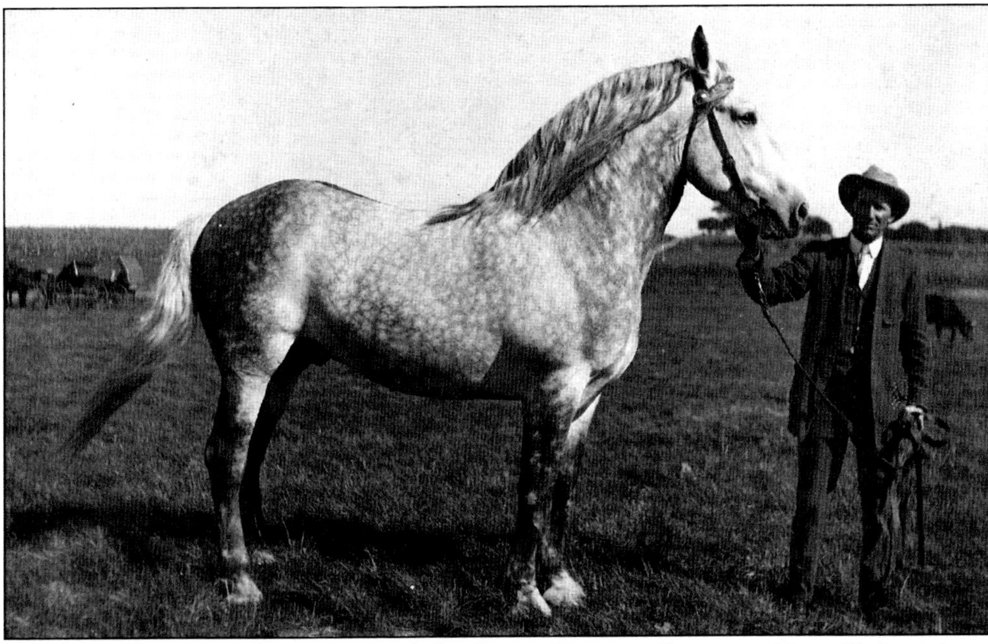

The legacy of James Prather was not only his famous Faustiana Farm near Maryville but interest throughout the county in finely bred horses. Price W. Calvert poses here with his prize stallion on his Bolckow Farm. Throughout the late 19th and early 20th centuries Nodaway County led the state not only in the quality of its stock but also in the quantity of production in horses, cattle, and hogs.

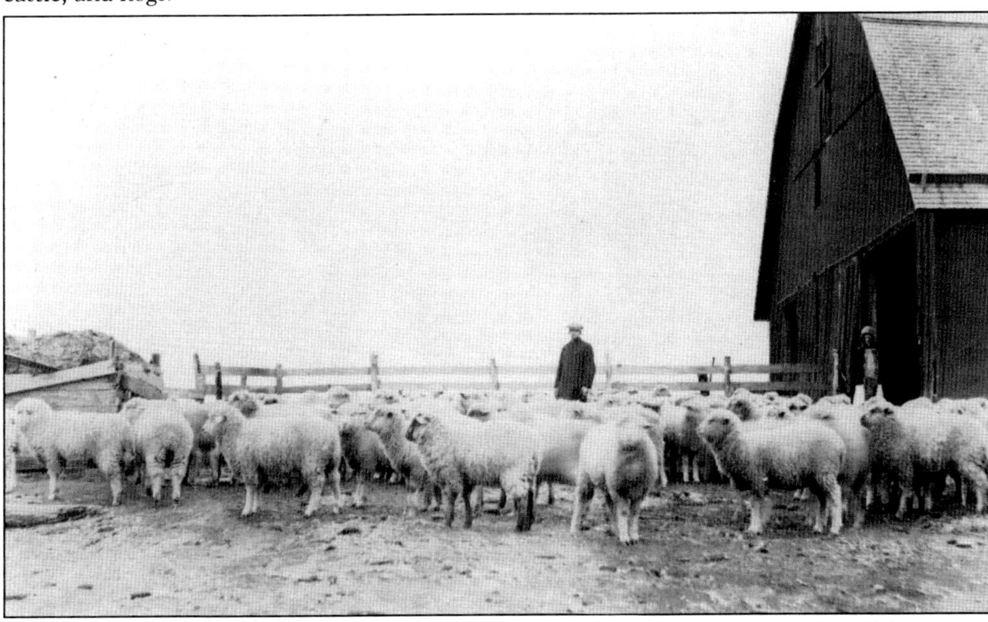

The migrants from Kentucky and Tennessee who served as the primary settlers of the county had much less interest in sheep. By 1902, of the 300,000 head of livestock bred in Nodaway County, only 5,000 were sheep. Like other herdsmen, those who raised sheep took great pride in the careful breeding and maintenance of their stock but likely at the cost of some sneering from their non-woolen neighbors. (Courtesy of Coby Lamb.)

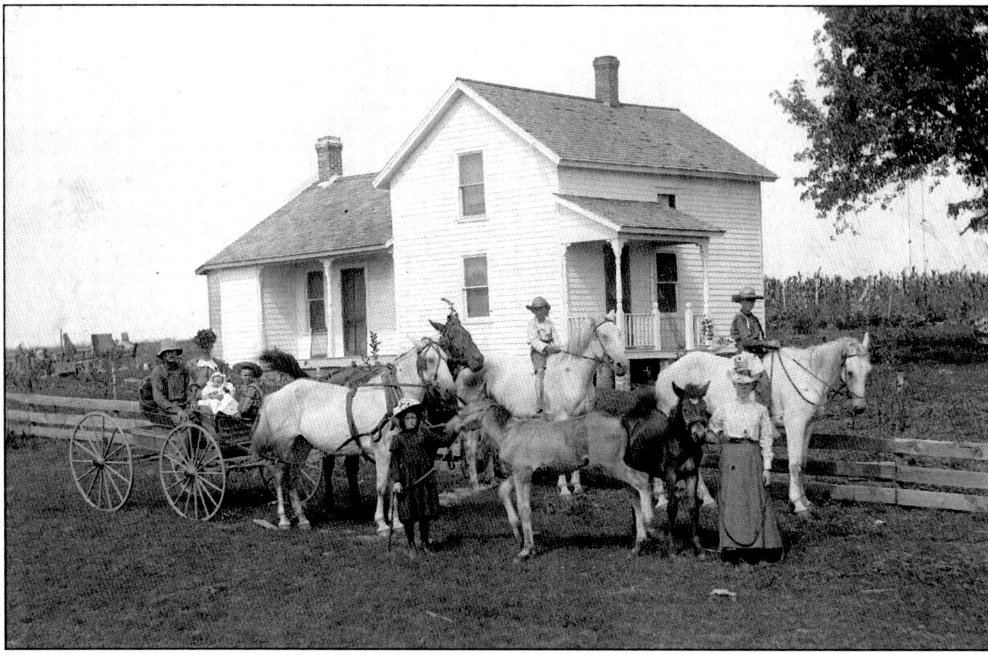

For many rural Americans a sense of prosperity often led to family portraits much like this one taken of a Hughes Township family. A freshly painted house and new hats for the ladies may have been the occasion for the family portrait that included the respectable buggy and fine animals in a celebration of success, which was repeated many times in front of similar farmsteads.

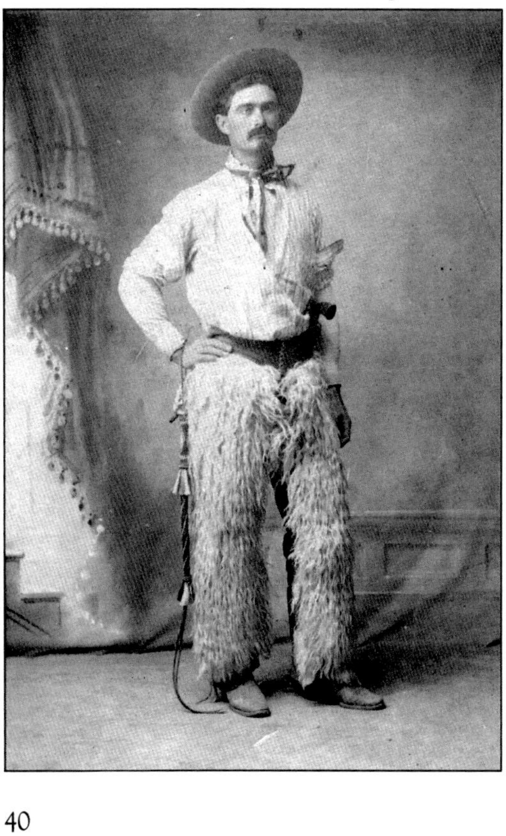

Land was still open enough through the last three decades of the 19th century for the men at the Bilby ranch to drive cattle from Omaha to Green Township to feed for a season and then ship on to Chicago. Roy Albright posed for the studio photographer in winter "woolie" chaps with his pistol tucked in the belt. His boots were modified from the army boots of Civil War issue and narrowed to fit his stirrups. His hat was likely a $5 Stetson "Boss of the Plains."

Three

Prosperity

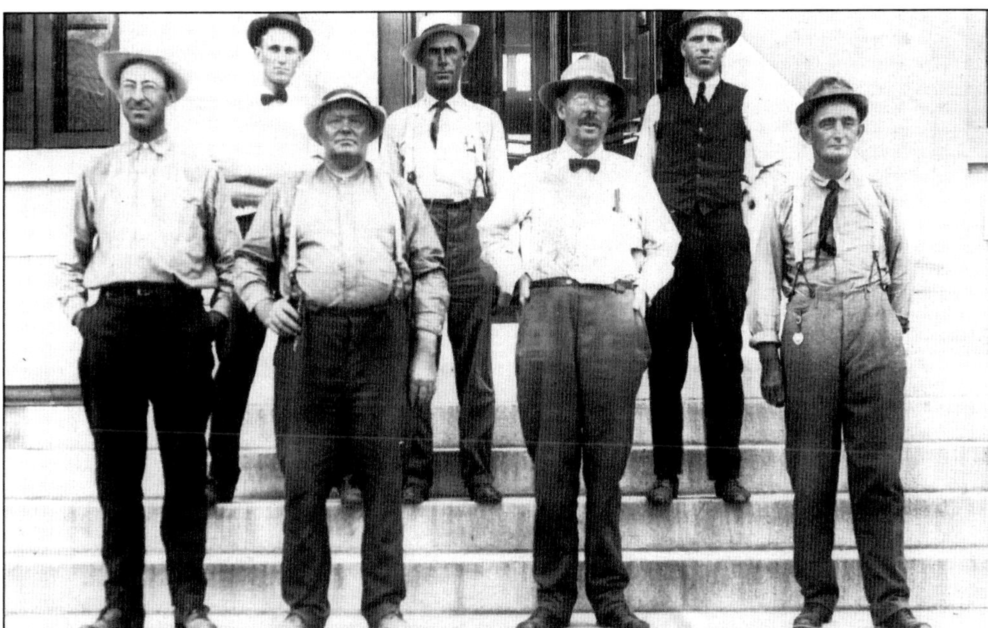

The most reliable link to the urban world for farmers was the rural mail carrier who brought them news by word of mouth, updates on construction in town, and a world of modern consumer goods. William Howard Watson (in the vest) is joined by the county's rural mail crew on the steps of the new Maryville Post Office. The front line of modernization, the first rural carriers delivered on horseback and wagon, but by 1910 they were switching to Ford automobiles. The linkages between the rural and urban economies were critical to prosperity, although the rewards were not always equitably shared.

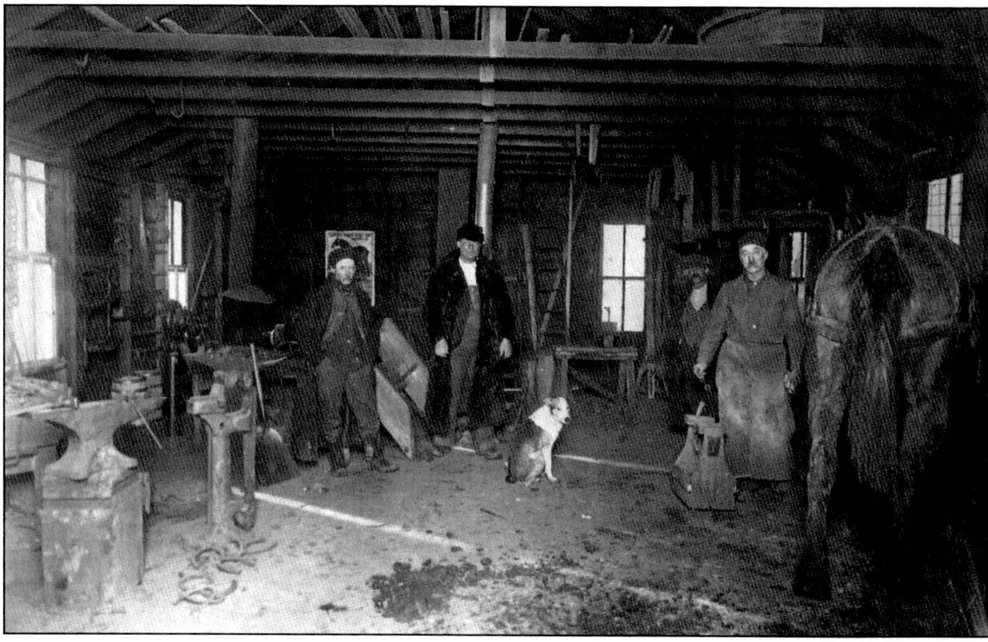

Paul Laipple, joined by Elmer Orme, John Sleep, and Elmer Beauchamp, takes a break on another day of hard work at Laipple's shop in Hopkins. Laipple moved to Hopkins from Bedford, Iowa, in 1905 and worked first with the Strawn Blacksmith Shop on South Third Street, and then he joined William French's shop before opening the shop shown here. (Courtesy of the Hopkins Historical Society.)

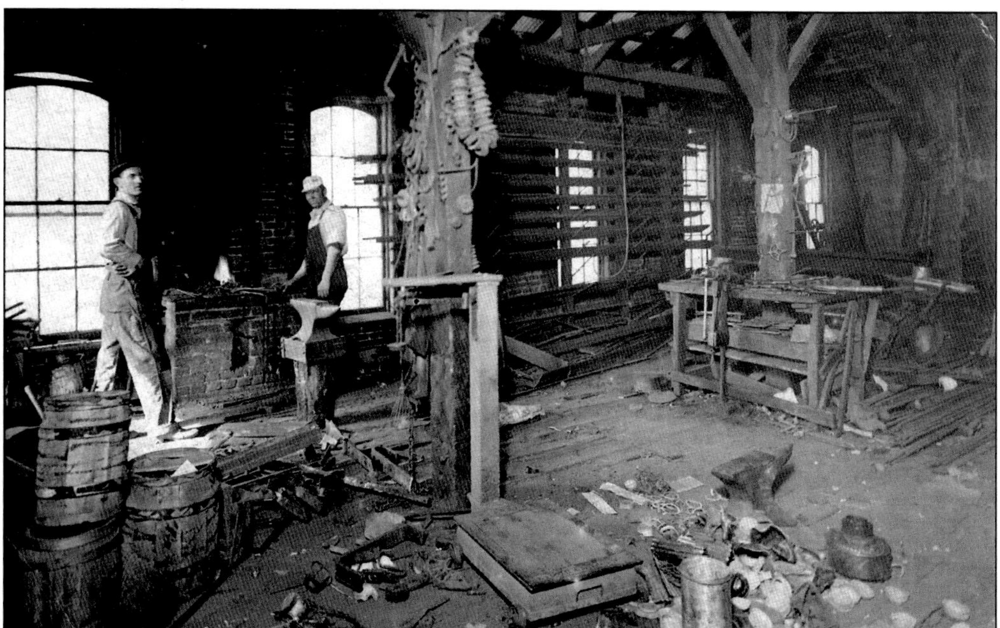

James A. Smith (in the white cap) works at the Armstrong Foundry in Maryville in 1910 using essentially the same tools and techniques that were used at the shop's founding in 1877. Owner William Armstrong inherited the foundry and machine shop from his father. It was located on Market Street between Fourth and Fifth Streets.

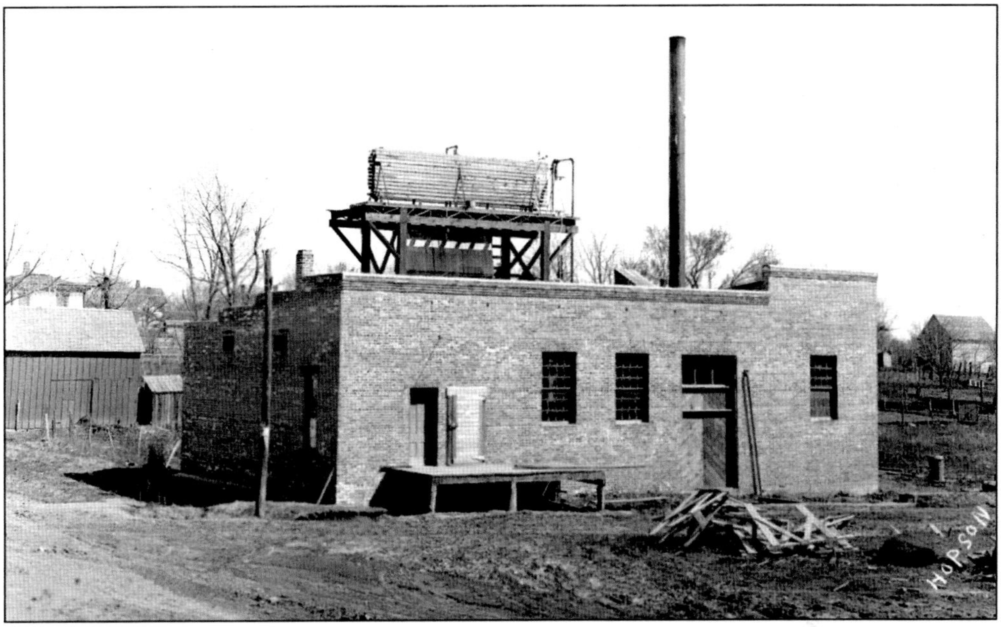

No longer dependent on storing winter pond ice in sawdust through the summer, providers of "artificial" ice proclaimed to skeptical consumers that the manufactured ice was purer and healthier. Rumors persisted among rural consumers, nonetheless, that pond and river ice was healthier. Lon Monk and a partner built the first ice plant in Burlington Junction, seen here in 1914.

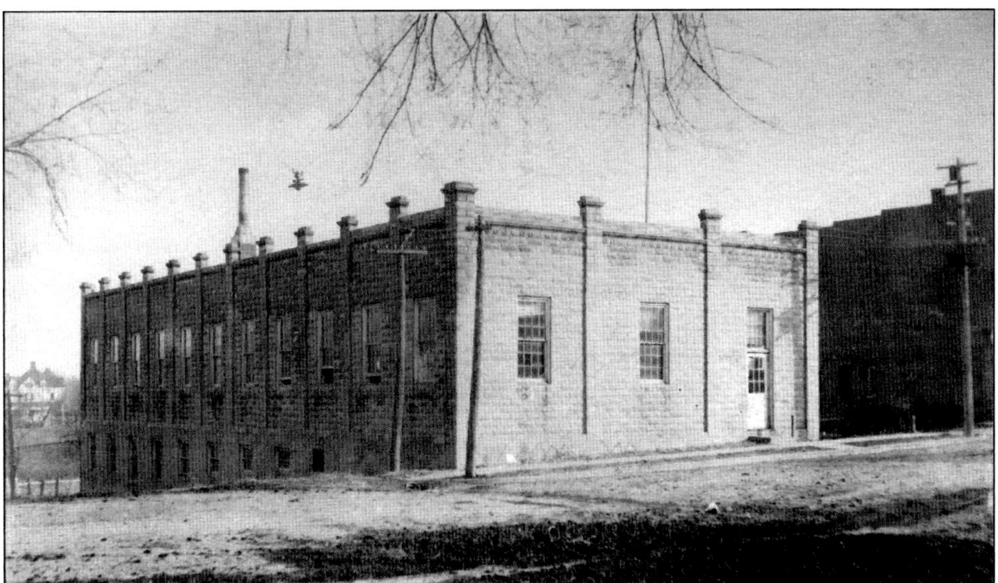

The McDonald Garment Company of St. Joseph located a manufacturing plant in Maryville in 1906. It is seen here two years later. The plant produced fine shirts for men under the brand names of Red Seal and Unicorn. The factory opened with 12 women working, and by 1912 it had 80 workers producing about 600 shirts per week. (Courtesy of Coby Lamb.)

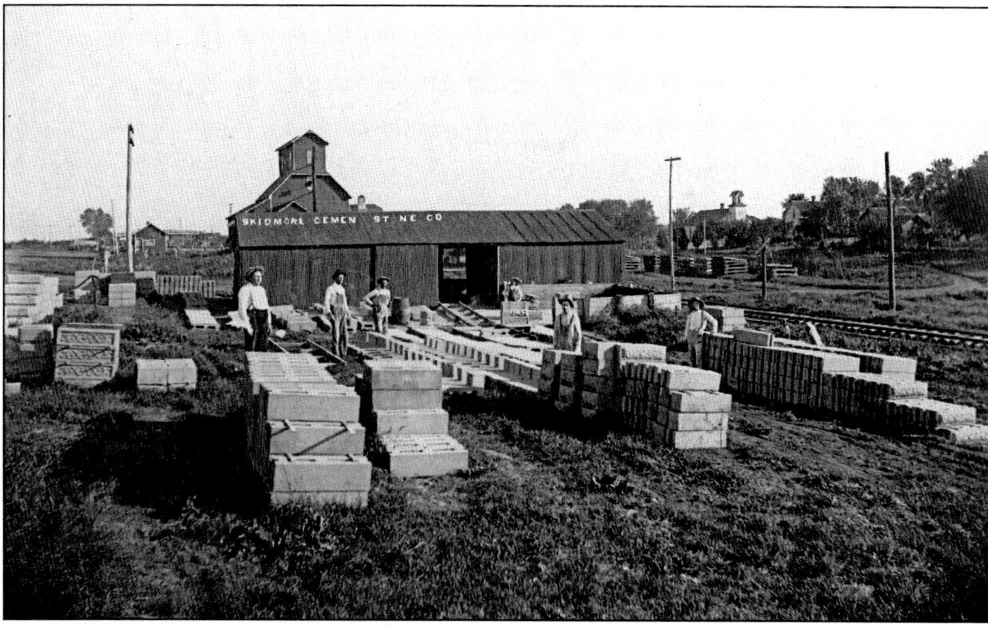

Walt Mitchell and Ed Strickler owned and operated this cement plant in Skidmore, seen here in 1905. Pictured from left to right are Mitchell, Jake Dawson, Strickler, Elmer Reese, and Charley Robbins. Among many other local jobs, the old boardwalks of Skidmore were replaced with concrete by the firm and the "M&S" mark was visible for decades in sidewalks that remained in good condition. (Courtesy of the Skidmore Museum.)

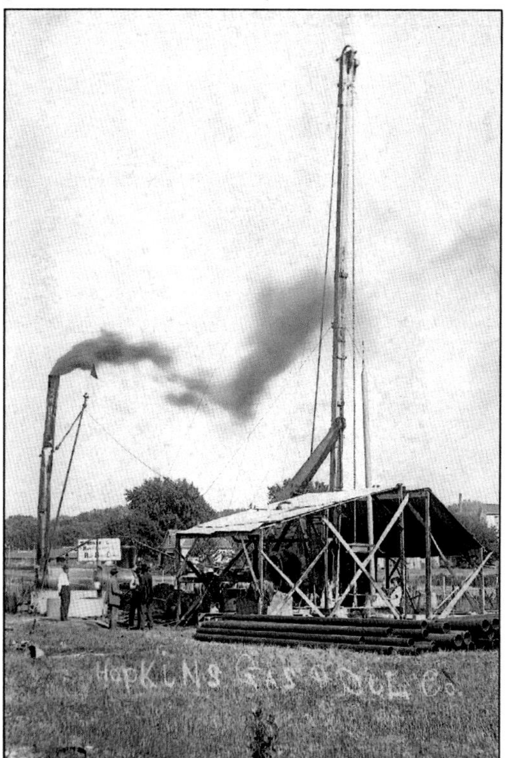

Residents of Hopkins were excited when Hopkins Gas and Oil struck a vein of coal about 60 inches thick at a depth of 920 feet, showing promise of gas reserves to fuel the town. (Courtesy of the Hopkins Historical Society.)

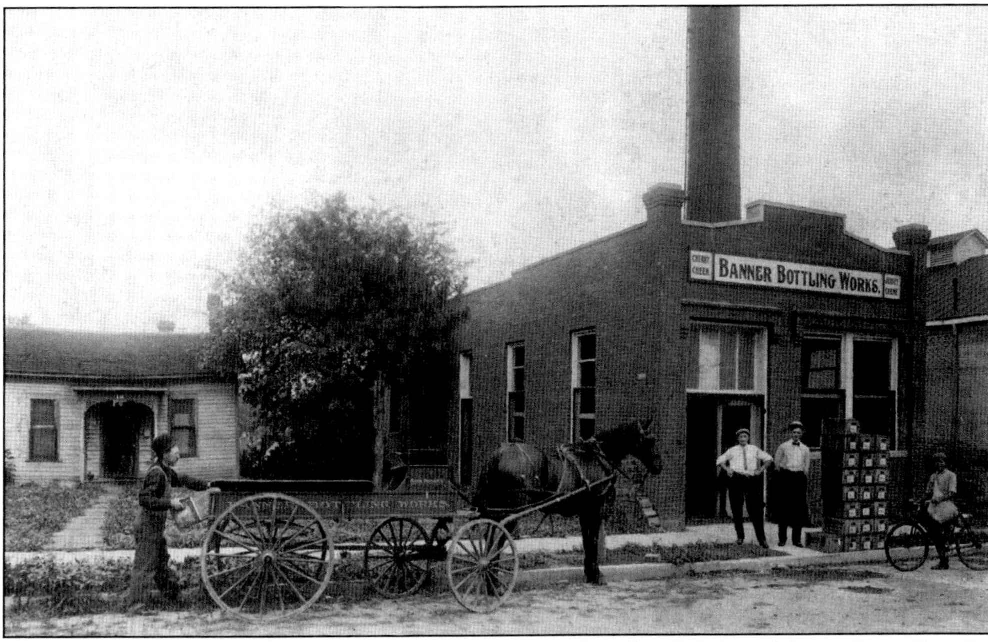

In 1910, L. C. and Henry Upschulte founded the Banner Bottling Works in Maryville and bottled a variety of beverages under several names, including those of the founders, local mascots, the company, and its flagship label, Gay Ola. The bottling ended in 1937, and Upschulte converted the facility into a tavern named the Palms, which is the name the establishment still bears.

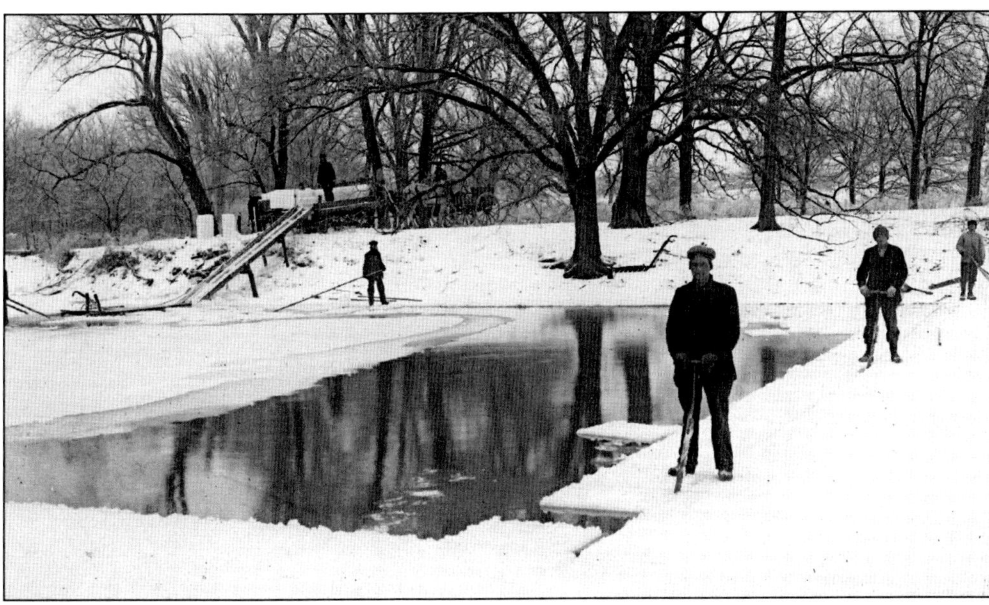

Without the luxury of an artificial ice plant, residents of Skidmore in the late 19th century purchased blocks of ice that were cut from ponds and packed in sawdust in icehouses. Cutting usually had to wait for January or February, when the ice neared a foot thick. Occasional labor was needed earlier to remove snow. Young men from the surrounding township usually took the work as a seasonal job when labor on the farm was slack and a little cash was appreciated. (Courtesy of the Skidmore Museum.)

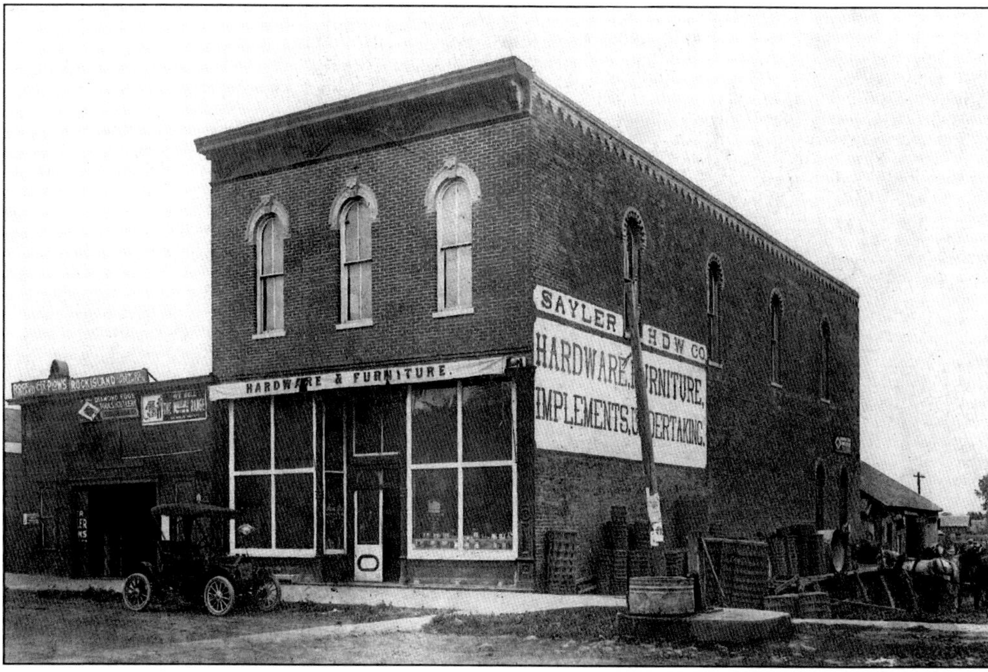

Ora Henry Sayler took over management of the hardware store when his father-in-law Stephen Wray passed away in 1901. The building, seen above in 1912, was erected by Dennis Jeffers for the hardware and undertaking business he shared with W. S. Frayne. A lover of the new automobile, Sayler bought one in 1916 that he converted into Hopkins's first automotive hearse. In 1920, he employed Roy Clark, who was educated in embalming, to run the funeral parlor on the second floor. Below, the crew from Sayler's Hardware shows off its current line of Rock Island farm implements on the streets of Hopkins. Sayler sold hardware, furniture, appliances, farm implements, and undertaking services until 1925 before selling to B. Wray Mahan, who moved the stock to Maryville in 1932. (Courtesy of the Hopkins Historical Society.)

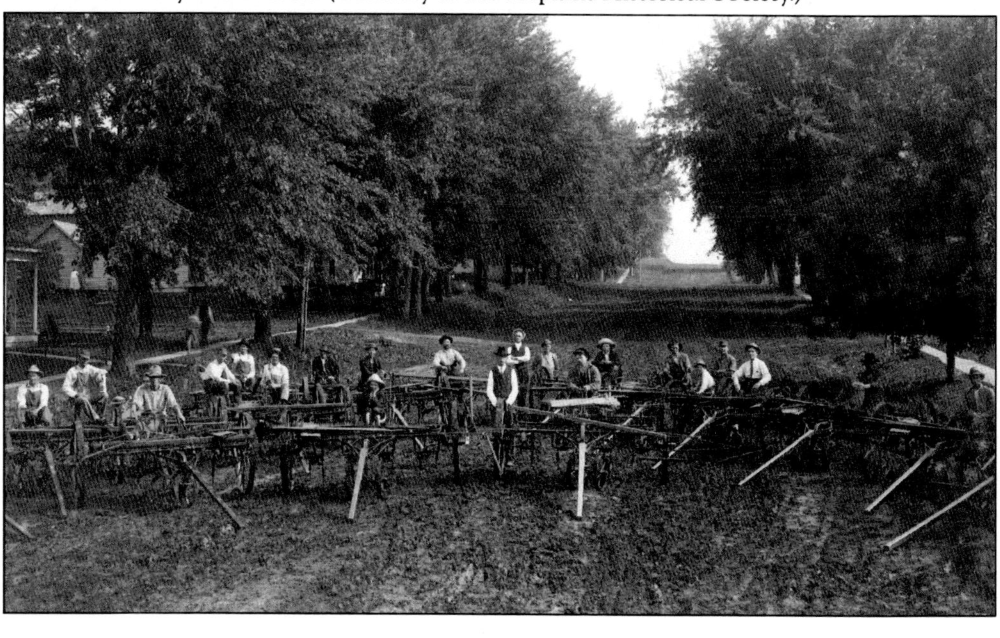

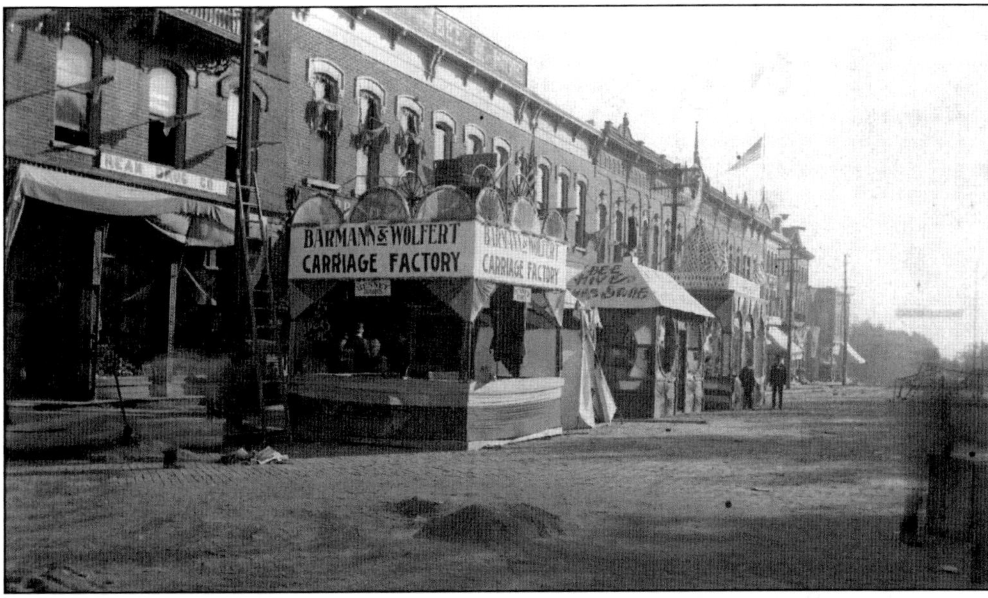

Among the firms advertising at the Maryville Street Fair, Barmann and Wolfert Carriage and Wagon Works boasted one of the more venerable positions. The firm opened a shop on North Main Street in the early 1890s and by the end of the century did most of the wagon work in town. While the street fair provided opportunity for local amusement, its elaborate booths represented fierce commercial competition between firms in a market that was already reducing the number of competitors.

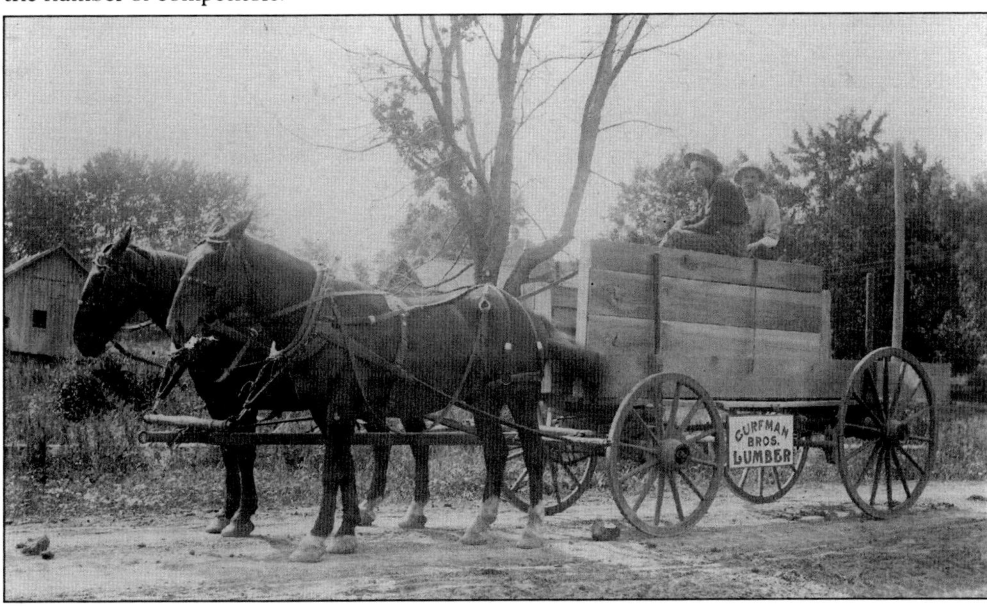

After working for years in area lumberyards, Edwin Curfman bought a yard of his own in Burlington Junction. Then with his brother Roy he bought out his former employer in Maryville and by 1910 had the largest lumberyard in the county. The Curfmans were also proud members of the International Concatenated Order of the Hoo-Hoo, a fraternal service organization of the lumber industry that mixed serious lobbying for the industry with a humorous parody of their numerous contemporary fraternal orders.

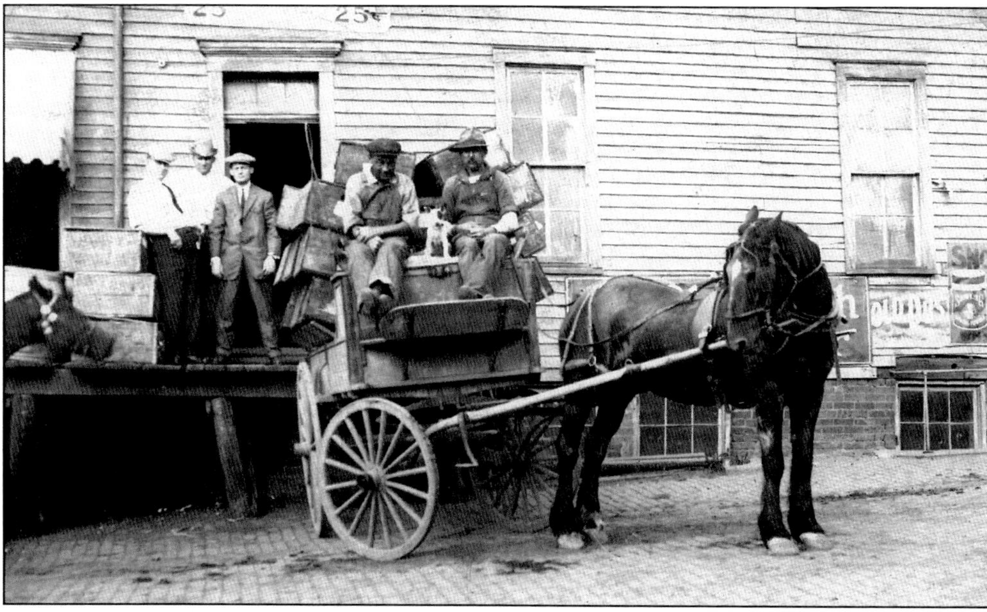

Joshua Sayster began a dray service from the railroad station in 1870, and well into the next century wagons brought consumer goods of all sorts to the general merchandise stores of Maryville. The buckboard wagon held advantage over most other vehicles for such service, but the brick paving under this fine rig rendered it increasingly obsolete as automobiles took over the job.

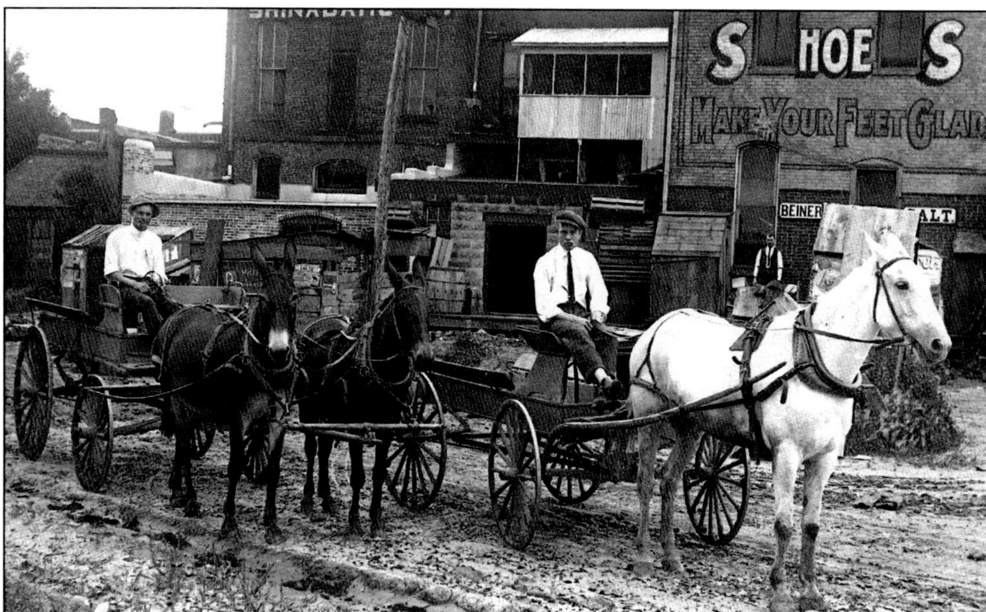

Charles "China" Wilson, at left, working for Kysar and Son Grocery, and Frank Bonham, working for W. G. Shinabargar, prepare to make the rounds in Hopkins. Grocery men still filled orders while patrons waited in the store or made regular deliveries. Seen here around 1912, Wilson's mule team soon faced competition from the Ford trucks and significant changes in the way customers were served. (Courtesy of the Hopkins Historical Society.)

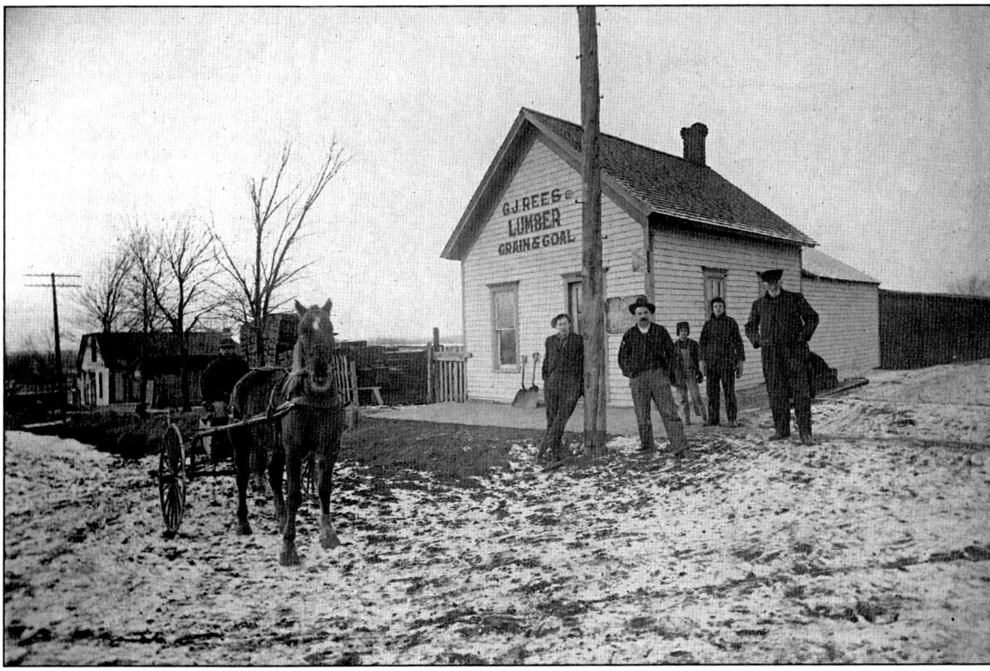

C. J. Rees, a Civil War veteran, purchased this lumberyard from Praisewater and McGee in the boomtown of Burlington Junction with his son Ed and helped to supply a community that continued to grow through the 1920s. (Courtesy of Skidmore Historical Museum.)

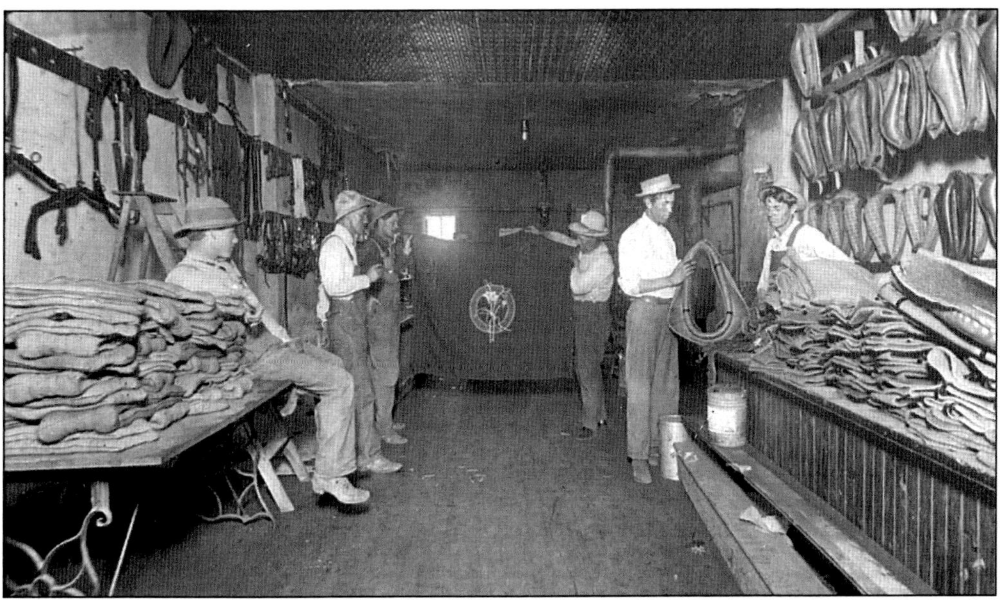

William Harrison Ralston moved his family from Brown County, Indiana, in 1883, settling first at Mount Pleasant in Gentry County and then moving eight more times around Gentry and Nodaway Counties. In 1908, he finally settled in Ravenwood, where he and his son Sie moved their harness shop. The shop is seen here about a year later. While harnesses were not the necessity they had been a decade earlier, harness makers continued to provide a vital service in rural communities at least through the 1930s. (Courtesy of Emily McLain.)

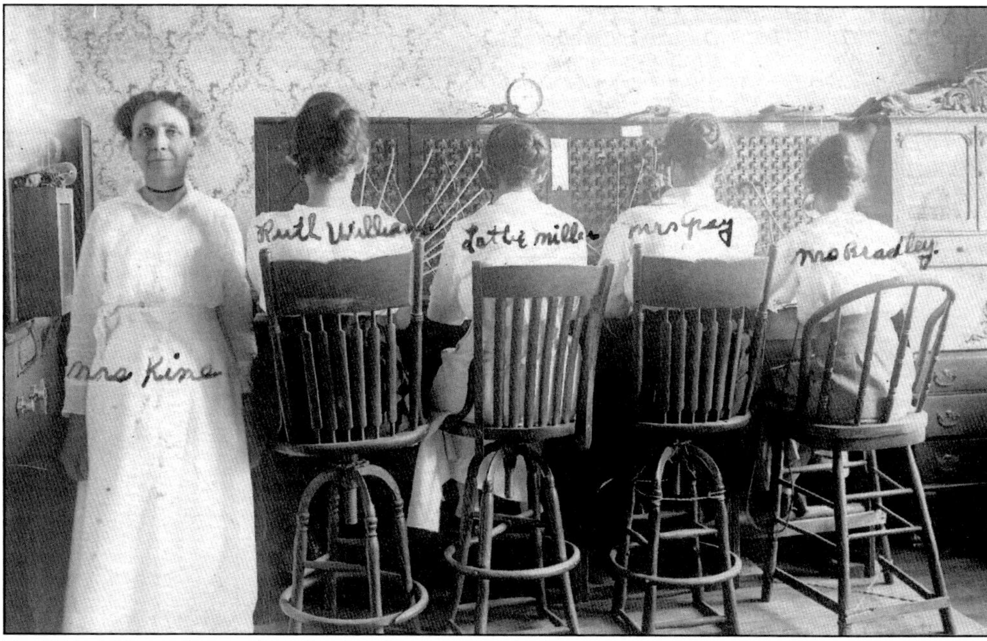

By 1918, 300 residents subscribed to Bowman's telephone service, which was served dutifully by Lettie Kime, Ruth Williams, Charlotte Miller, Temperance Gray, and Lela Bradley. Invented in 1877, the telephone exchange required operators to answer a subscriber's call and patch it through to the jack of the called party, if local, or to a trunk line that sent the call on to a long-distance operator.

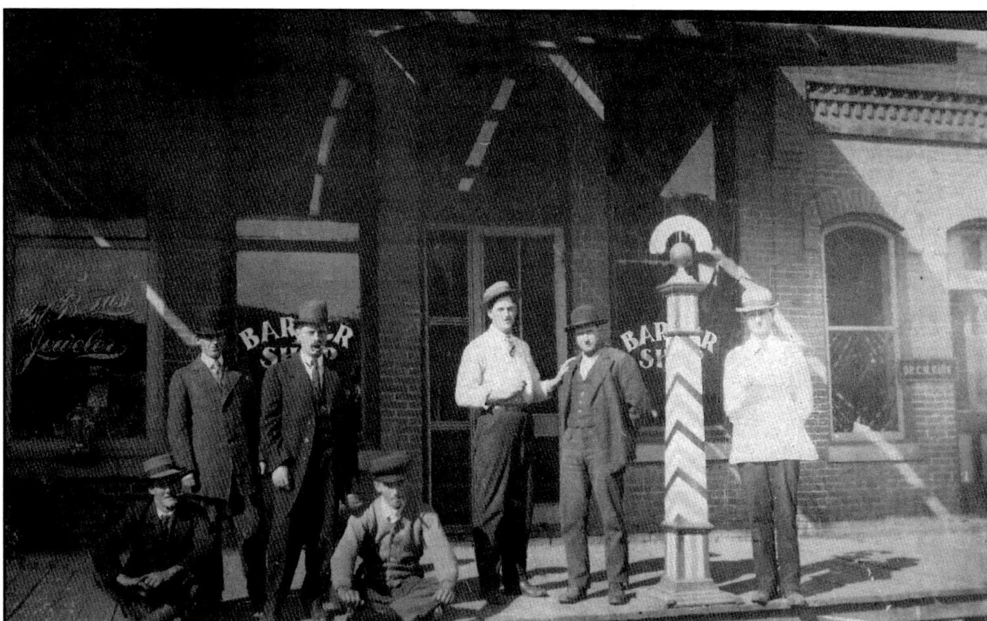

The barbershop was an essential service and meeting place in every community. This group of freshly trimmed gentlemen in 1906 moved out to the wooden walk in front of Charlie Broyles's barbershop in Hopkins for a photograph. (Courtesy of the Hopkins Historical Society.)

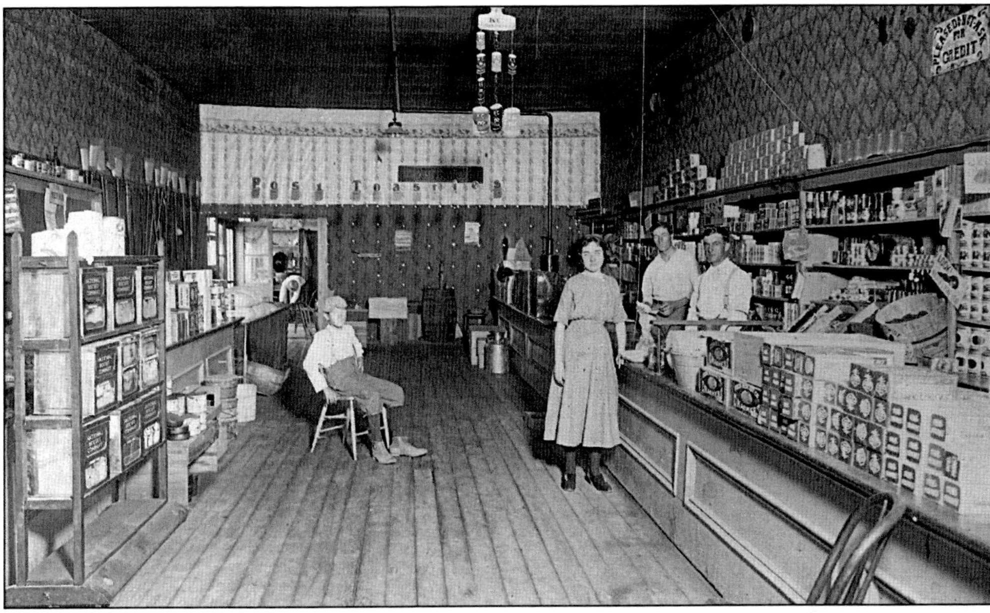

A mercantile store in Barnard provided the residents of Grant Township with early-20th-century food conveniences like Post Toasties, boxed crackers from the National Biscuit Company, and Jell-O, but unlike county merchants a generation before, they could not offer credit. In the chair is Dean Campbell, nearby is Flossie Haselwood, and behind the counter are Buzzy and Elmer Sell. (Courtesy of the Barnard Community Historical Society.)

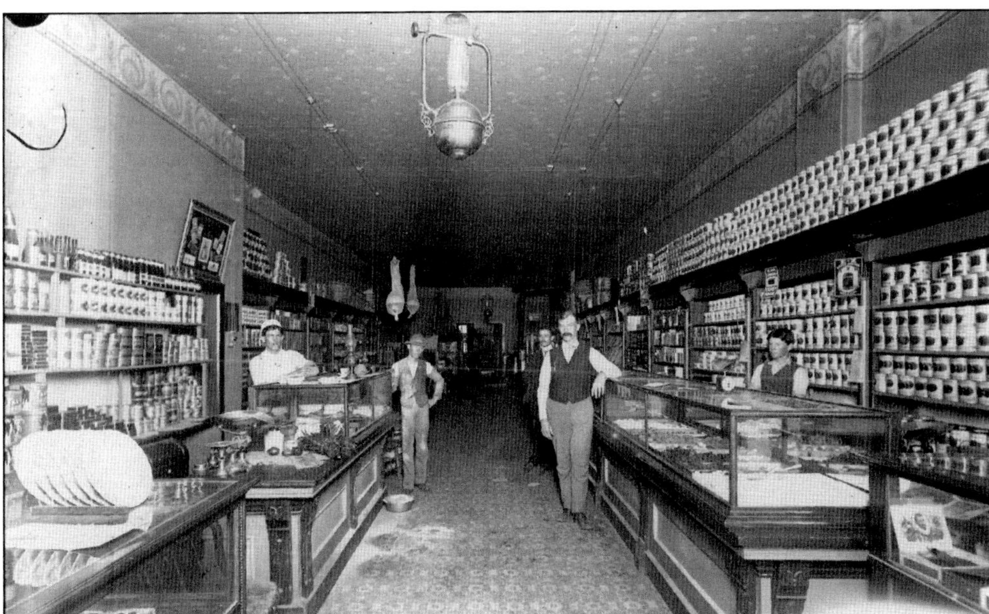

During the summer of 1900 the proprietors of Airy and Roseberry Grocers on West Third Street in Maryville display the array of brand-name goods that brought national marketing to local stores. Here ready to serve canned and fresh goods to customers are (from left to right) Arch Frank, Ed Thompson, J. B. Roseberry, J. W. Airy, and young Emery E. Airy, who grew up to become one of Maryville's most productive mayors.

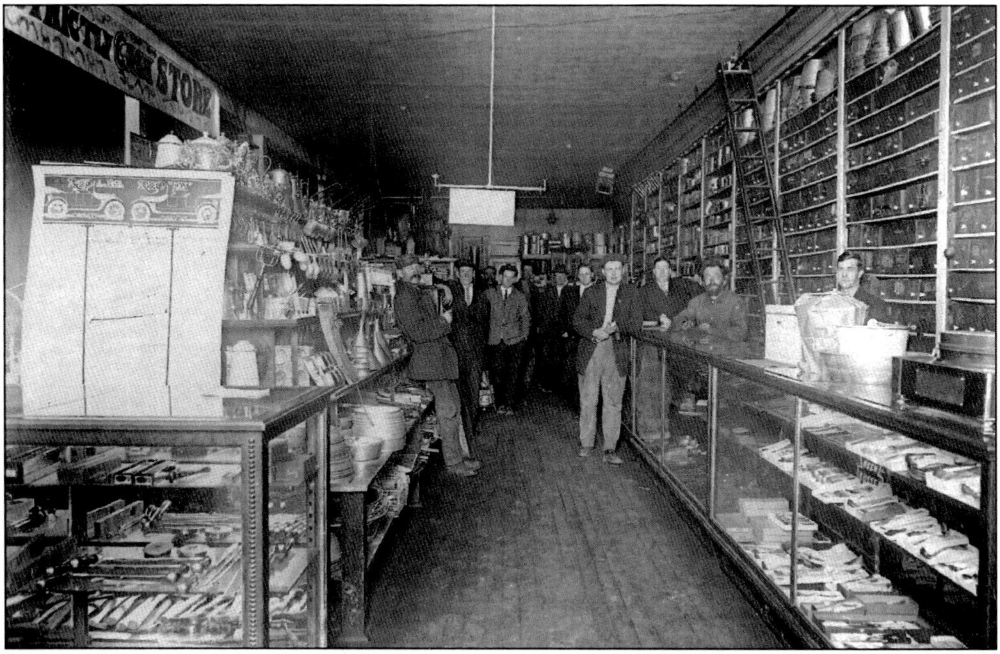

New products abounded in the well-stocked interior of the hardware and furniture store in Barnard owned by James Campbell and his son Lowell. While the Campbells were reportedly trusting and neighborly, the large sign on the left wall announces that theirs was a "strictly cash store."

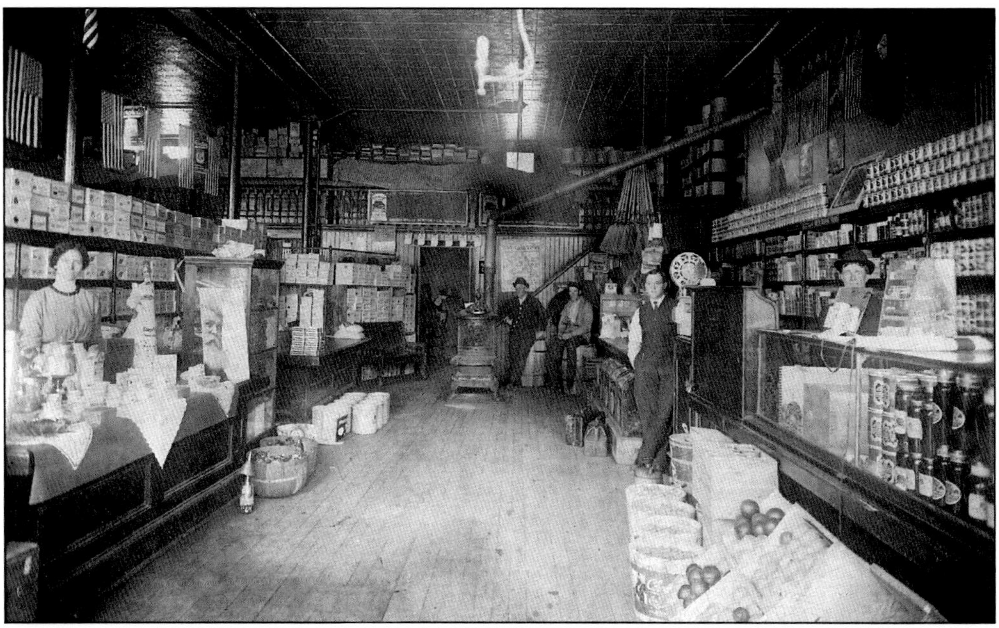

Six sons and one of three daughters of Edmund and Matilda Barrett moved from Pennsylvania to northwestern Missouri in the late 1870s in search of cheap farmland and opportunity. After first farming in Monroe Township, Henry T. Barrett opened this grocery and general merchandise store in Skidmore. He stands at the rear by the stove, and his son Frank Barrett is by the cash register. (Courtesy of the Skidmore Museum.)

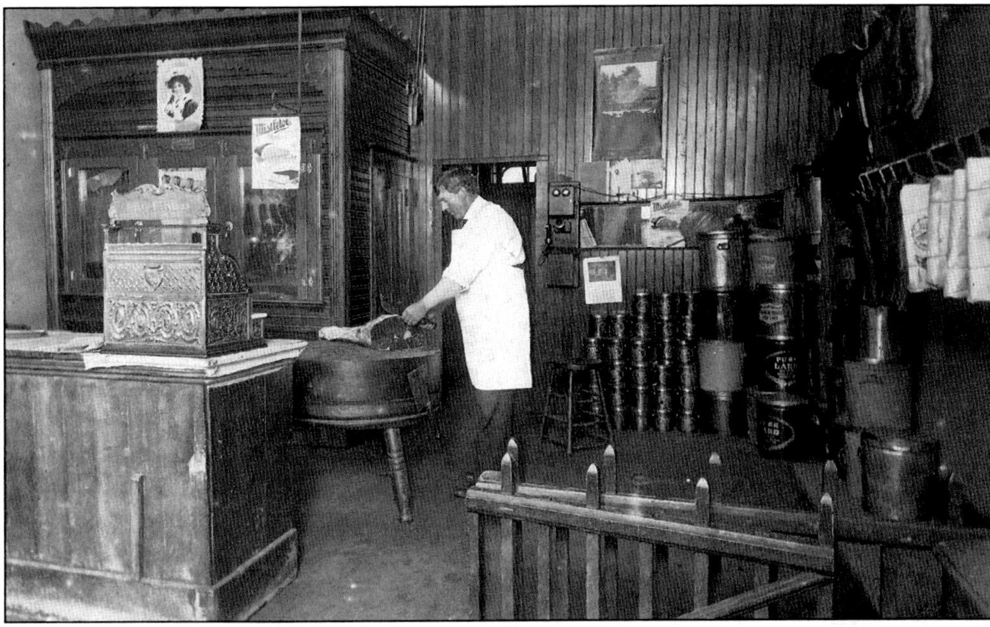

Frank Bloomfield works in the Parnell butcher shop owned by E. F. Klaas in 1897. A Western Electric box telephone stands ready for taking orders, and buckets of pure lard await purchase for local kitchens. Modern packing and refrigeration and demands for federal meat inspection (often by the large packing firms competing with Bloomfield) made business more difficult for local butchers in the decades that followed. (Courtesy of Emily McLain.)

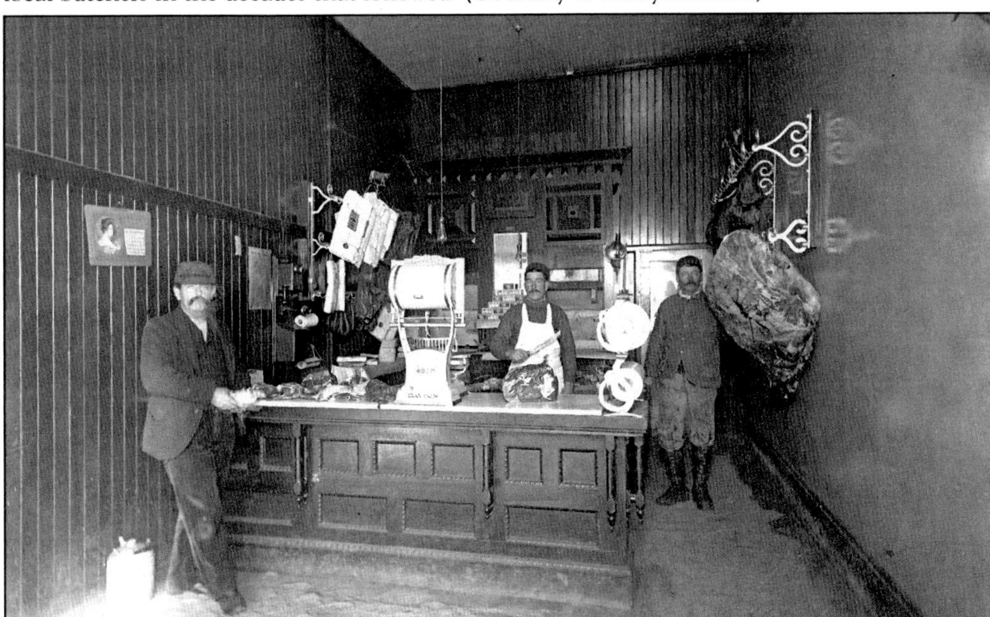

William R. Linville, born to Nodaway County pioneers in 1848, farmed in several locations in Monroe Township for over 20 years before settling in Skidmore. From there, he prospered in a variety of business enterprises, including land and livestock speculation, commercial real estate, and ownership of the Bank of Skidmore and a meat shop, likely the one pictured here in the 1890s. (Courtesy of the Skidmore Museum.)

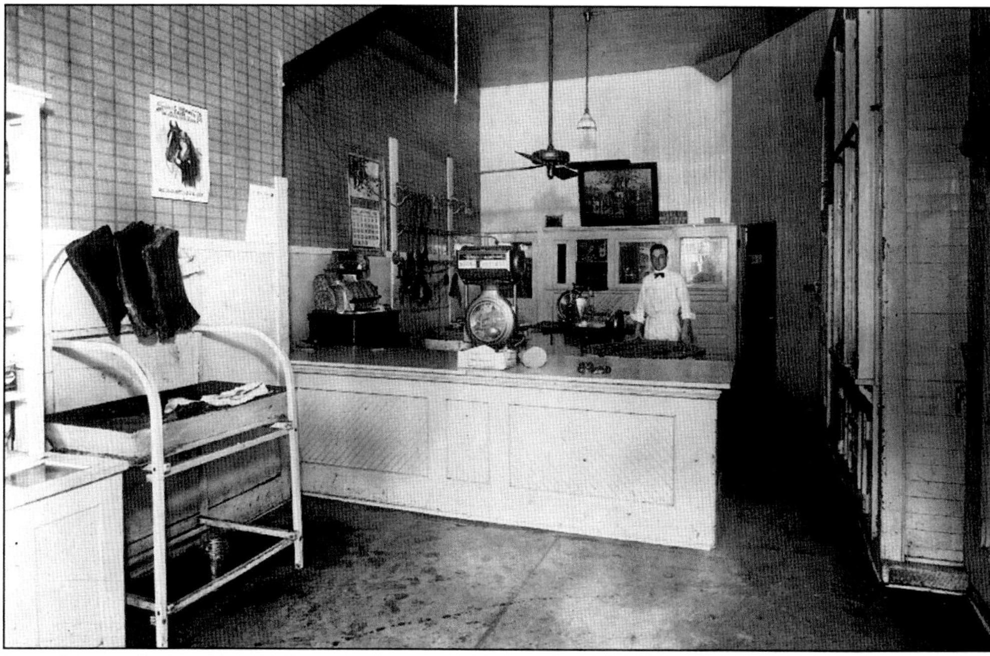

June brings the problems of warm weather and raw meat for a Maryville butcher shop in the summer of 1915. On the wall hangs a banner for the Nodaway County Fair and Agricultural Association, and on the counter sits a Toledo Electric Scale with its trademark slogan "No Springs, Honest Weight."

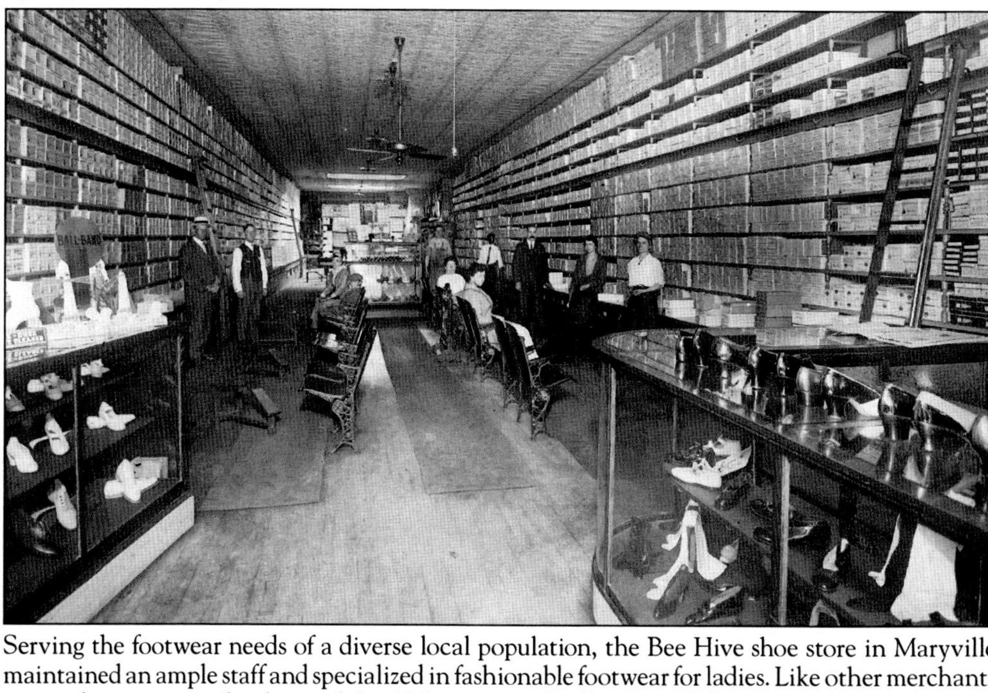

Serving the footwear needs of a diverse local population, the Bee Hive shoe store in Maryville maintained an ample staff and specialized in fashionable footwear for ladies. Like other merchants across the county at the dawn of the 20th century, the Bee Hive fed a growing demand among rural consumers for ready-made brand goods. Its stiffest competition came from the catalogs of Montgomery Ward and Sears.

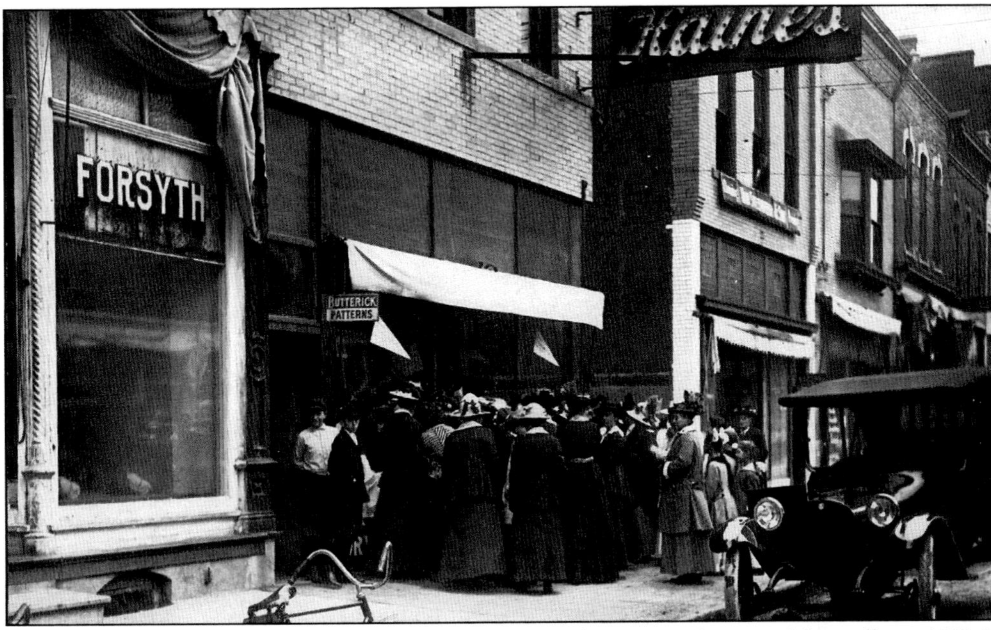

Ladies rush the door for the third anniversary sale at the Haines Store in Maryville in 1917. It carried the latest in brand goods for ladies, and the *Maryville Daily Tribune* announced that the store's stock was "from a maker of quality goods, as instanced by Phoenix and Radenoor hosiery, the guaranteed kind, the dependable, rust proof, service giving Gossard corsets, a leader the world over; Globe tailored underwear, non-shrinkable and form fitting."

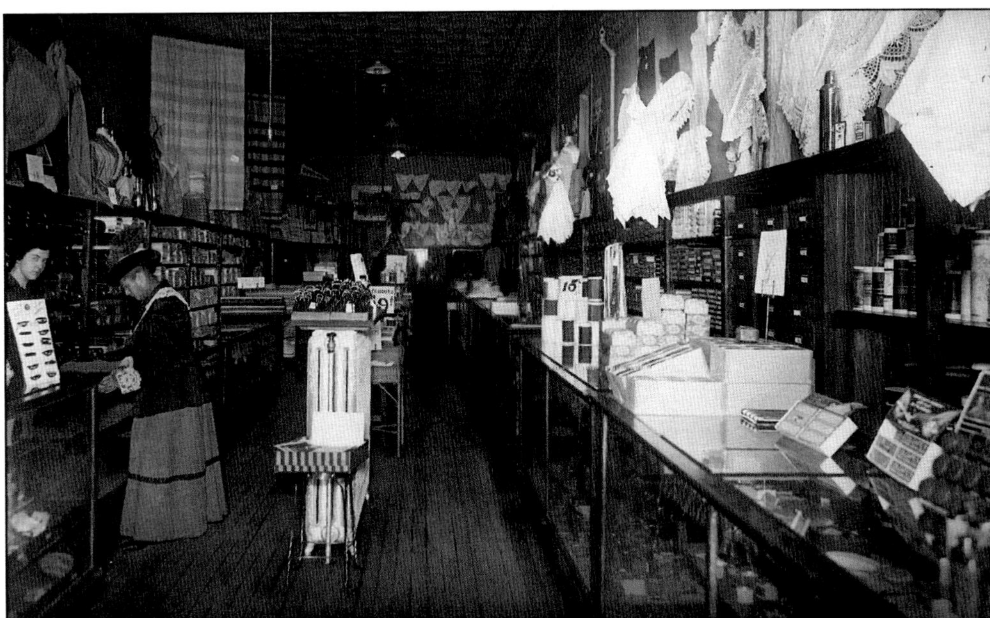

Anna Dougan tends to a customer in the new Haines Store in 1914. In addition to the demands of local women, the arrival of the normal school and the Maryville Business College promoted a steady trade in goods and accessories for women. Upstairs women could find a full selection of undergarments and overcoats.

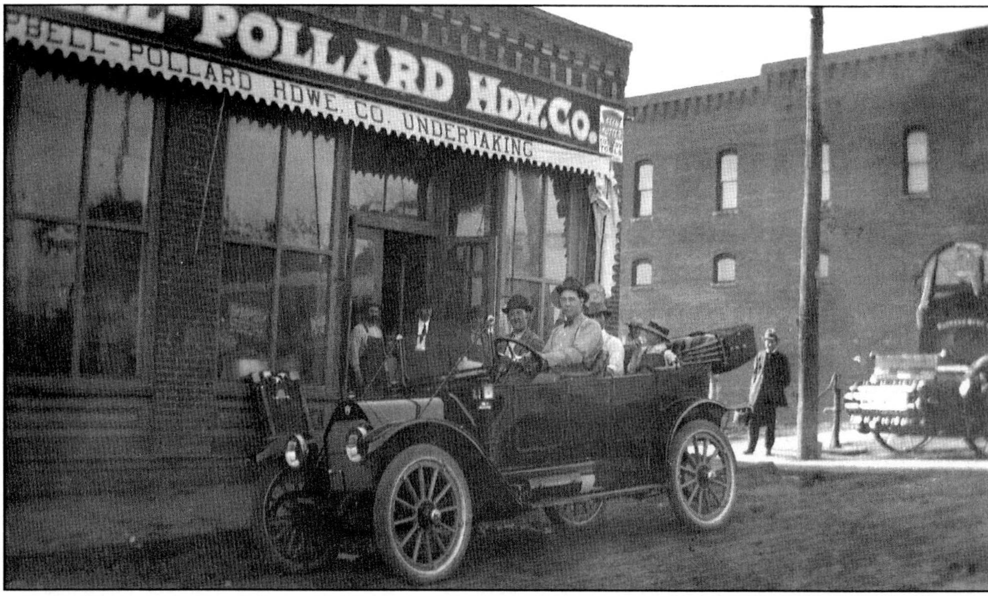

Lowell Campbell, the son of prosperous Barnard hardware businessman James Campbell, turned heads in town with his shiny, new Ford Model T. Lowell bought a garage from Earl McLeave in the early 1920s from which he built his own career and became one of the county's prominent citizens. Like those in other towns, the hardware stores in Barnard provided a wide range of products and services, including undertaking, which in most Nodaway County towns was not conducted as a separate business.

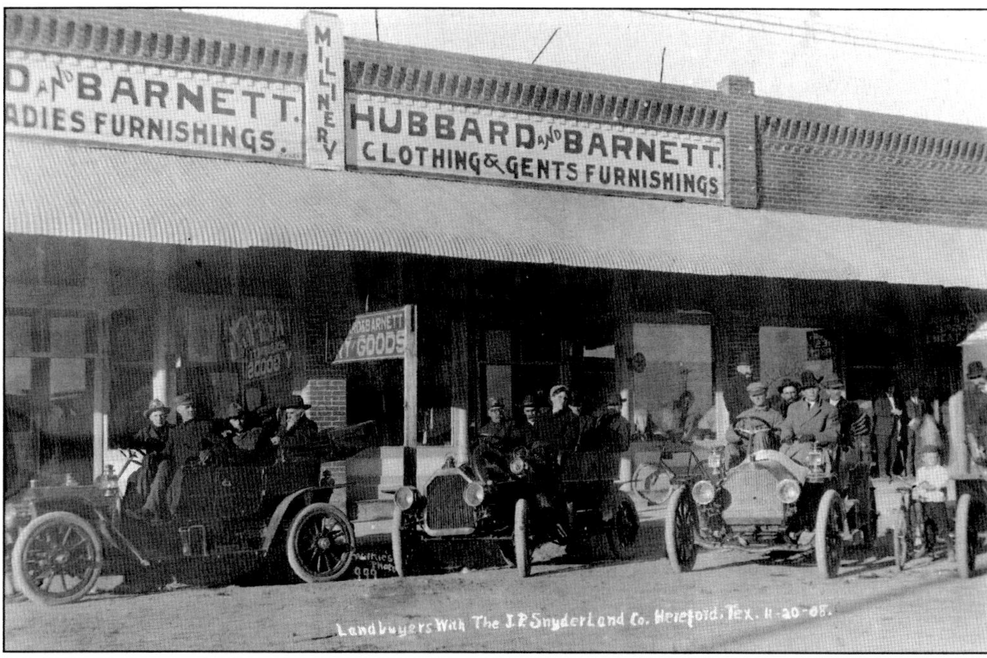

By about 1900 Nodaway County was a commercial success and demand for real estate in the county drove up land prices, fueling speculation. George Hamilton and company are pictured here in January 1908 in the town of Elmo with land buyers from the J. P. Snyder Land Company of Hereford, Texas.

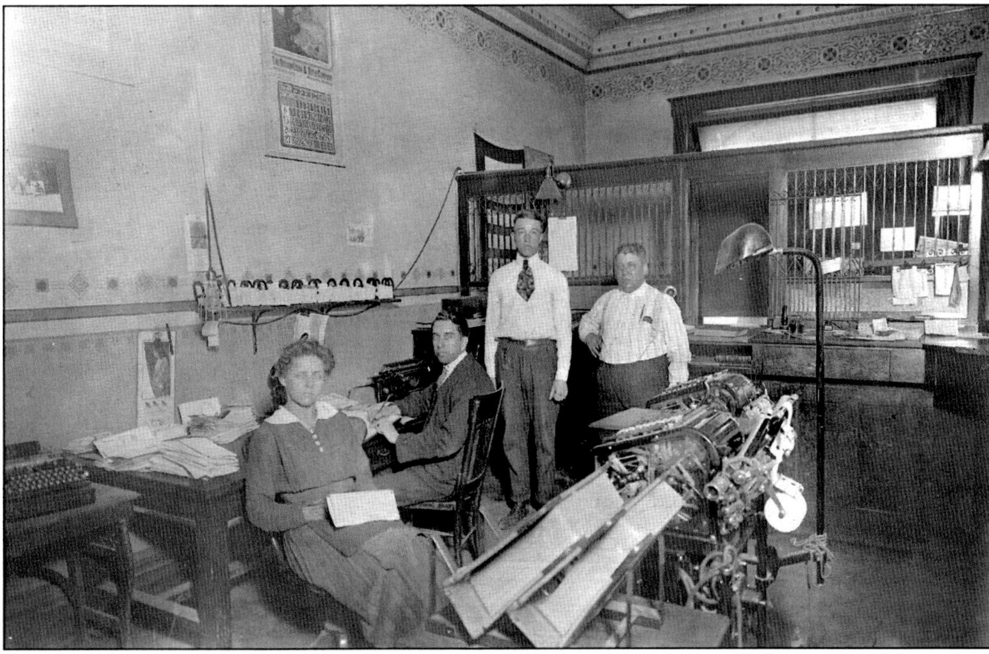

The Barnard State Bank was organized in 1892. By 1910, it held deposits of over $150,000 and was doing healthy business in 1919 at the time this photograph was taken. Pictured from left to right are Anna Matheny Thompson, Clay Burns, P. D. Stalling, and head cashier John Fields managing the accounts.

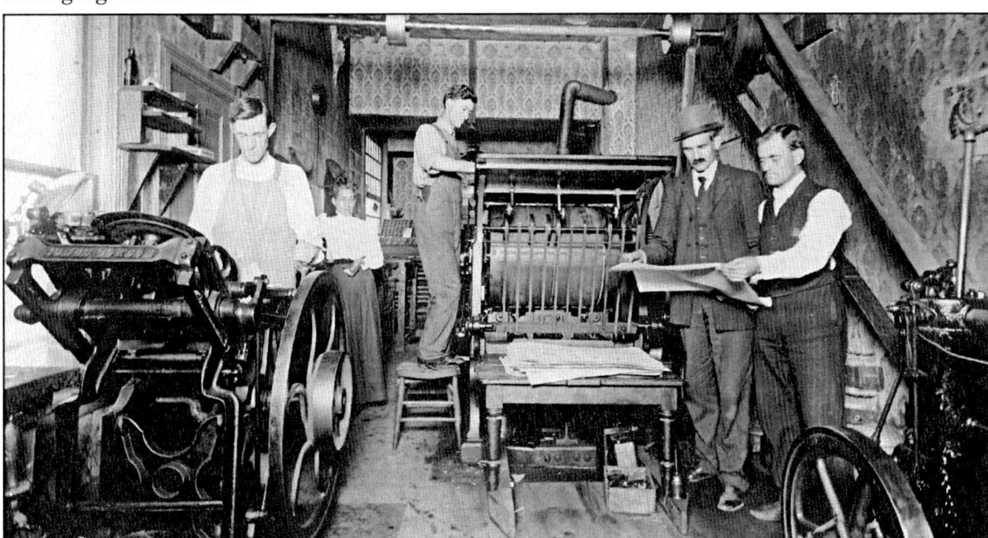

The staff of the *Skidmore New Era* poses with its presses in 1908. Ellwood Barrett stands near the large gas-powered cylinder press on the right, and Claude Stults is near the small press. Others on the staff included Mrs. Dan Baker, Ray Strickler, and Dan R. Baker (with moustache). Born in Nodaway County during the Civil War, Dan Baker taught school for many years and served as principal of the Elmo School. After a stint as an accountant with a lumber company in St. Louis, Baker purchased the Democratic-leaning *Skidmore New Era*. (Courtesy of the Skidmore Museum.)

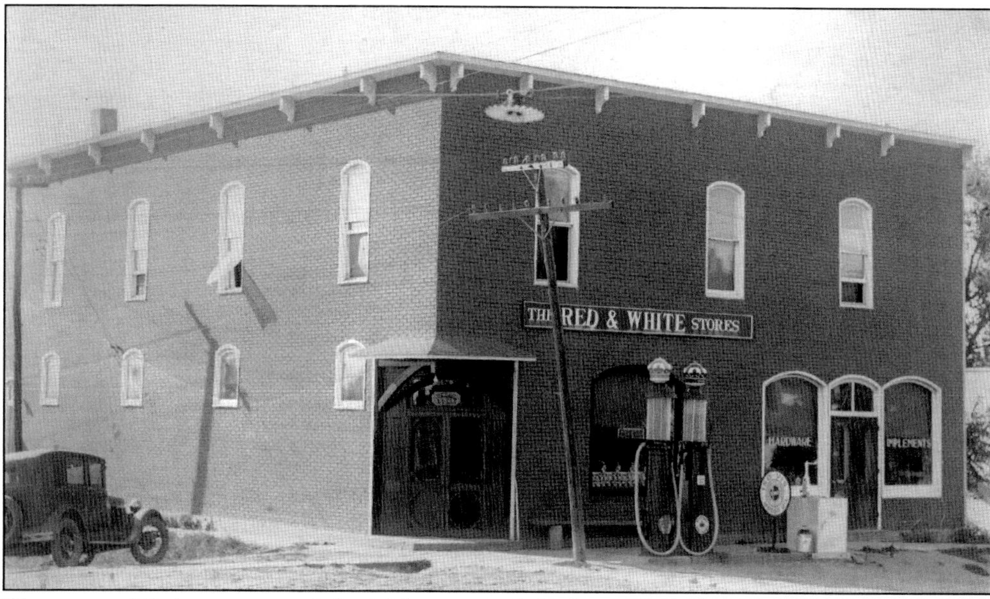

The town of Quitman entered the 20th century full of commercial potential, which was based heavily on the cattle empire built near the town by John Sliker Bilby and traffic on the Burlington line. But like others towns, the population after 1910 began to decline. Commerce held on, as attested to by the C. E. McDonald's Community Cash Store in Quitman about 1930. The store was part of the Red and White "no-frills" grocery franchise and served the inexpensive Red and White brand goods almost exclusively. The interior of the Community Cash Store testifies to the immense value of commercially canned and boxed goods to rural consumers by the late 1920s. The irony for merchants in the smallest towns was that such conveniences were also making these small commercial centers obsolete. Goods purchased on driving trips to larger towns could be purchased in bulk and used much later.

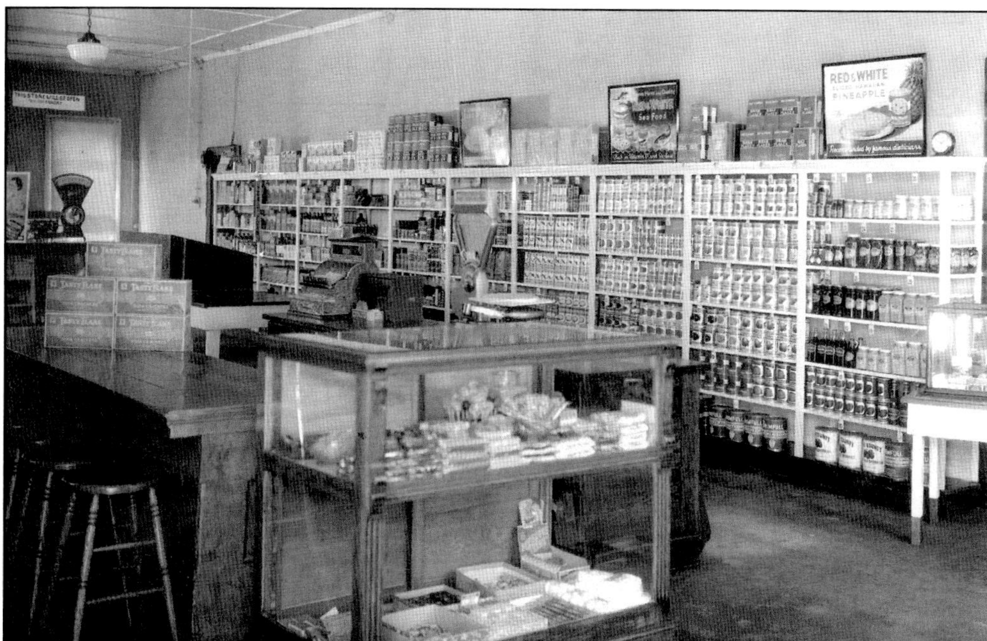

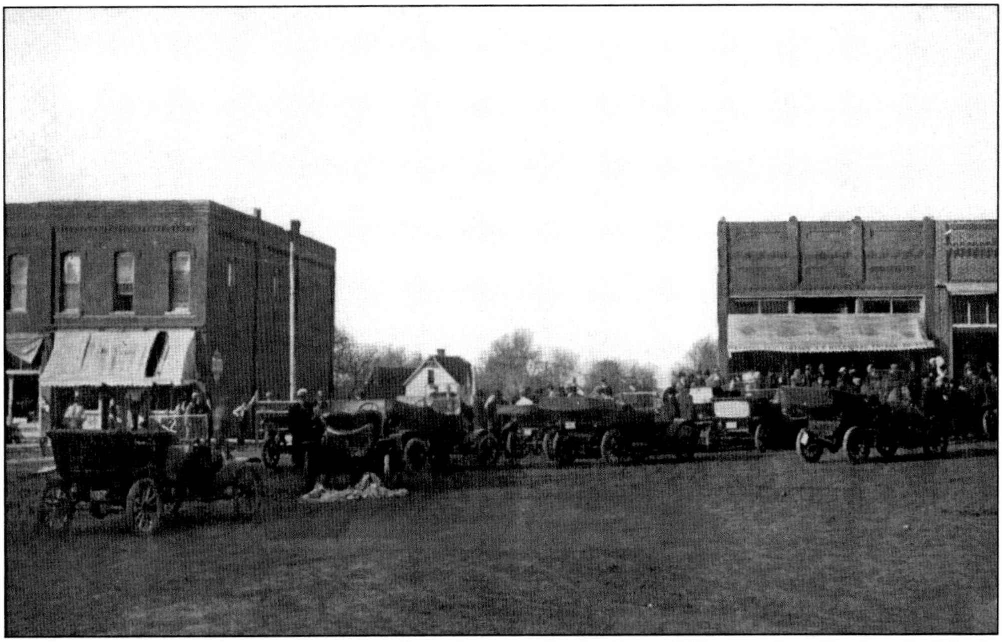

Parnell was born as a water stop on the Chicago, St. Paul, and Kansas City Railroad's Maple Leaf line and like many others saw its fortunes decline with the proliferation of the automobile. Automobiles are clogging the intersection of Main and Grand Streets about 1915, where a gathering assembles in front of A. F. Hall's general store. (Courtesy of Emily McLain.)

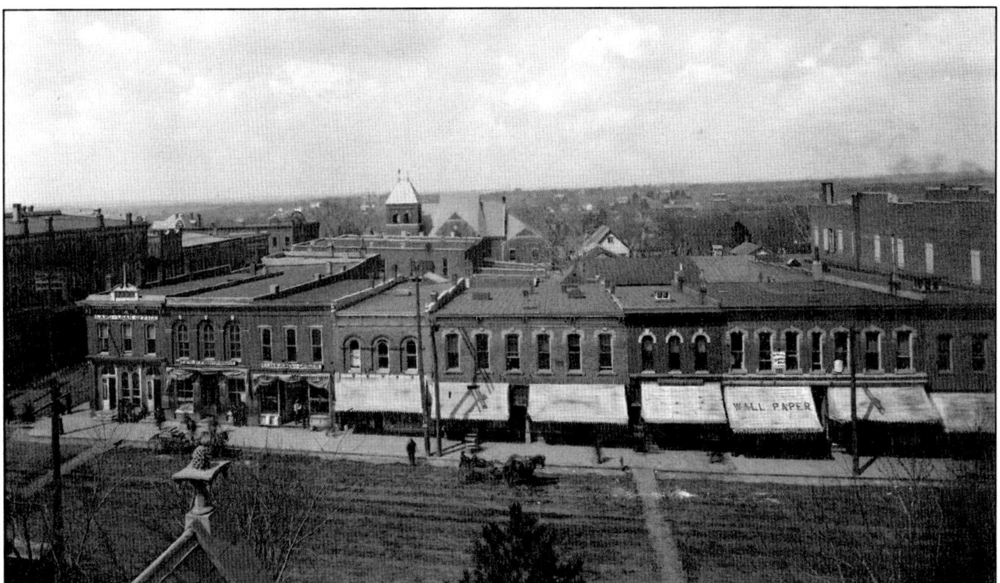

The explosion of commercial activity that followed the arrival of the railroads began in the mid-1870s, and by the mid-1880s full brick commercial blocks appeared seemingly overnight. By the time of this photograph in the early 1890s, Maryville's commercial center boasted an impressive array of brick commercial houses. The photographer may have taken his perch high in the courthouse building to get a shot to the west of the impressive new Christian Church raised above the houses of commerce.

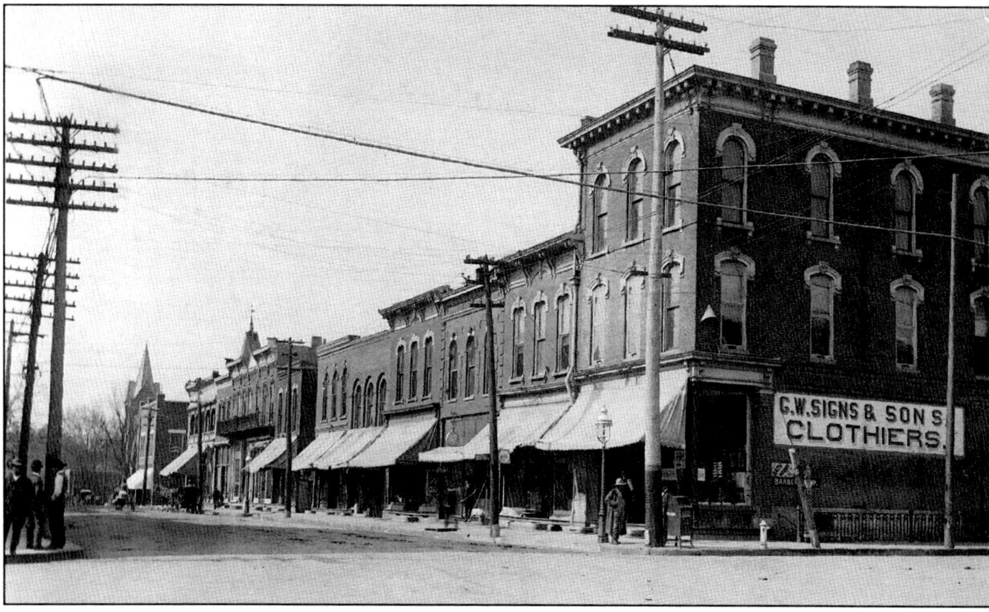

The Smith brothers building anchored the corner of Third and Main Streets in Maryville with C. W. Signs and Sons clothing store at street level. Plate glass allowed businesses in the late 19th century to display consumer goods and create inviting entrances but required awnings to shade buildings that were cooled only by belt-driven ceiling fans. (Courtesy of Coby Lamb.)

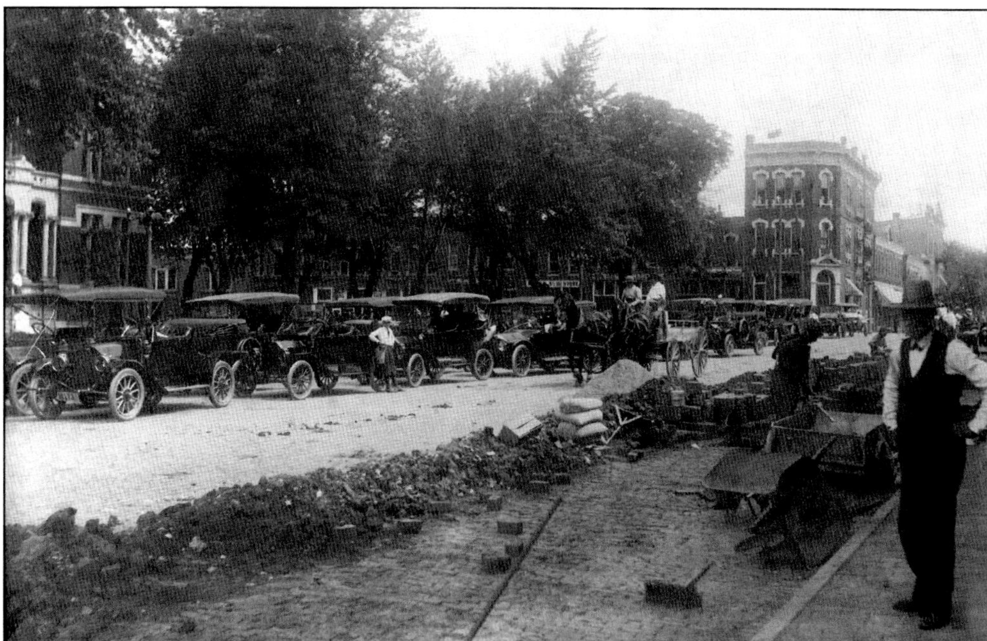

Among the more significant signs of prosperity in town were brick streets, although hard paving in the age of horses presented its own problems. F. G. Shoemaker of Maryville outbid contractors from Kansas City and St. Joseph with the contract to brick the streets around the square beginning in August 1892. In 1915, workers had to remove and then replace brickwork following the improvement of sewer lines.

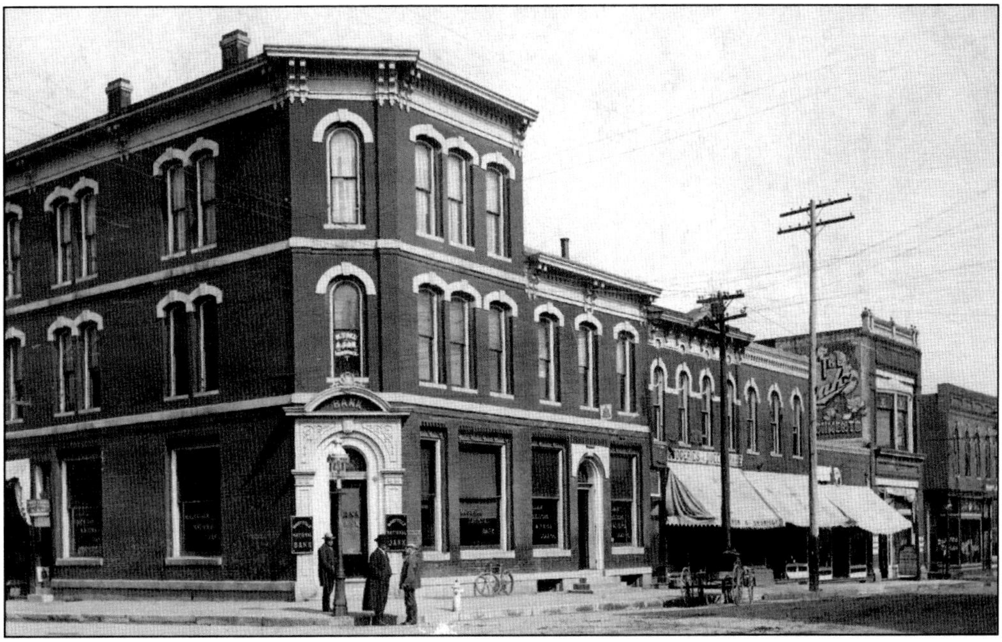

The Maryville National Bank, on the corner of Fourth and Main Streets, was one of four banks that anchored street corners on the square. Maryville National Bank competed for investment capital with the Nodaway Valley Bank, First National Bank, and the Real Estate Bank of Maryville. Twenty-two other banks, located in other towns, served Nodaway County customers at the end of the 19th century. (Courtesy of Coby Lamb.)

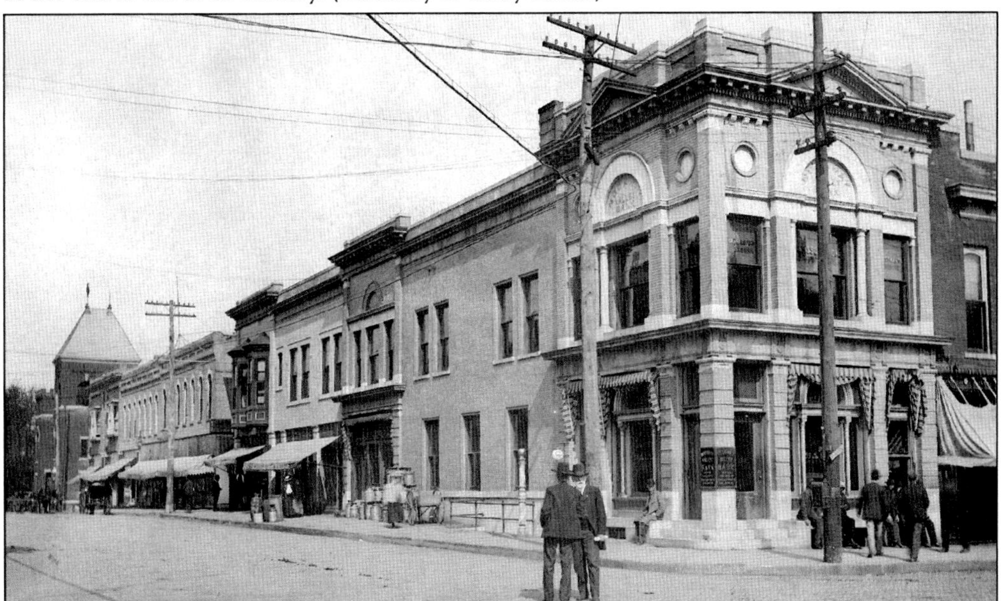

At the corner of Main and Third Streets in Maryville stood the Nodaway Valley Bank with its capital value of $100,000 emblazoned on the corner sign plates of its second building on the site, which was constructed in 1901. Established in 1868 by James Prather, E. S. Stephenson, Joseph E. Alexander, and William Orear, the bank continues to serve customers on the same site today. It is the oldest bank in the county. (Courtesy of Coby Lamb.)

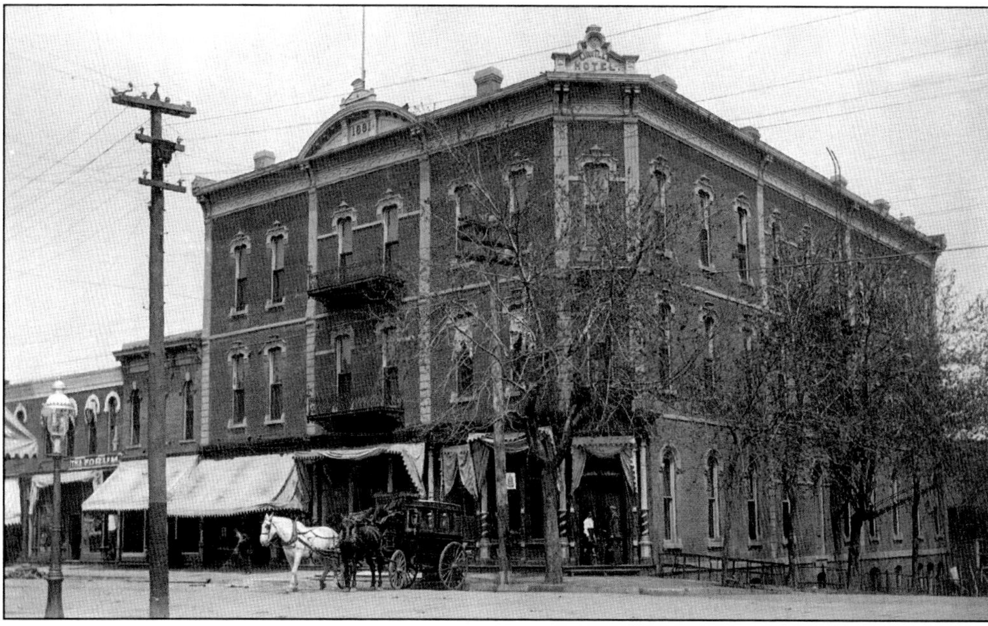

The first two brick hotels in Maryville were the Arlington Hotel and the Luona Hotel. They were followed in the early 1870s by the City Hotel, National Hotel, American Hotel, St. Johns House, and the Central Hotel, which were all located on Main Street or in the square. The stately three-story Linville Hotel followed in 1881 on Main Street as one of Maryville's fine establishments and outlasted most of its competitors midway into the next century. Aside from being a fine hotel, the Linville provided Maryville with one of its finest restaurants. In the 1890s, the kitchen of the hotel restaurant was spacious but limited in the equipment available to the cooks. Offering fine dining in the evening, the hotel's lunchroom became a dining option for college students when the normal school arrived.

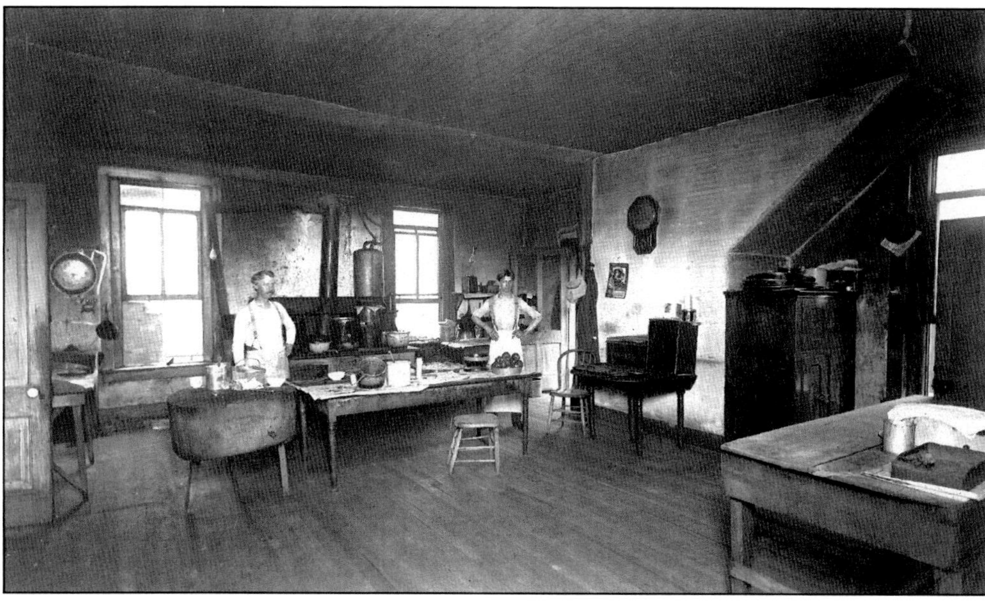

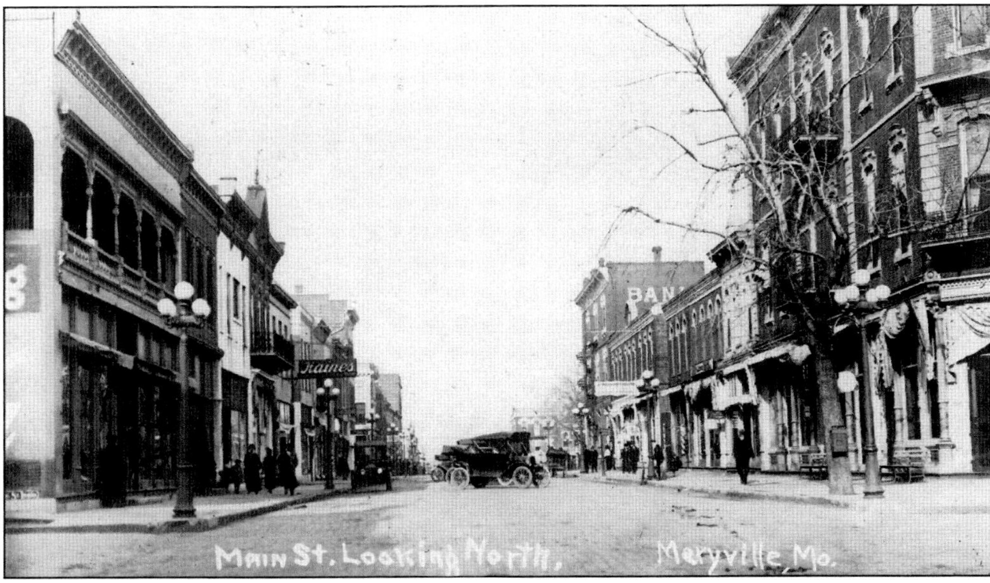

Main Street in Maryville was a bustling commercial center. In the span of a decade the traffic of horses and buggies dissipated, new streetlights appeared, and a host of businesses crowded multiple floors of its brick commercial blocks. Seemingly designed to last about a century, the commercial buildings seen here between Second and Third Streets are nearly all gone, having collapsed, burned, or been torn down. Despite the dangers, the Borrusch Brothers building of 1906 (below) at Third and Buchanan Streets still stands today in good shape.

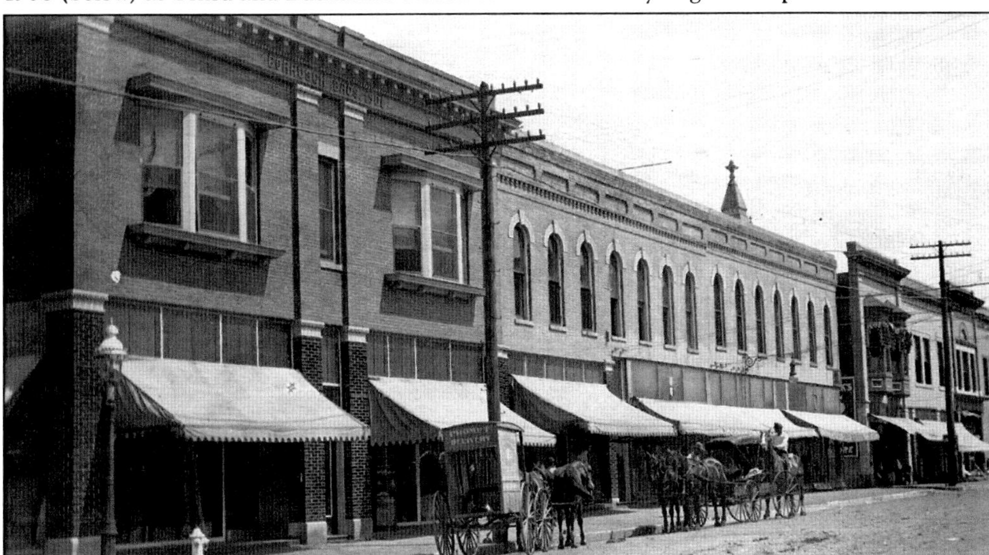

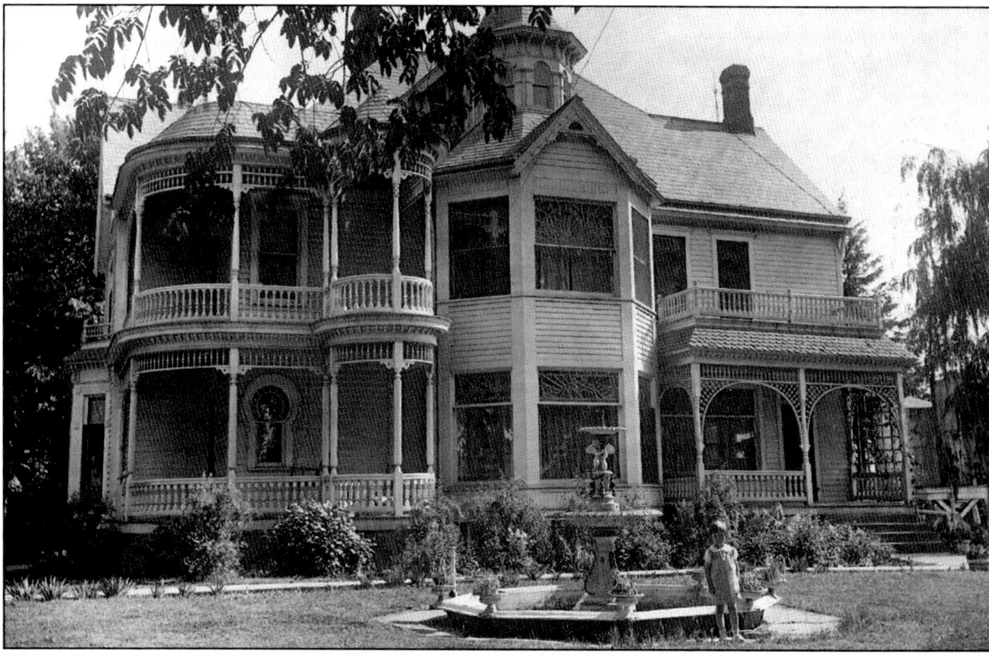

One of the finest homes in Nodaway County served as the Clearmont residence for banker Henry Weber and was later occupied by the Rhodes family. Seen in the 1890s with Janice Rhodes, the house featured slate roofing, imported plate-glass windows, parquet floors, and extensive woodwork throughout the 14 rooms of the home. The ample lawn around the home added to the demonstration of local prosperity.

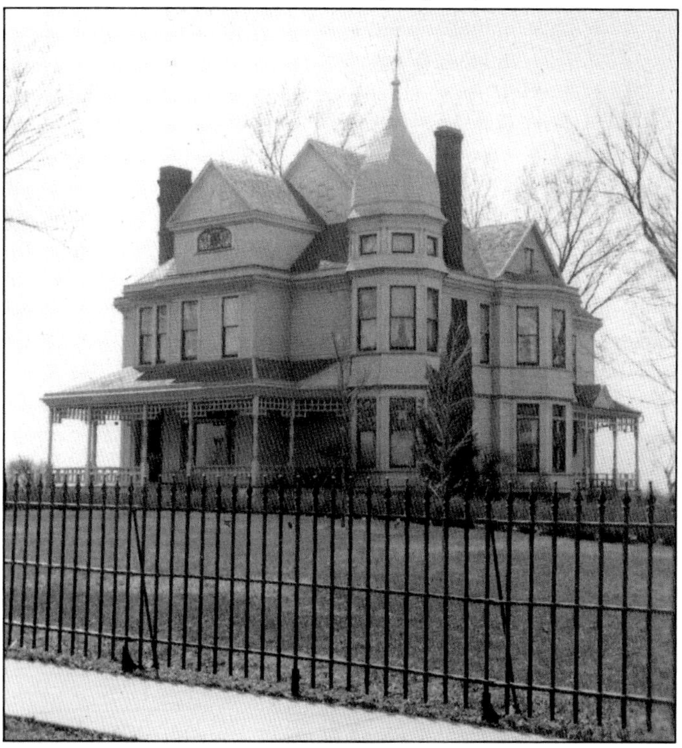

Built in 1890 at the corner of Walnut and Lincoln Streets, Joseph Jackson's 14-room home served as another example of the success of Maryville's business leaders. The fence around the property, which included a separate home for his daughter Mary, originally encircled the county courthouse. The original square tower was replaced by the onion-domed cupola seen here.

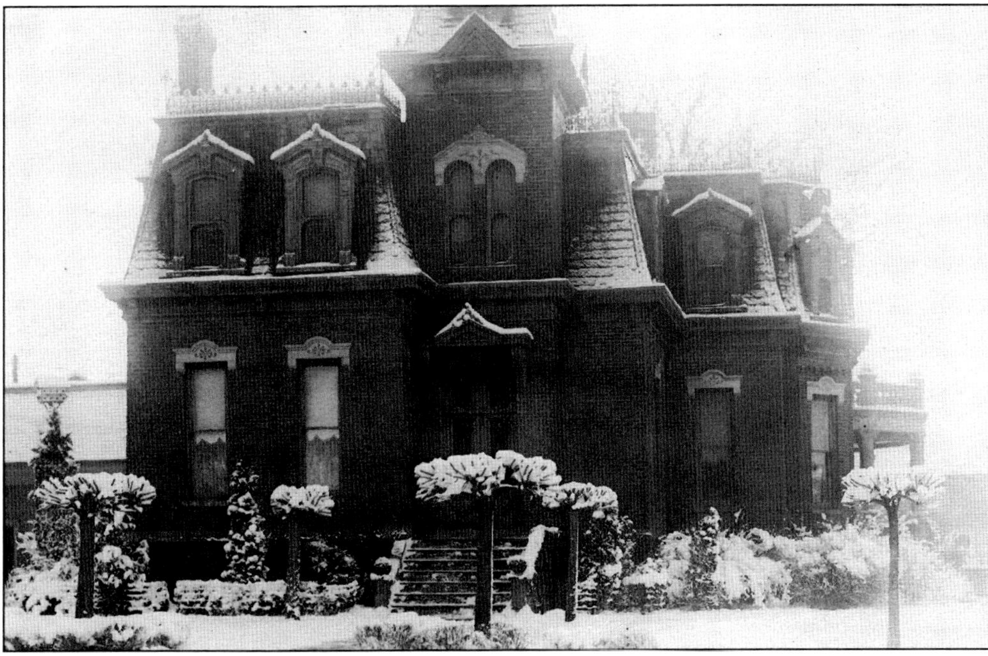

The home built for Albert Ellis, known for much of its history as the Forsyth Place, was among Maryville's early showplaces. Built in 1883, the French Colonial home was designed by J. M. Gile, who also designed the Nodaway County Courthouse. The brick and sandstone structure featured six bedrooms, two bathrooms, a kitchen, a dining room, a parlor, and a sitting room.

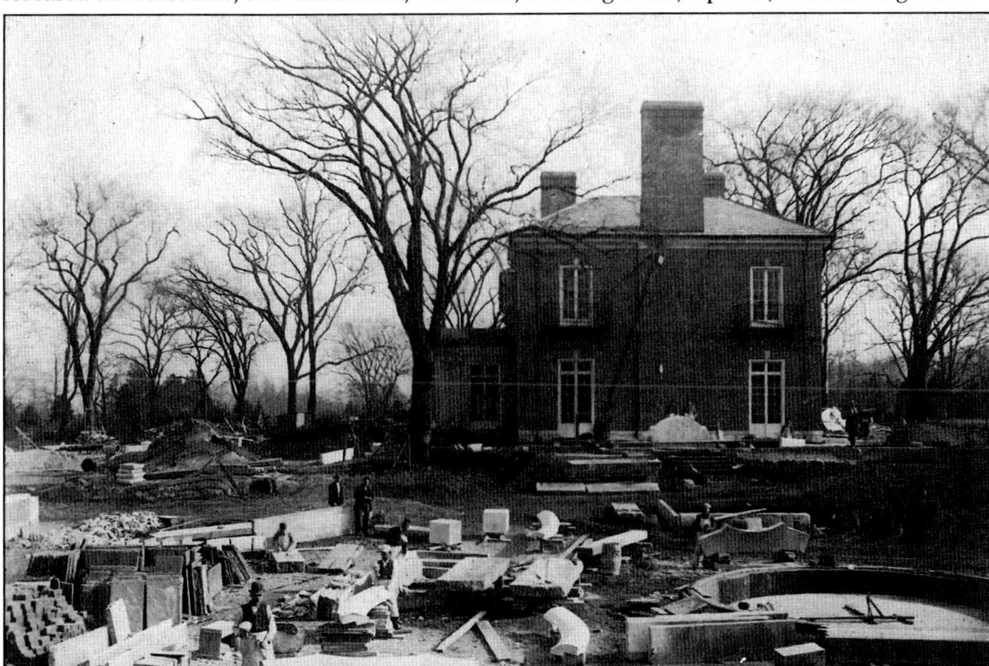

Stone masons use hand tools and expert skill to shape pieces for one of Maryville's fine homes in the 1890s. Workers in the rear prepare an arched stone near the heavy block and tackle used to lift the heavy masonry into position, much as builders had done for centuries.

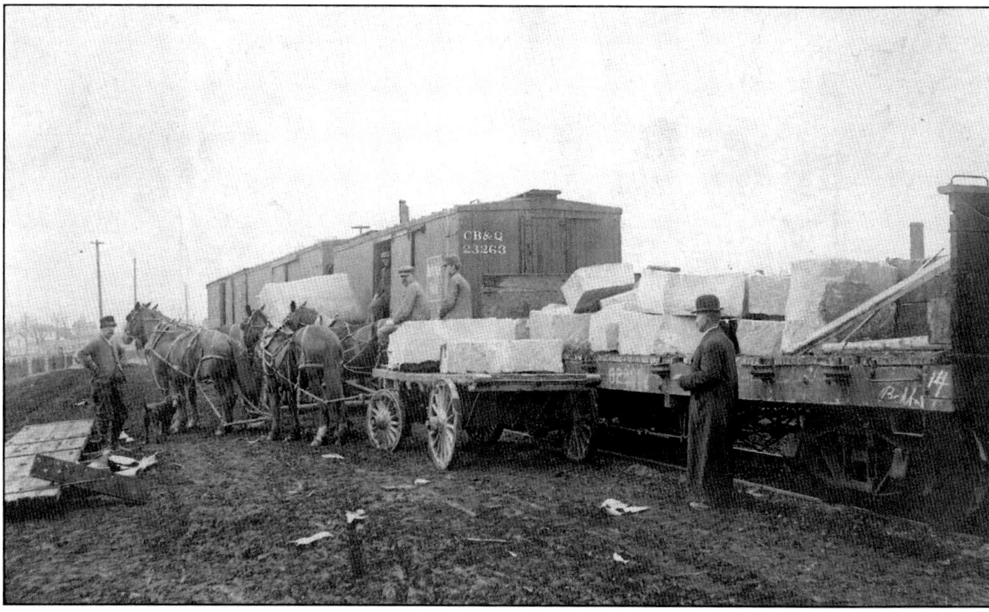

Prosperity in the 1890s brought with it the construction of large homes and commercial buildings, prompting the importing of stone for fine construction work in the county. The Iowa and Missouri Granite and Marble Company brought stone into Maryville via the Burlington line.

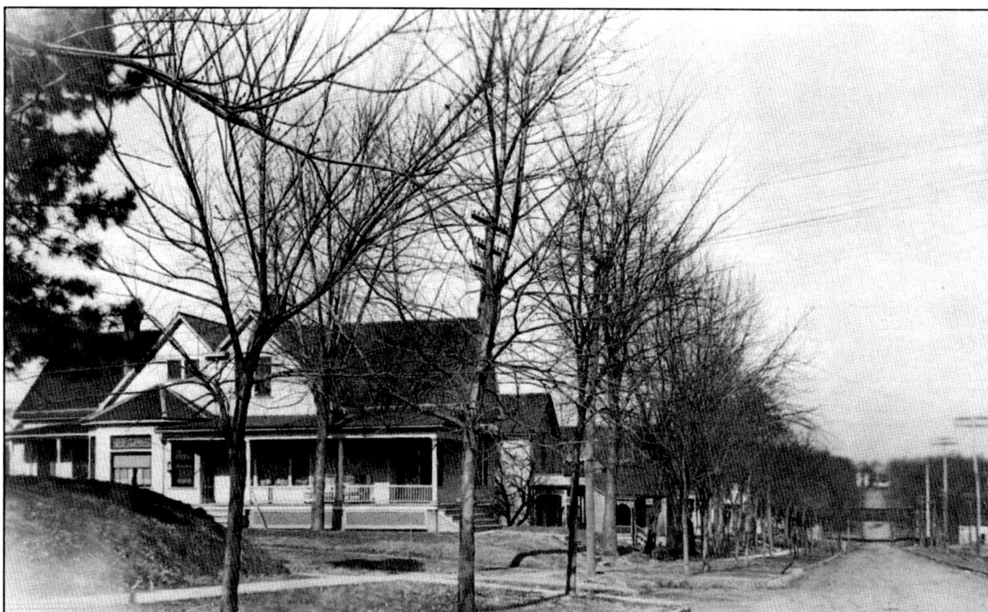

While the *Maryville Daily Tribune*'s 1899 *Maryville Illustrated* displayed a good number of spectacular homes, it was streets lined with comfortable bungalows like these on North Main Street that offered stronger evidence of a community's economic success. Despite occasional setbacks, wages in most trades grew handsomely as the agricultural economy and local light industry enjoyed their golden age in rural America.

Four

GETTING AROUND

The essentials of farm life in the prairie included windmills to pump water, fences to protect crops, and roads to access markets. This county road scene from about 1910 suggests prosperity for neighboring farms on all three counts, although the owners of automobiles quickly found the new technology wholly inadequate on rural roads. For much of the year, animals pulled wagons up rural roads like these far more effectively.

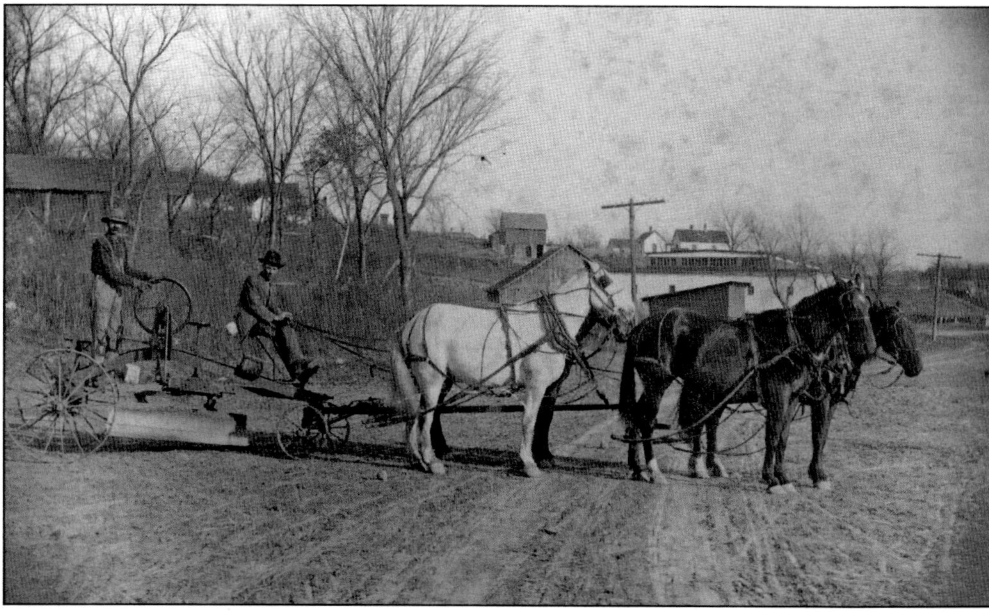

Hundreds of miles of rural road in Nodaway County required constant maintenance. Jim Lucas and Fred Bare (driving) pause near Barnard amid the endless task sometime during the 1890s. Over the next 20 years, the road graders found themselves in the middle of a battle between farmers who wanted to maintain local control over the roads and the towns that wanted more assistance from the state and federal government. (Courtesy of the Barnard Community Historical Society.)

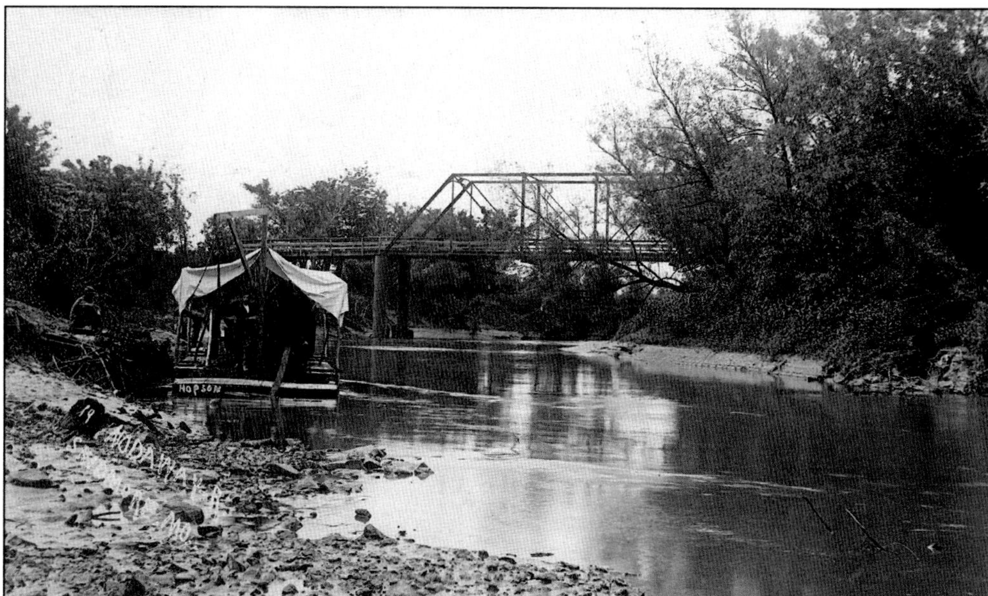

A sand-pump crew takes a break while working along the Nodaway River near Skidmore. Along with significant straightening of the rivers, the channels were made deeper with sand pumps. The clean sand pulled from the river bottom was sold for a variety of uses, including as a base for the bricked roads in towns. (Courtesy of Coby Lamb.)

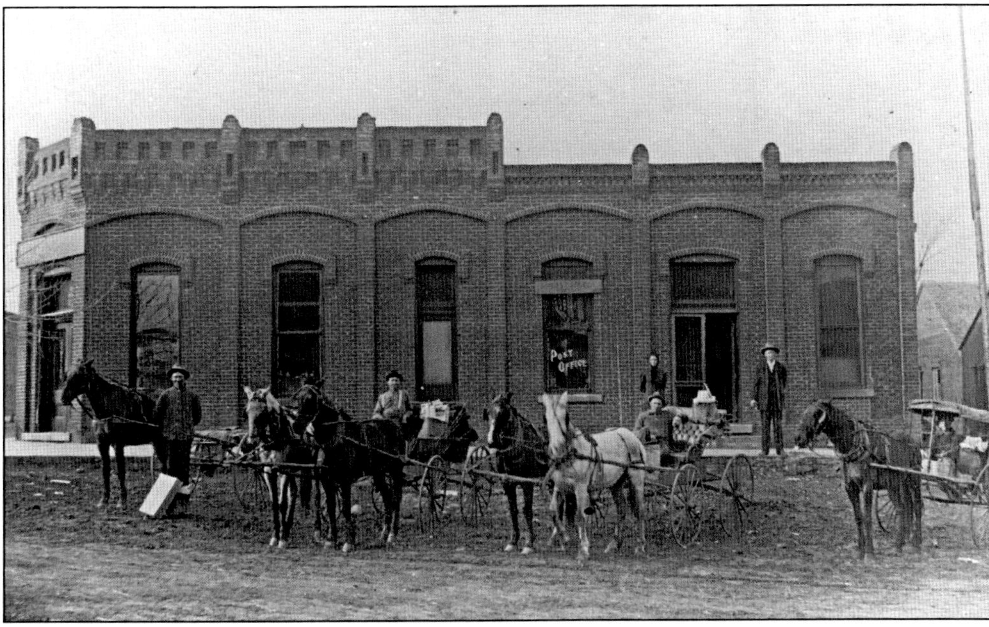

J. T. Logan (left) and company prepare to deliver the rural mail out of the Parnell Post Office in 1908. Riding an assortment of buggies and sulkies, the carriers were responsible for maintaining their own equipment under conditions that certainly tested them. While automobiles were gaining popularity in replacing horses on rural routes, many rural carriers still preferred animal power until there was considerable road improvement in the late 1920s.

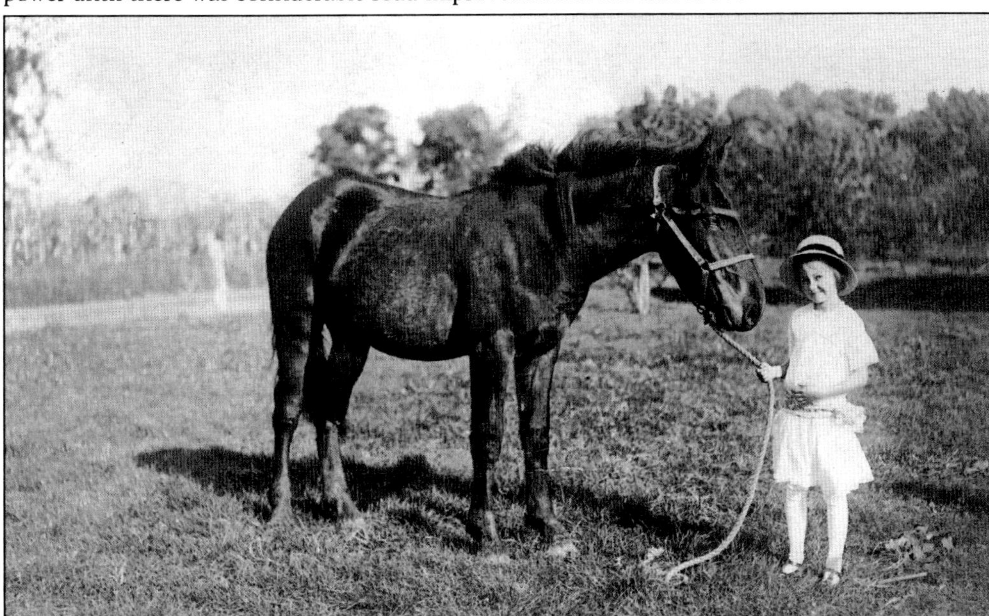

While Nodaway County gained recognition for its finely bred horses, mules of Missouri fame were often more valuable to the work done on area farms. Here young Ruby Norris poses with a family mule. Life with animal power provided an entirely different type of excitement and danger than what young people experience today, and newspapers offered regular accounts of children being thrown or kicked by animals. (Courtesy of Coby Lamb.)

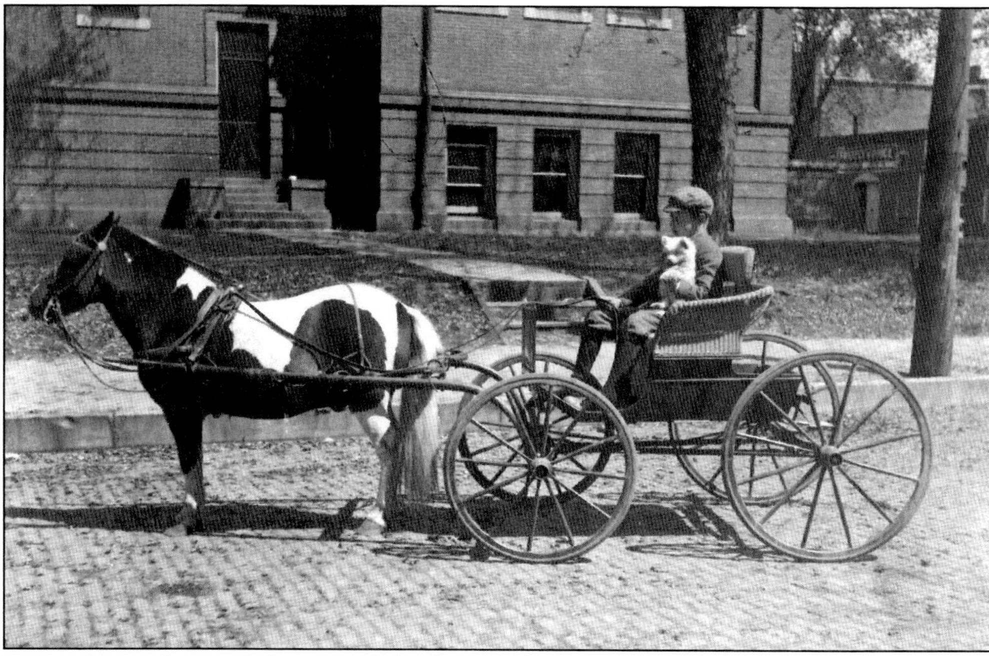

Before the revolution of the automobile, the pony buggy offered transportation that was easy to operate and safe for youngsters like James Robinson, who pauses with his cherished rig near the side door of the Maryville Public Library. Robinson, of course, had the advantage of a prosperous family, while most young men were not as fortunate.

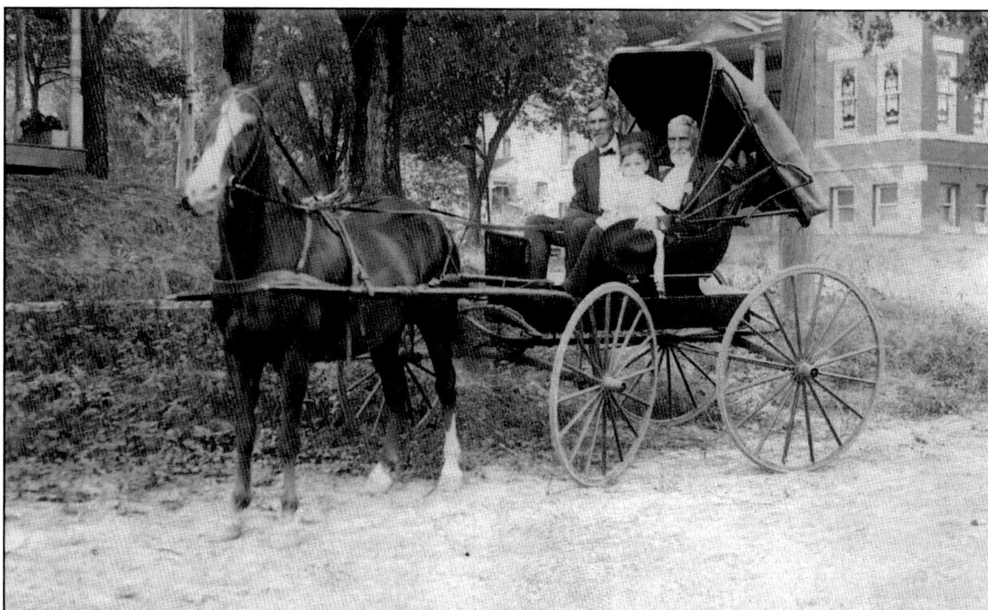

In 1900, three generations of Maryville men make their way around town in the type of buggy that served as the most popular form of transportation from the Civil War to World War I. Hundreds of small companies across the Midwest built and repaired buggies, including Weddle and Parrish in Skidmore and Barmann and Wolfert in Maryville. Residents could also always rent transportation at the livery in every community. (Courtesy of Coby Lamb.)

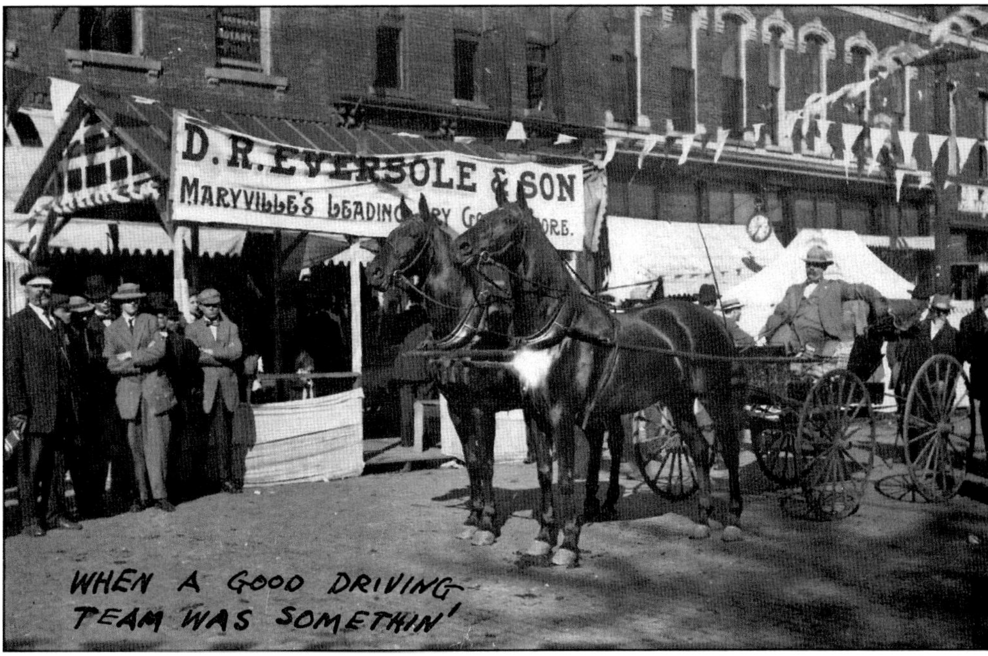

The breeding of fine horses in Nodaway County stimulated local competition for the best transportation. John Sprague poses quite proudly here with his prize-winning team in October 1900 at the Maryville Street Fair.

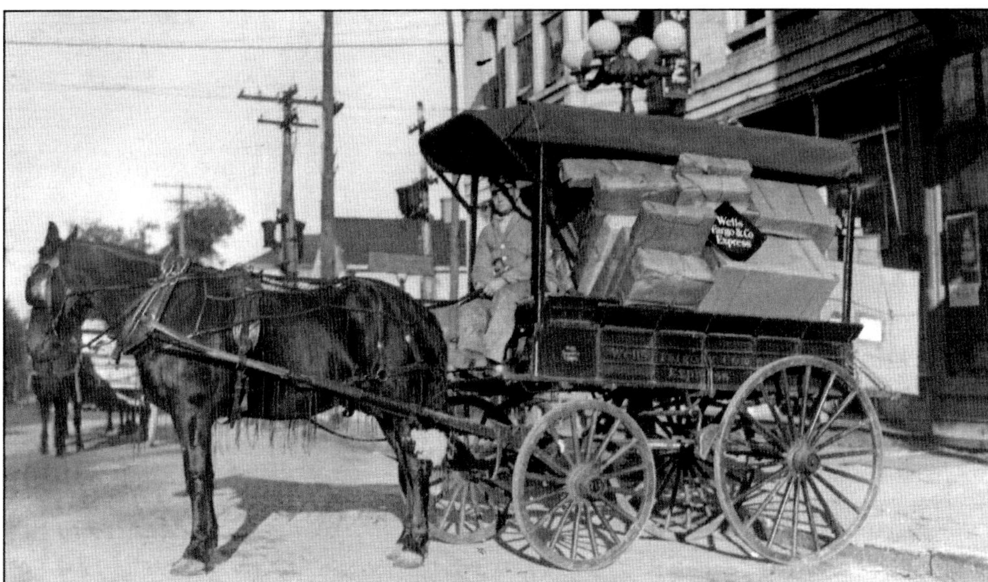

Roy Mays prepares a delivery for Wells Fargo and Company along West Fourth Street in Maryville. Founded in 1852 to provide banking and overland mail service to the California Gold Rush, Wells Fargo triumphed over considerable competition in the express package service. At the time of May's employment, Wells Fargo was still flush with prosperity from the considerable capital it handled funding the reconstruction of its hometown of San Francisco following the earthquake of 1906.

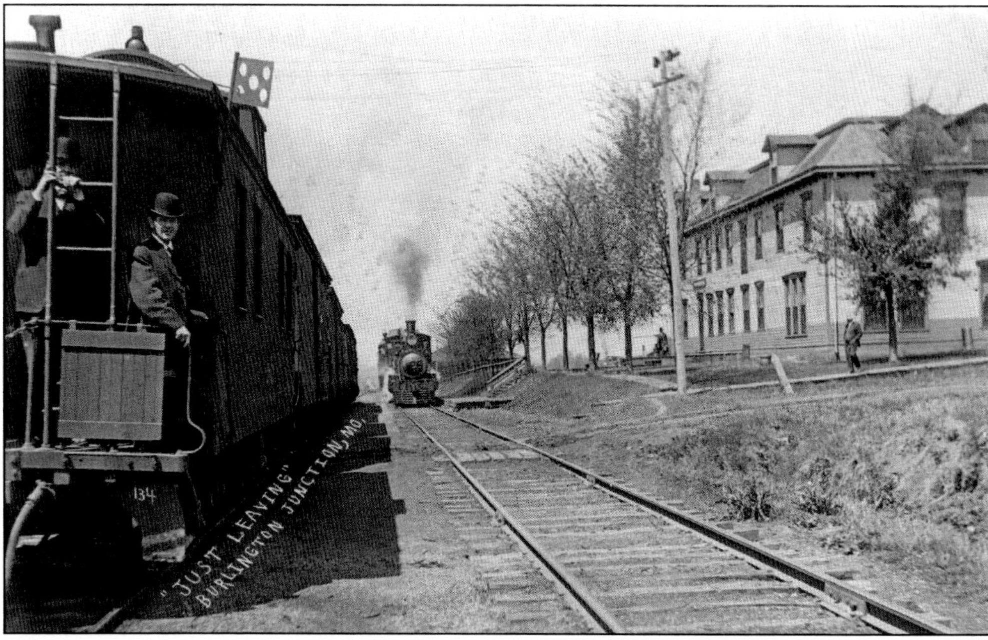

The crossing of the Chicago, Burlington, and Quincy Railroad and the Wabash Railroad lines made Burlington Junction, and the first Burlington train rumbled into the crossing in 1879 and left two days later with a load of grain. The Wabash Railroad ran passengers and freight through the county from Clyde to Elmo and on to Council Bluffs.

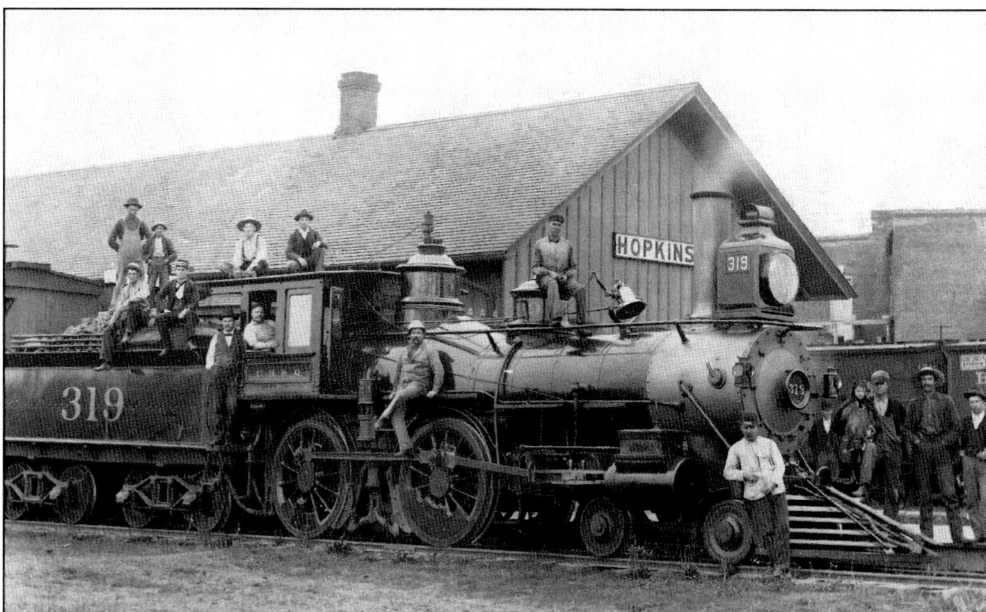

A variety of folks, including rail workers, local businessmen, and others, joined aptly named station agent Ed Goforth (seated on the coal tender) to meet the Chicago, Burlington, and Quincy Railroad's No. 319 train as it arrived in Hopkins station on its initial run. The arrival of a photographer proved an irresistible opportunity to pose with an impressive specimen of locomotive power.

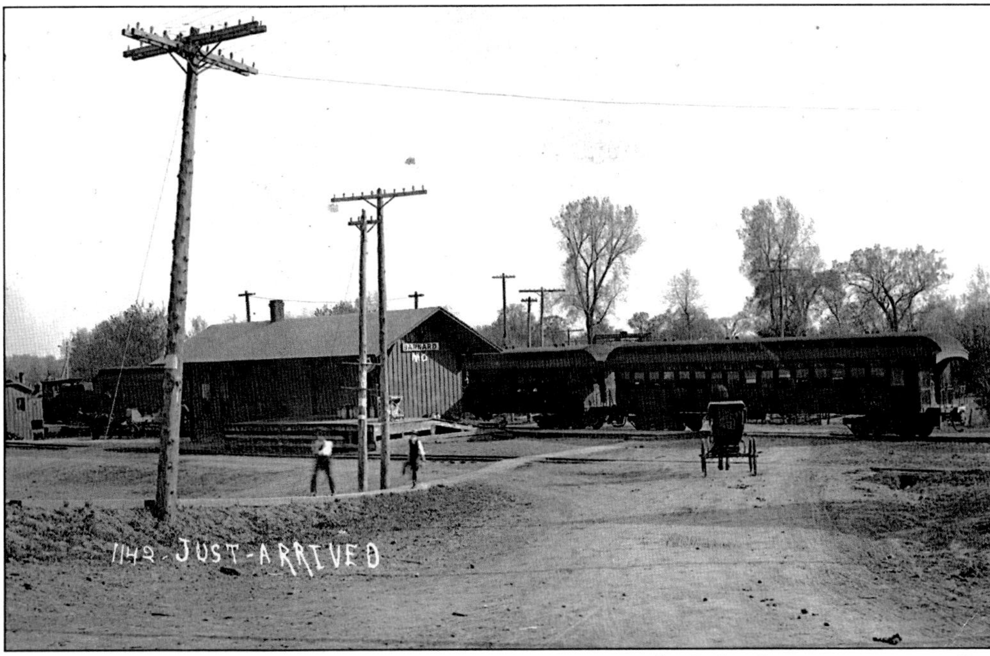

By the early 1880s the depot at Barnard was shipping 20,000 bushels of grain a year as well as providing transportation for livestock, people, and all the goods necessary to supply its diverse mercantile interests. Passenger cars prepare to load in 1910 for the run south to St. Joseph and perhaps on to the metropolis of Kansas City.

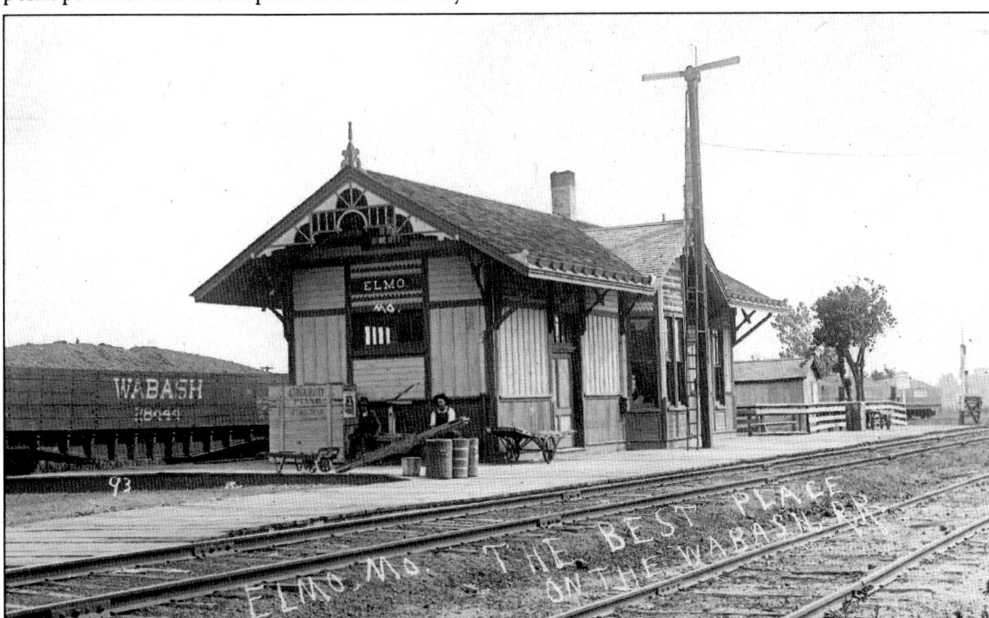

A Kingsbury piano, manufactured by the Cable Company of Chicago, arrived on the platform at Elmo's Wabash Railroad station in 1913. While the combination of mail-order firms in big cities and regular rail service brought all the commodities of civilization within the grasp of small towns and farmers, cutting local merchants out of the deal was often a source of tension in small communities.

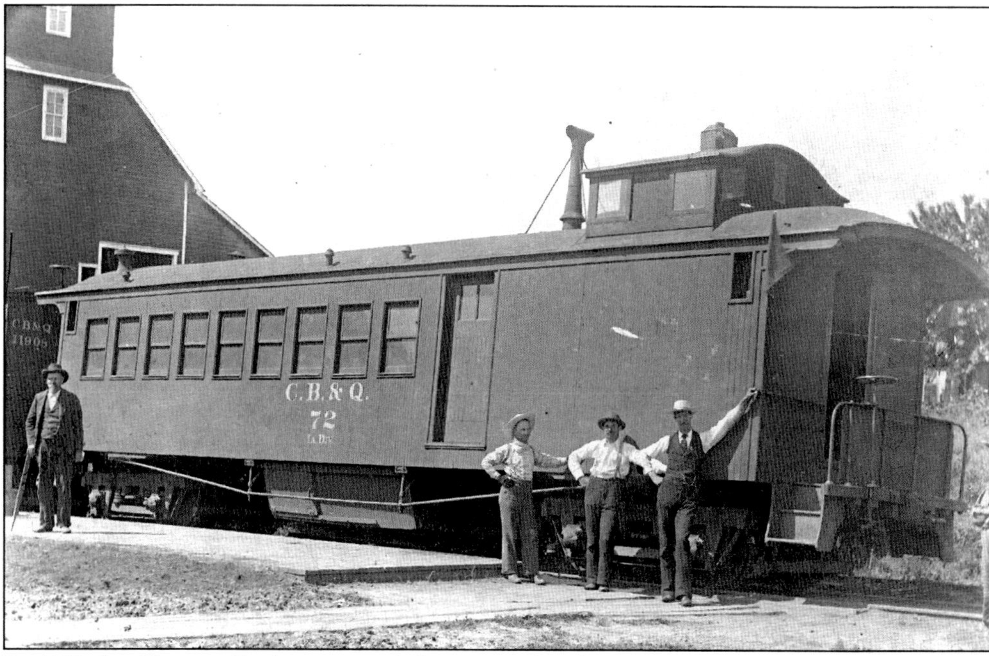

By 1910 the Chicago, Burlington, and Quincy Railroad sent a half-dozen trains a day through Skidmore, including one passenger, one freight, and one mixed going each direction. Local business speculator William R. Linville, on the left, and company pose next to one of the railroad's coach-cabooses used on local mixed trains in its Iowa division. (Courtesy of the Skidmore Museum.)

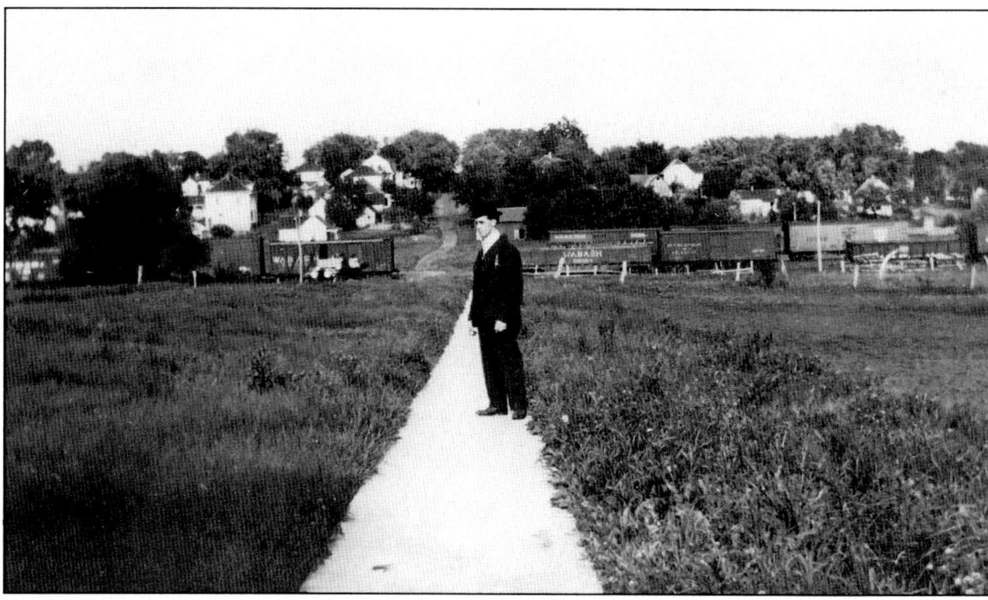

The Wabash Railroad yard on the eastern side of Maryville, seen at its Seventh Street crossing, served a handful of enterprises between the college campus and the town. It allowed for storage of rolling stock in an area whose current mixture of parking lots, apartments, and fraternity houses have erased all vestiges of a rail yard, except for the depot, which still stands. (Courtesy of Coby Lamb.)

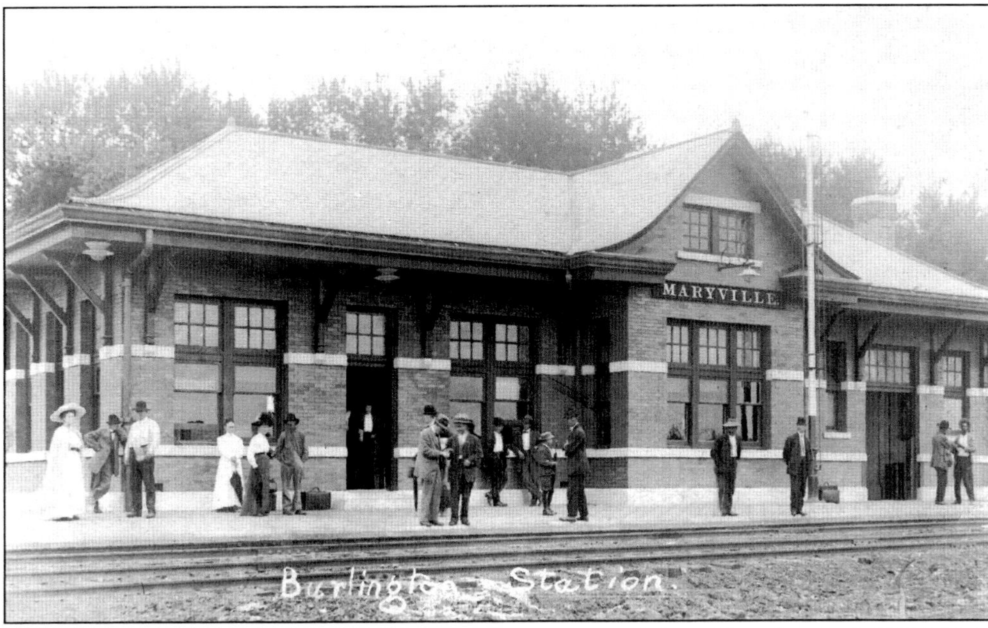

Following a failed deal in 1867 with two rail companies, Maryville subscribed $125,000 in 1869 to entice the Missouri Valley Company to construct the line that eventually became the Burlington's Maryville division. The brick station at the east end of Third Street in Maryville was completed in 1910 to replace the already dilapidated wooden station. With its two waiting rooms, it served several trains per day.

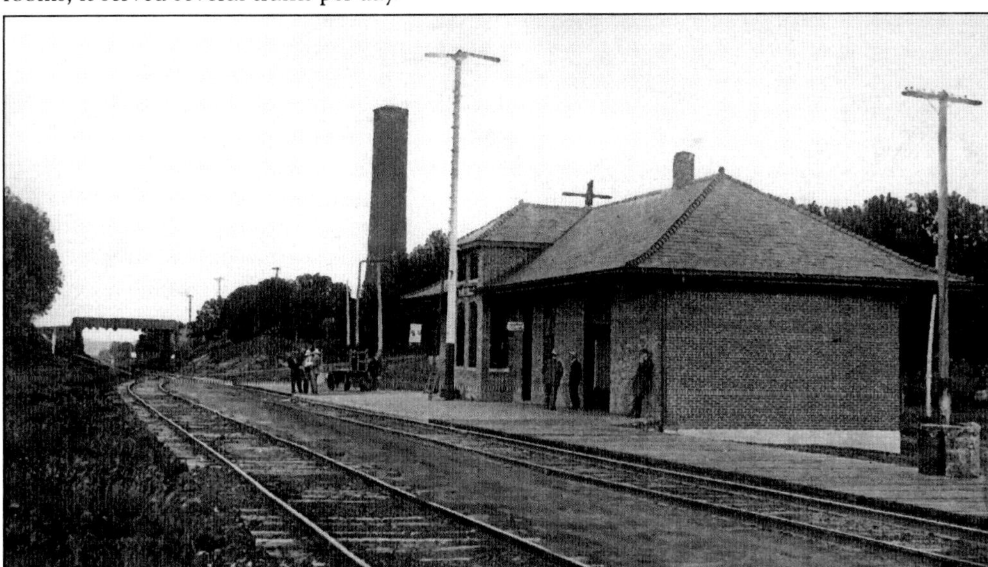
After securing the Burlington line in 1869, Maryville was fortunate to also get a stop in 1879 on the Council Bluffs and St. Louis Railroad, which soon became the Wabash, St. Louis and Pacific Railroad. The railroad required that the city and county raise a subscription of $125,000 with the county's $75,000 share to be paid in produce. Early concerns that the center of commerce in Maryville would drift eastward toward the Burlington depot and away from the courthouse were for naught, as the town's depots sat with the business district halfway in between.

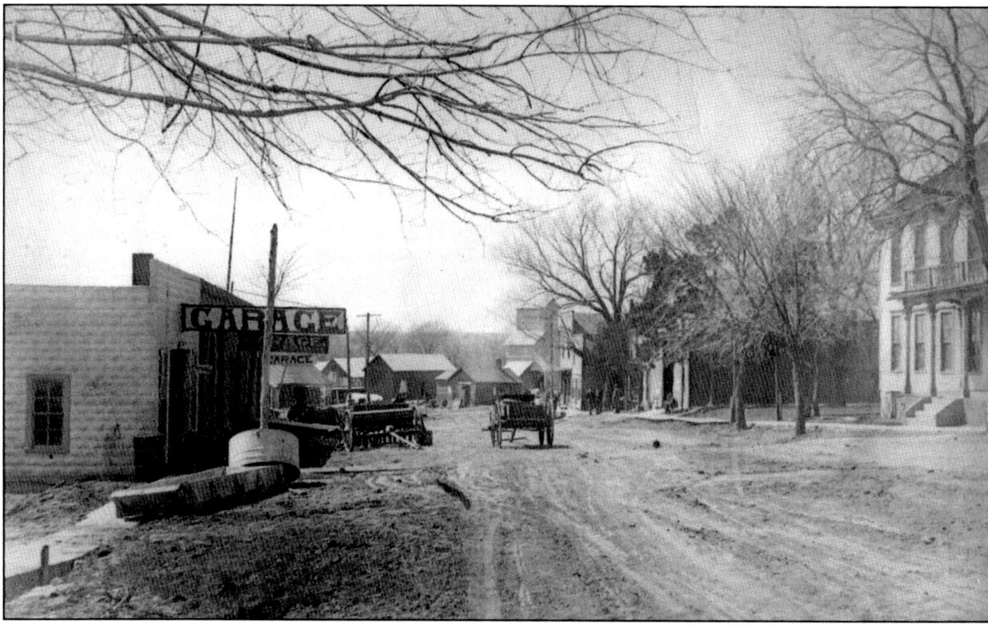

The horseless carriages of the 1880s that became automobiles by the dawn of the 20th century needed constant repair, and wainwrights and farm implement repairmen filled the need. The word *garage*, which was French in origin, came into fashion in the United States by 1900 to distinguish a shop that repaired automobiles. This early garage/livery repair shop on McKenzie Street in Barnard made the offer clear with its redundant signage.

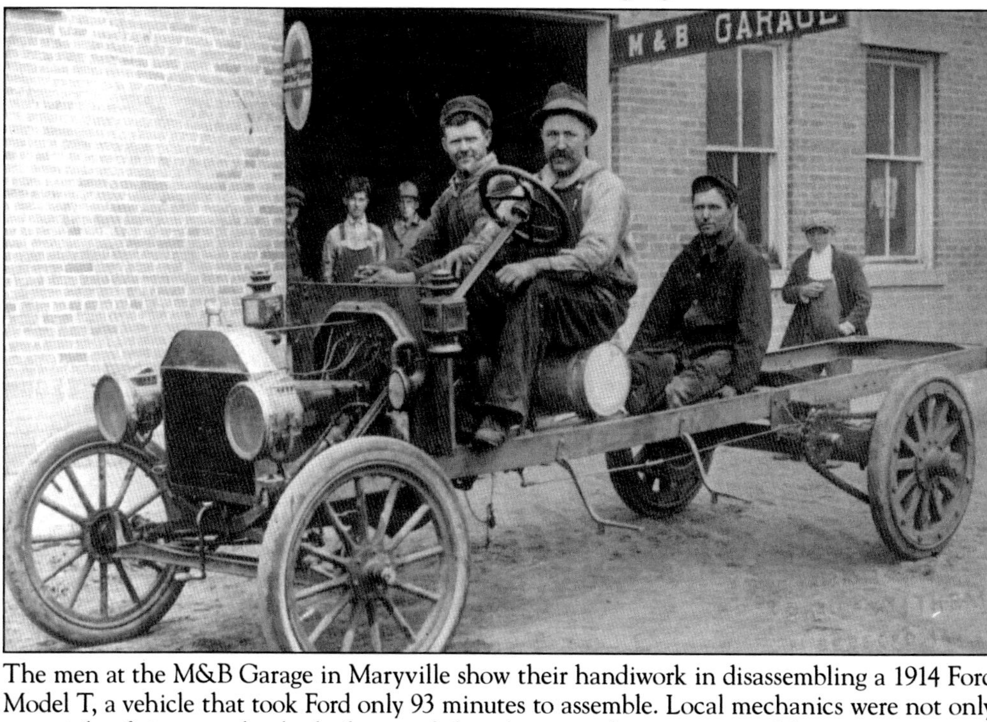

The men at the M&B Garage in Maryville show their handiwork in disassembling a 1914 Ford Model T, a vehicle that took Ford only 93 minutes to assemble. Local mechanics were not only essential to fixing cars that broke frequently but also to teach new owners of the inexpensive cars how to drive them. The car had rear-wheel drive with a planetary gear two-speed transmission.

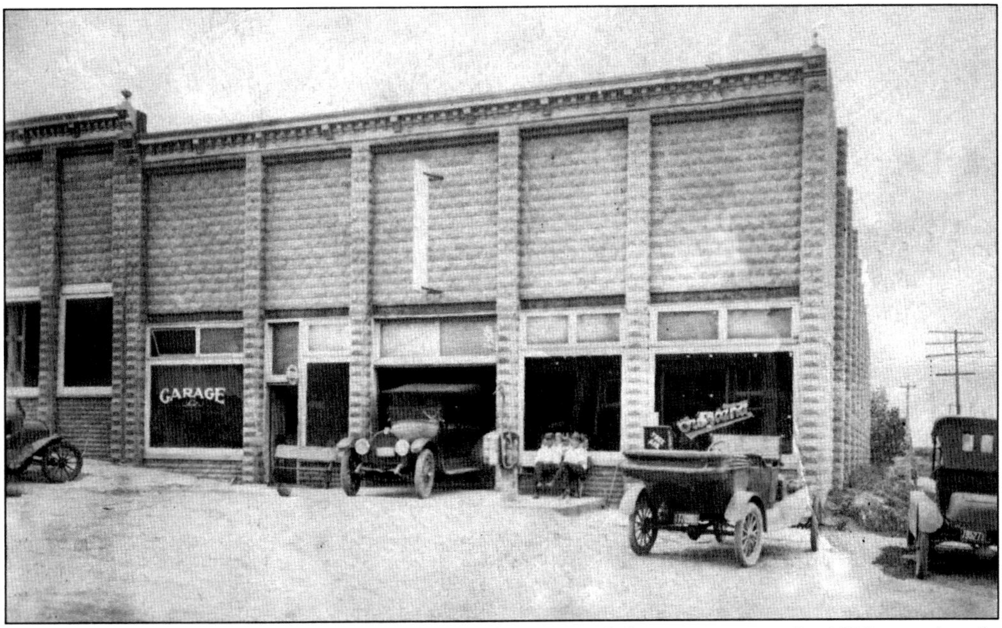

Like the barbershop and livery barn before it, the automobile repair garage by 1920 was already a place not only for business but also for socializing among men. This is Nick Garnett's Garage in what was later known as the Floyd Nelson building in Skidmore.

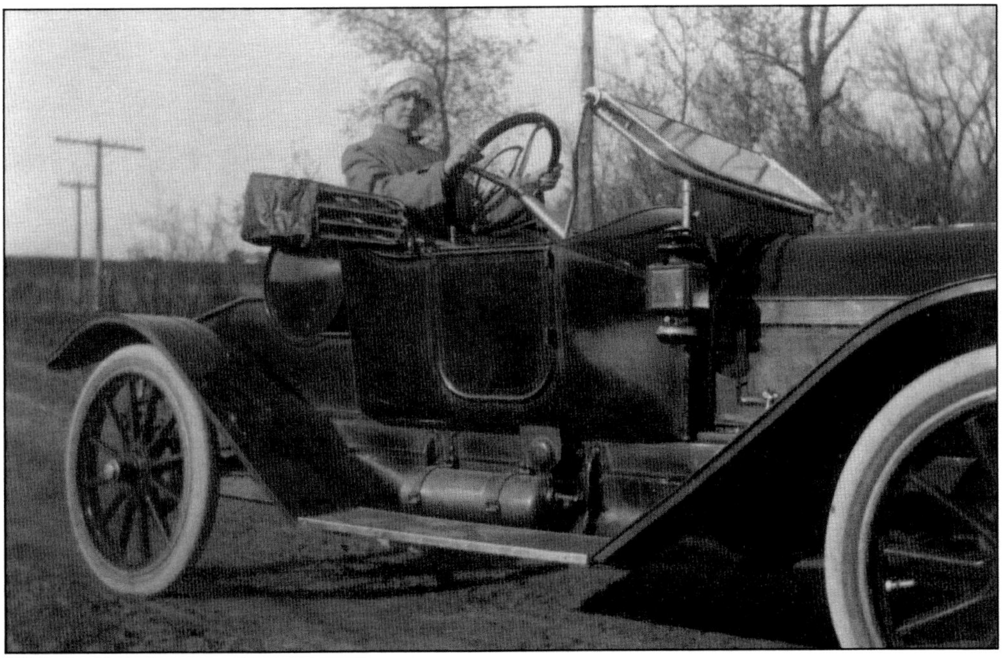
Virginia Morgan of Skidmore had the distinct luxury as a young woman of owning a car and having a family that encouraged her to drive. In 1927, the high school senior recorded in her scrapbook about driving the Hudson with three other young ladies to Maitland and boasted of having repaired a flat tire on the return trip.

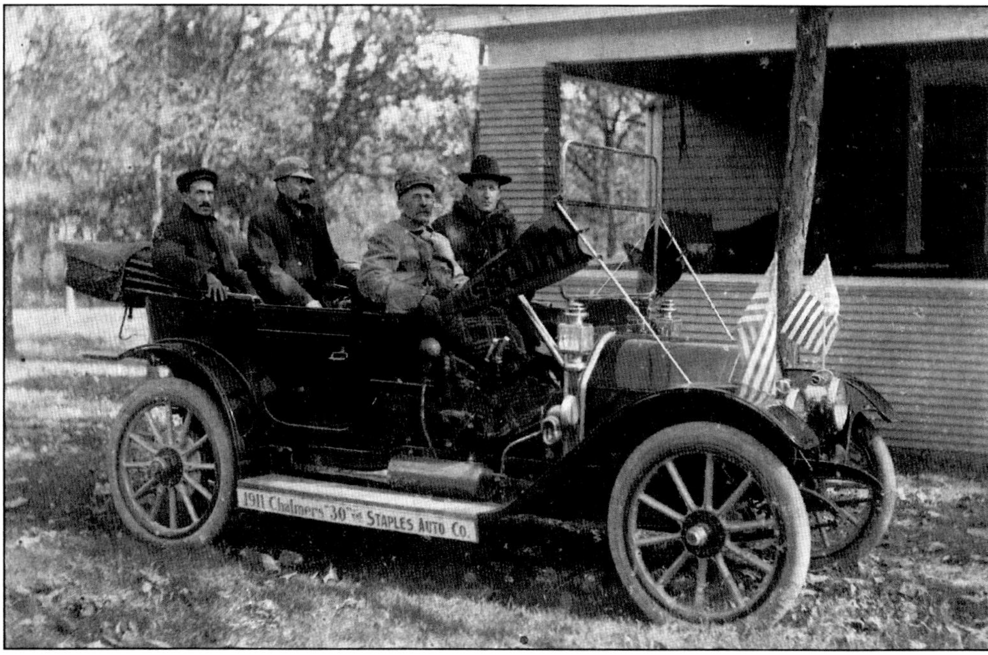

Curtis Wray, Cat Pierce, Willis Staples, and E. E. McJinsey, from left to right, pose in the elegance of a 1911 Chalmers "30" motorcar. An agent for Western Union Telegraph and later Bell Telephone in Maryville, Staples (at the right-side steering wheel) kept residents of Maryville on the cutting edge of communication and transportation.

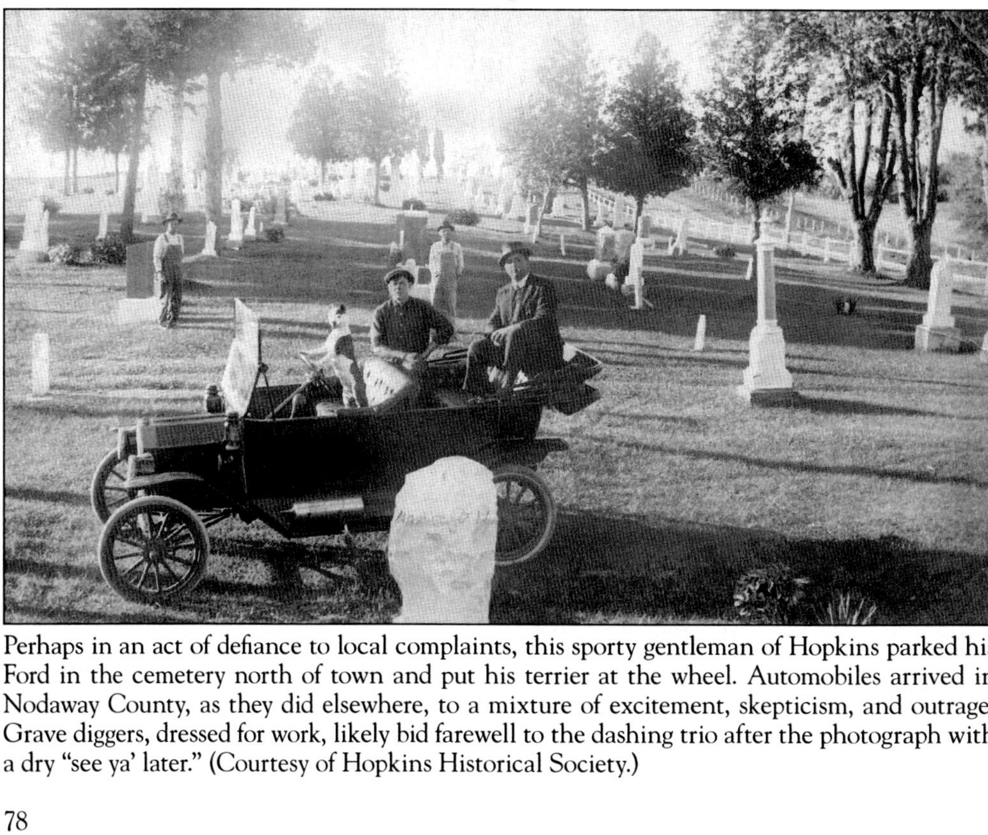

Perhaps in an act of defiance to local complaints, this sporty gentleman of Hopkins parked his Ford in the cemetery north of town and put his terrier at the wheel. Automobiles arrived in Nodaway County, as they did elsewhere, to a mixture of excitement, skepticism, and outrage. Grave diggers, dressed for work, likely bid farewell to the dashing trio after the photograph with a dry "see ya' later." (Courtesy of Hopkins Historical Society.)

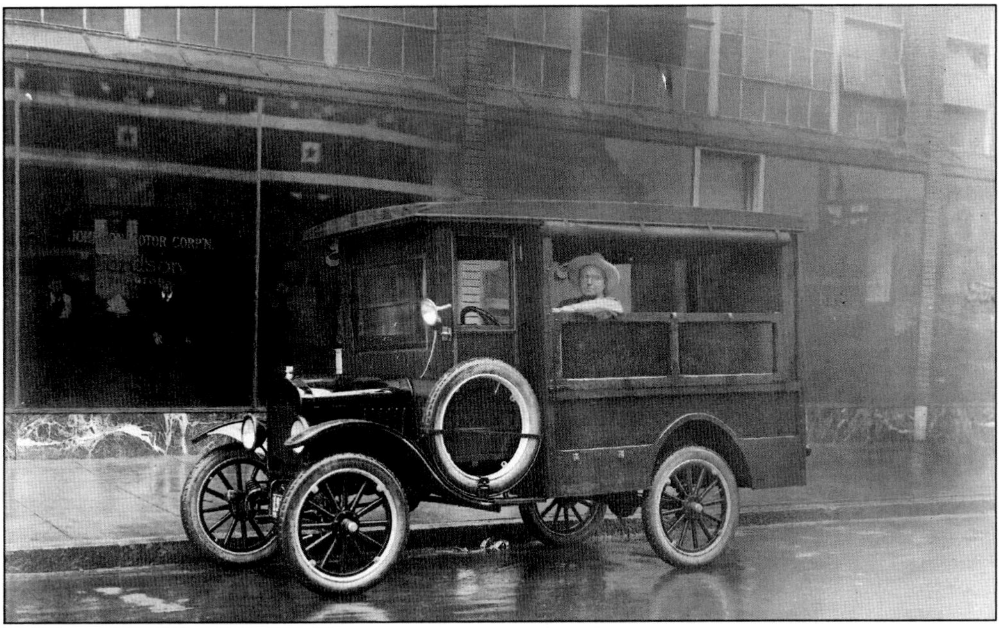

Gladys Ford's brother Stanley rolled into Maryville in 1922 in one of the nation's first campers. Having constructed the body in Panama, he shipped it to Virginia where it was mounted on a Ford Model T with modifications that allowed it to sleep four. Ford drove the car cross-country to Maryville, where he paid a publicity visit to Johnson Motor Corporation for a photograph opportunity.

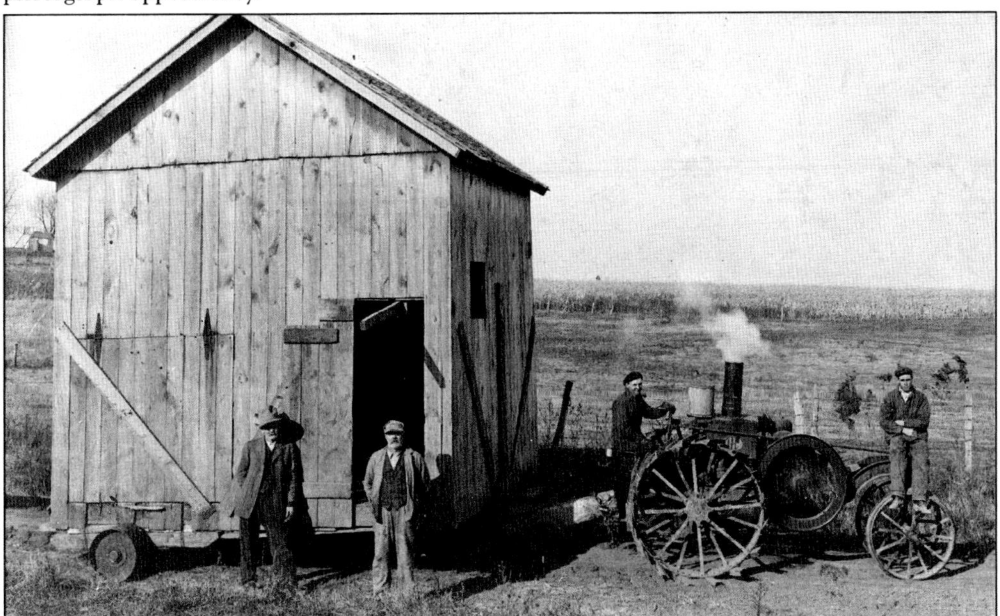

Joe Logan and "Poppa" Jim Newton, with two unidentified helpers manning the tractor, make use of modern power to move a house near Skidmore in 1917. The men are using an International Harvester Mogul 8-16 kerosene tractor for the job. While the machine appears effective, Newton was also inclined from time to time to go back to animal power for his moving jobs. (Courtesy of the Skidmore Museum.)

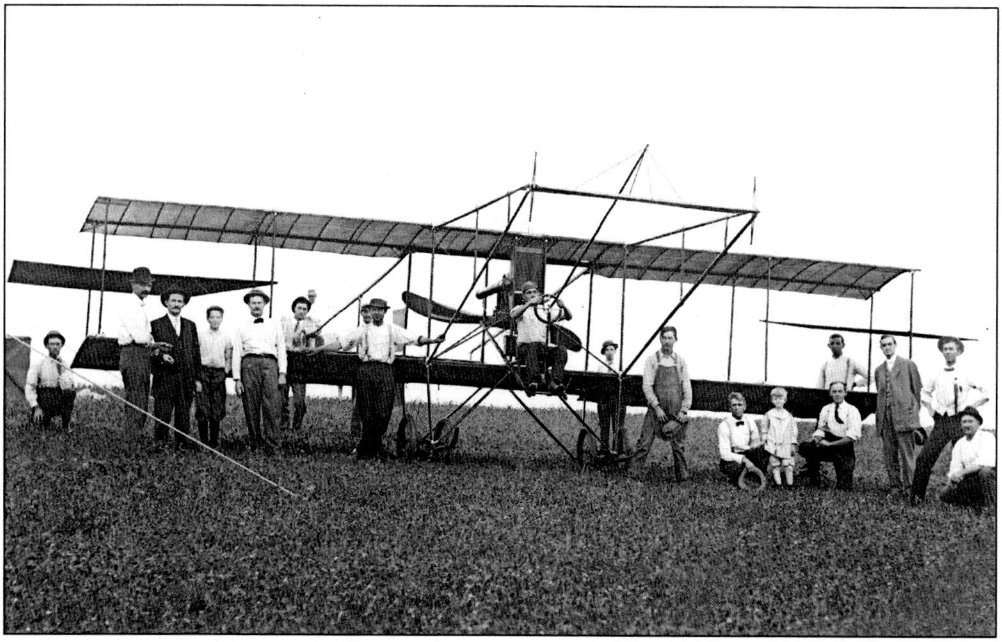

Flying was just entering the national conscience in 1910 as Americans read news of a series of races in the United States between pilots in the first practicable aircraft designs. Landing his Curtiss-styled biplane at the Skidmore Punkin Show in September 1910, Prof. William Evans faced considerable danger, as the casualty rate among these first exhibition pilots was high. While the Skidmore Punkin Show never failed to entertain and was often the occasion of an amazing sight of some sort, the arrival of Evans in his craft surely ranked highly as one of the most unusual and remarkable events for residents at the time. (Courtesy of the Skidmore Museum.)

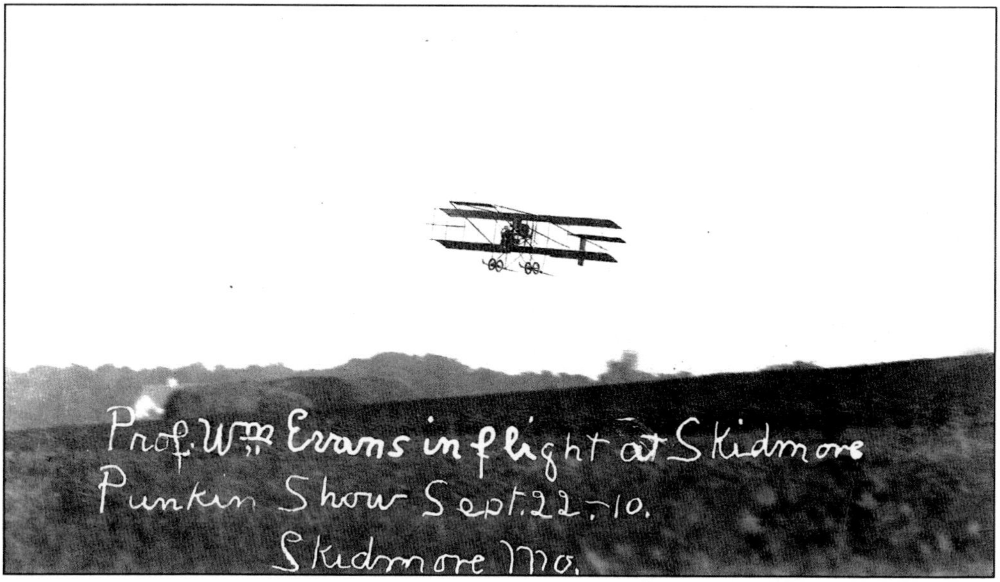

Five

CIVILITY

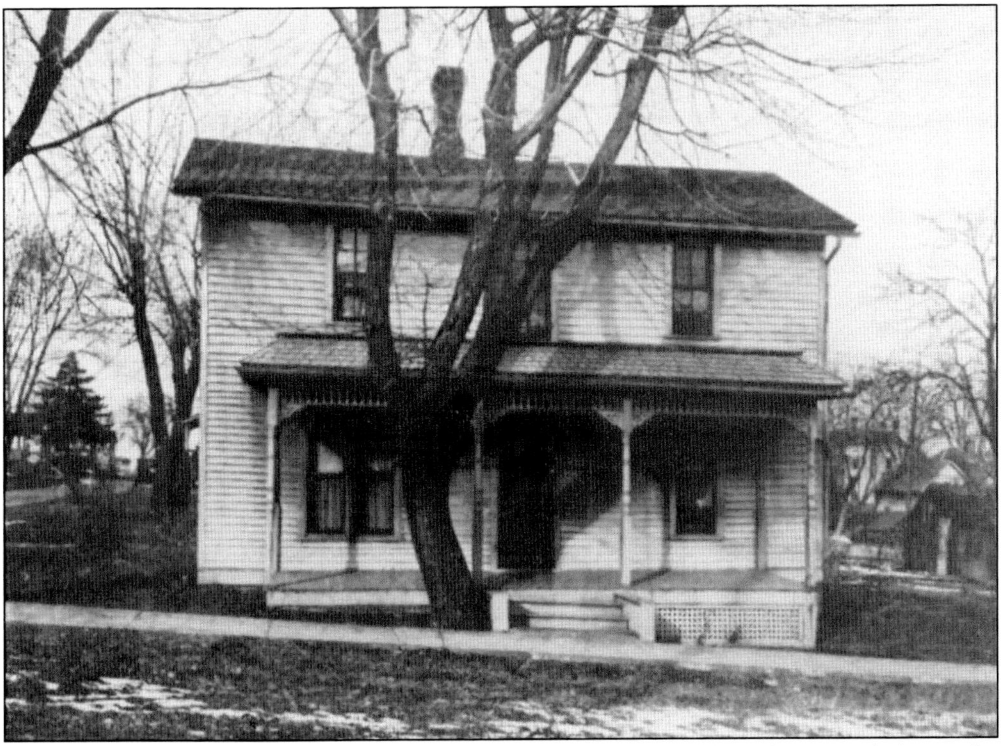

The first school commenced in Maryville in 1847 in the log building that served also as the courthouse. In 1857, the lower story of the structure shown here became the new school with a second story added soon after. Located at the corner of Market and East Fifth Streets, the school offered a more advanced curriculum under the tutelage of at least four different teachers over the next 10 years. A more substantial brick structure at the corner of Vine and First Streets replaced the old subscription school in 1867 with a fully public institution. The school was used as a private residence at least until the 1940s.

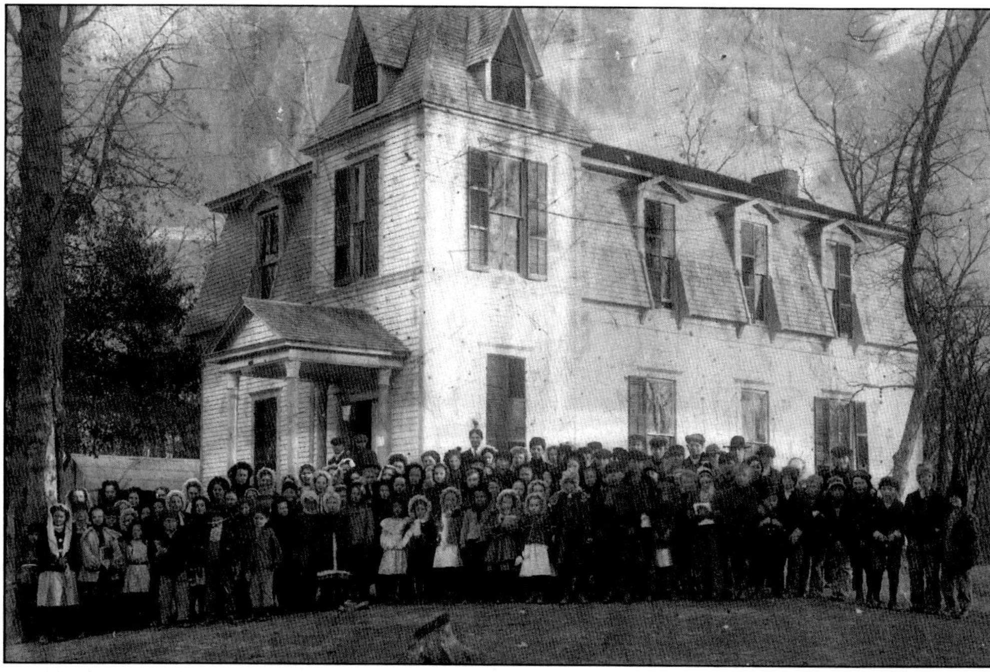

Guilford's first school met in a log cabin starting in 1856 but was replaced by a frame structure that accommodated 60 students. Built in 1898, this third school contained one large room on the first floor for the primary grades and one large room on the second floor for the grammar-level students. A later addition allowed for further division into intermediate and high grades.

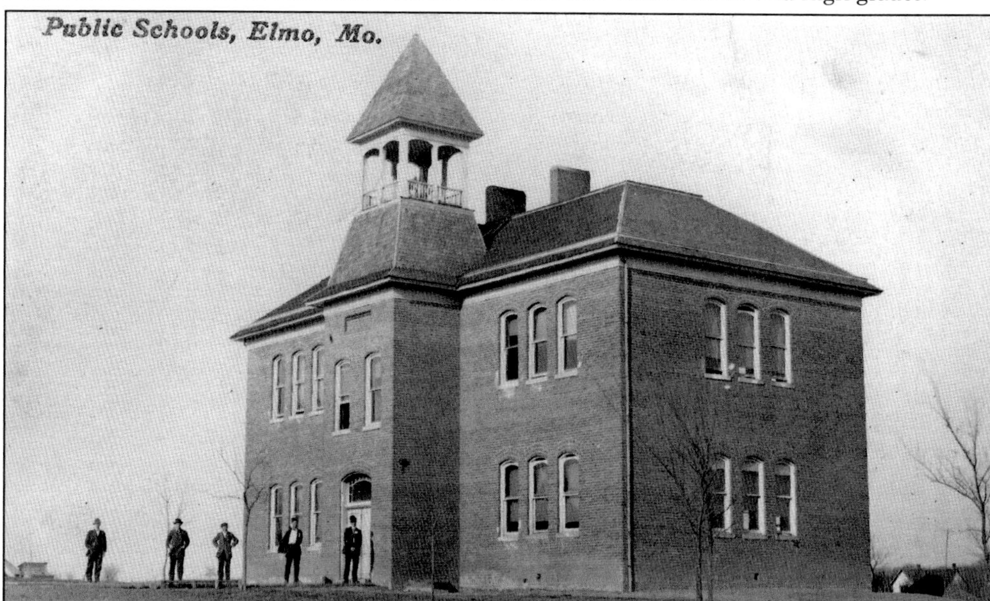

The Elmo School consisted of four large classrooms divided by central halls on the first and second floors. Growth in Elmo by 1916 required a two-story addition on the east side of the building. In 1918, Elmo expanded its three-year high school program to four, graduating its first state-approved four-year class in 1920. By the 1920s the rural schoolhouses were already closing and the Elmo School became Consolidated School District No. 38.

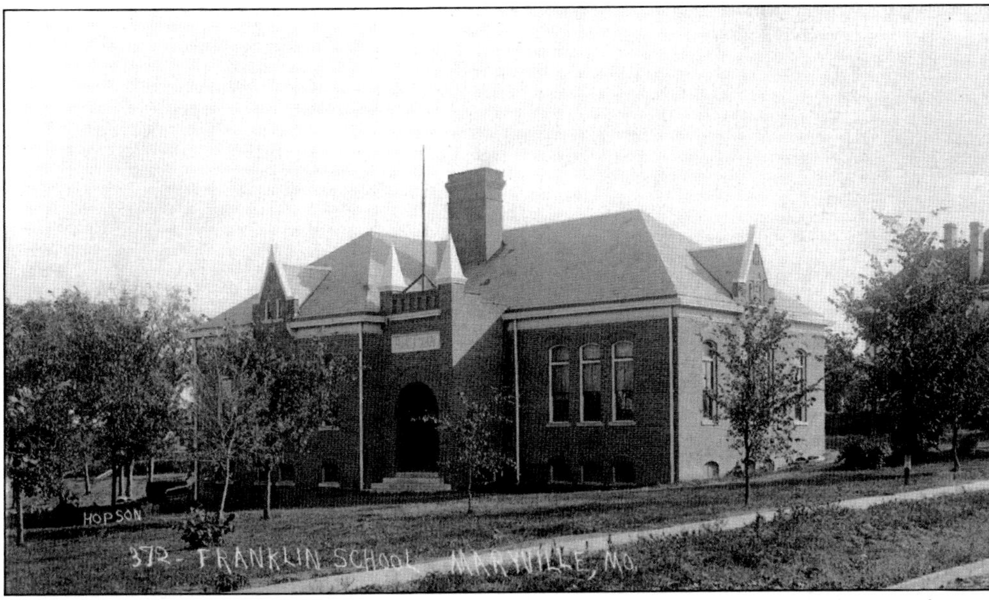

Maryville Public Schools constructed three ward schools in 1892 to relieve the crowding in the central school building. The new schools included Jefferson School, Garfield School, and Franklin School (shown here). A separate school for black students operated from 1870 to 1921, known eventually as the Douglass School. The land for the Franklin School building, now called Franklin Park, was donated by the Scott family with the stipulation that the site always be used for public purposes.

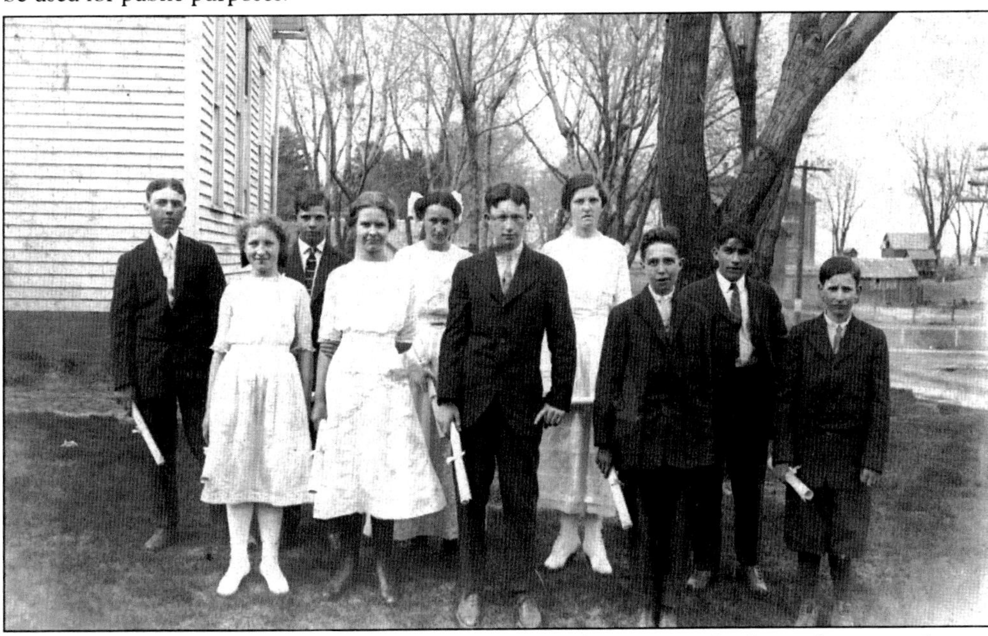

The eighth-grade graduates of Pickering School in April 1914 were the first to have a graduation program and to get diplomas. Photographed on the east lawn of the Christian Church, the students, from left to right, are (first row) Lucy Busch, Annice Neal, Clifford Moon, Claude Moon, Floyd Fakes, and Allen Burks; (second row) Alva Lett, Loren Hackett, Stella Burr, and Opal Birkenholtz.

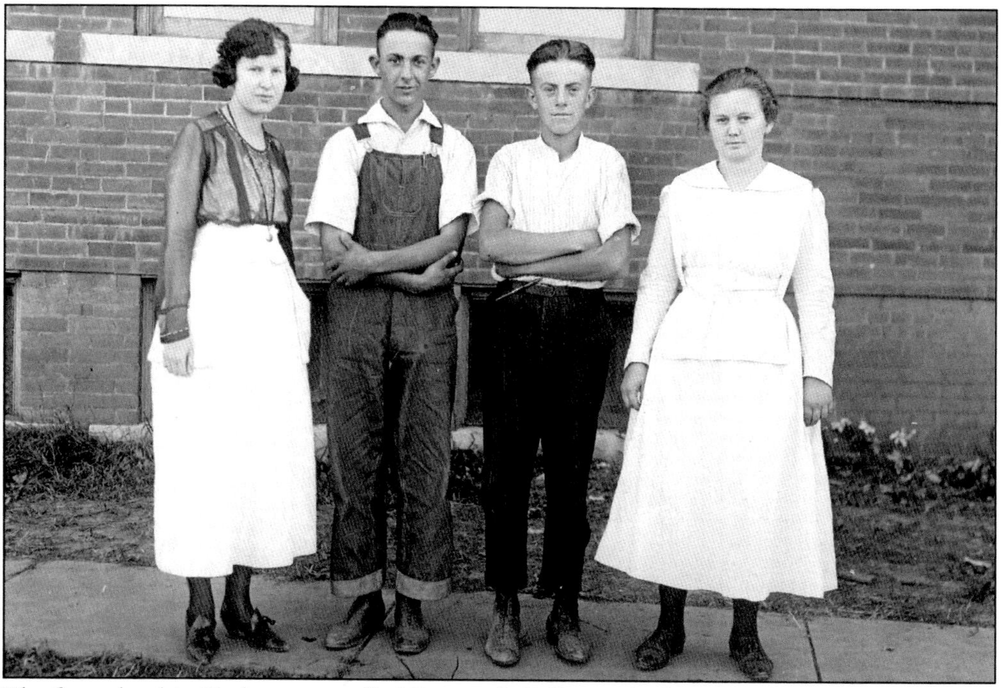

The first school in Graham was called Simpson's College, which was established in a log cabin built in 1843. A frame public school building was erected in 1892, and a brick building followed in 1904. For their last three years, the 1921 graduating class at Graham School had the luxury of electricity in the building, and they were no longer required to attend on Saturday. Pictured from left to right are Vera Long, Earl Bratcher, Joe Gex, and Harriet Wright.

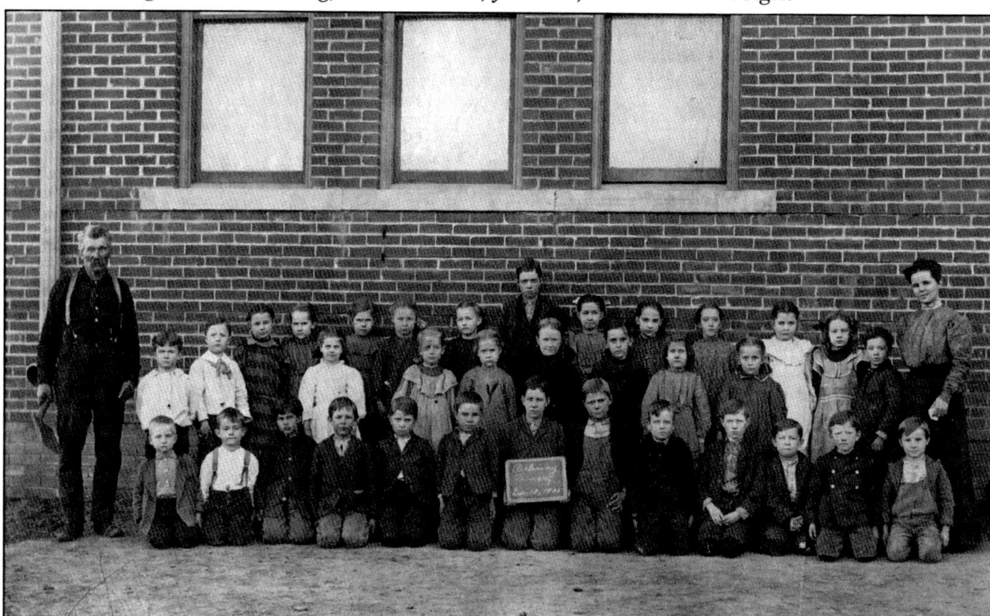

The first room at Pickering School poses for a photograph in 1905. Custodian A. J. Sturgil is on the left, and teacher Julia Roach stands at the far right. Three grades learned together in the first room under Roach's tutelage.

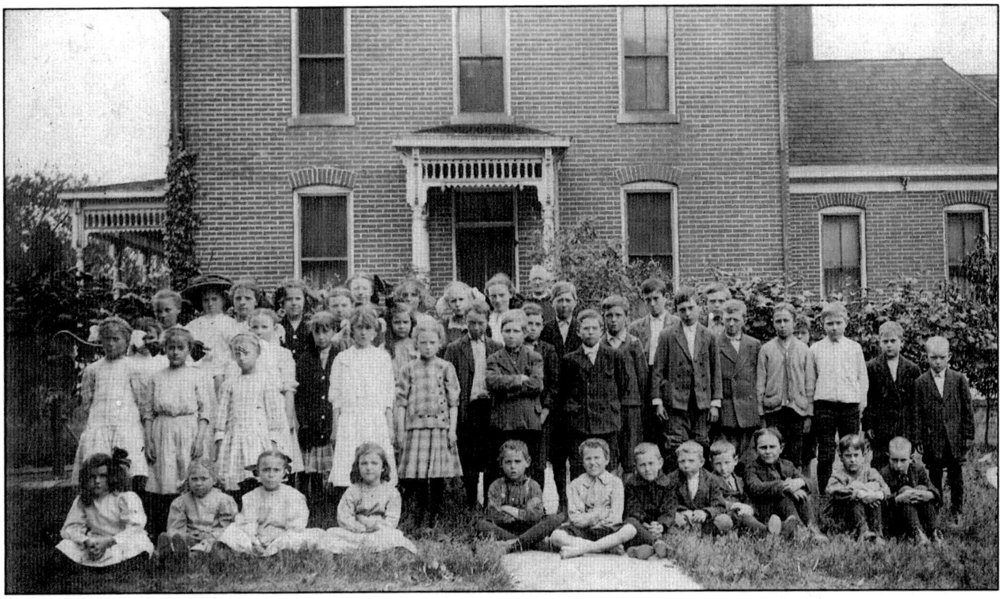

St. Mary's Parish in Maryville organized its first regular school in 1874 when Rev. Adelhelm Odermatt, OSB (Order of St. Benedict), secured the arrival of Benedictine sisters for Maria Rickenbach in Switzerland. The students here pose in the 1890s with Fr. Anselm Ineichen, OSB, who had guided the parish through a difficult split when the Irish families of the community separated to form St. Patrick's parish. The parishes reunited in 1959 as St. Gregory's Church and School.

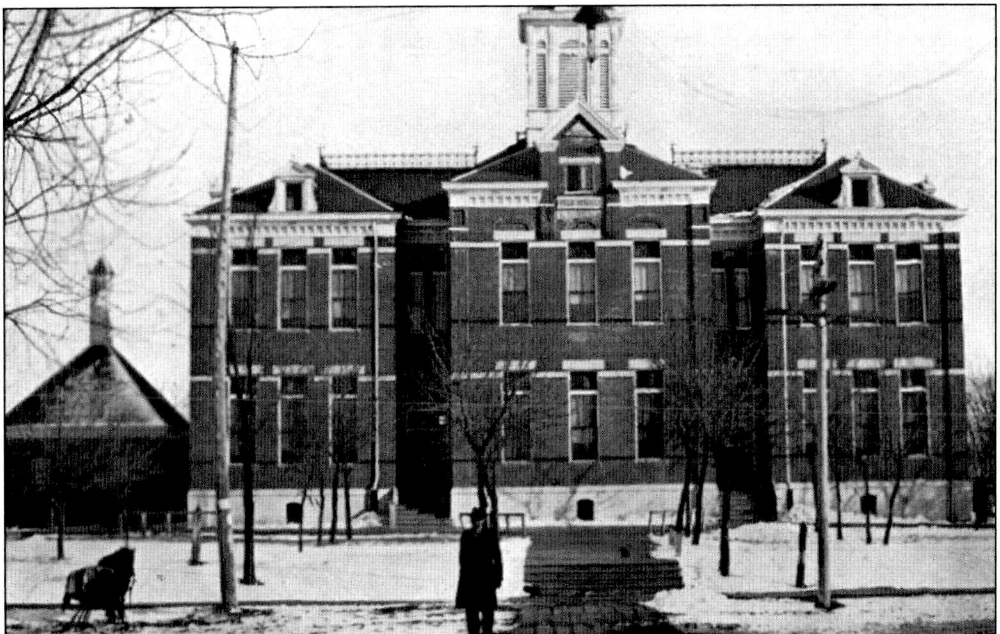

Anxious to erect a modern school building, the Maryville Public School District erected a generously proportioned brick school in 1883. Warmed by steam heat, the building was comprised of 12 rooms with 6 serving the high school and 6 serving the lower grades. The fine structure served Maryville students for only 25 years before being demolished in 1908 to make room for a new school built on what became the Washington School site.

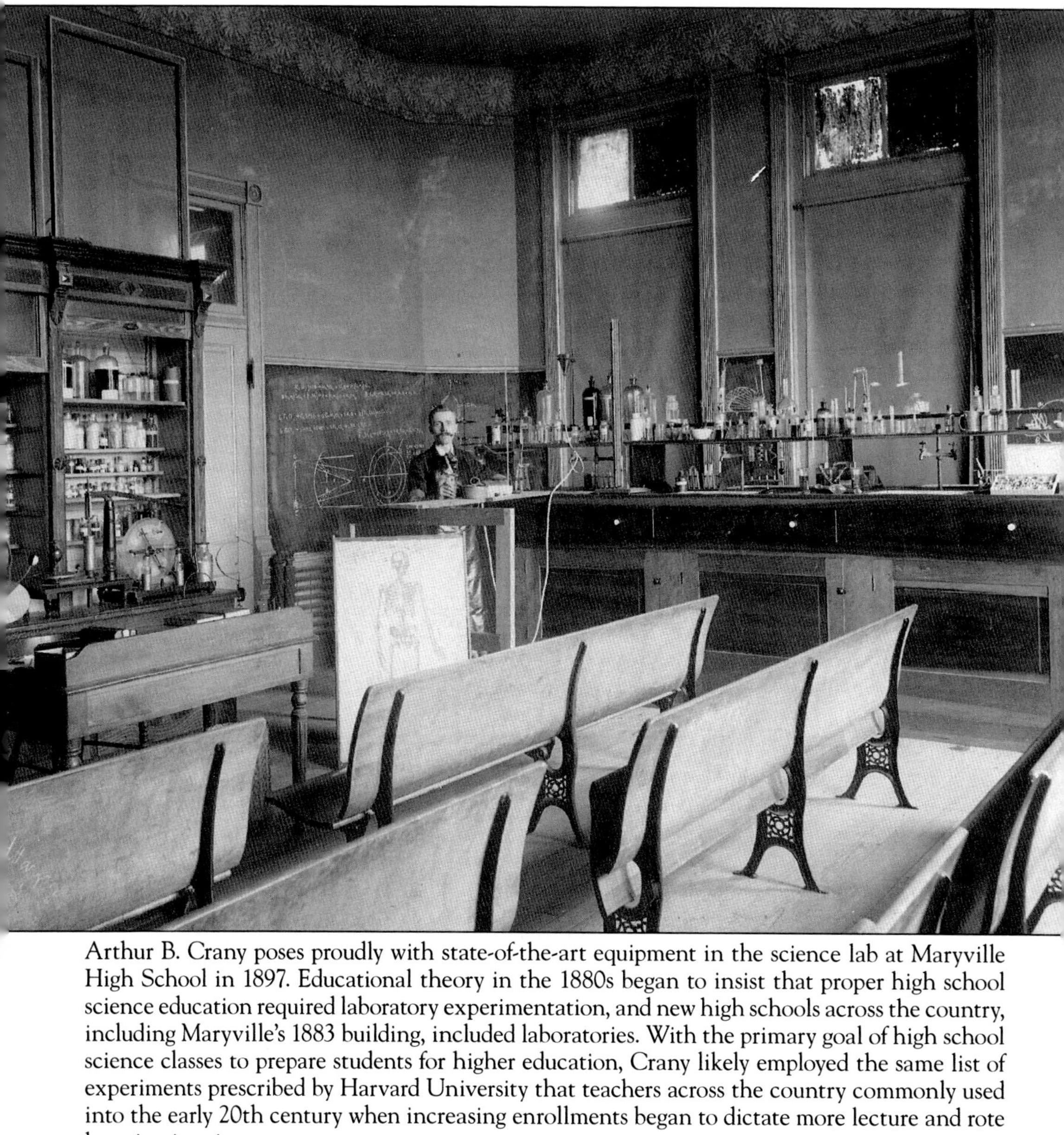

Arthur B. Crany poses proudly with state-of-the-art equipment in the science lab at Maryville High School in 1897. Educational theory in the 1880s began to insist that proper high school science education required laboratory experimentation, and new high schools across the country, including Maryville's 1883 building, included laboratories. With the primary goal of high school science classes to prepare students for higher education, Crany likely employed the same list of experiments prescribed by Harvard University that teachers across the country commonly used into the early 20th century when increasing enrollments began to dictate more lecture and rote learning in science.

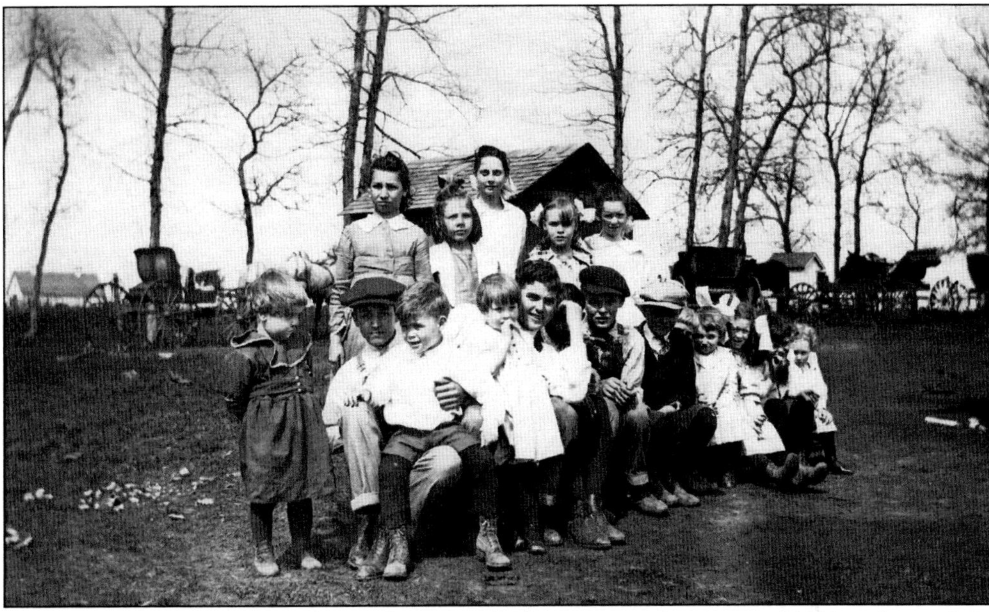

Hickory Grove School opened near the town of Clearmont in the spring of 1883 and served the students of Atchison Township until 1946. Students gather for a class photograph on the school year's last day of classes on May 1, 1919, like those at over 160 other school districts in the county at the time. The school was moved in 1970 to the campus of Northwest Missouri State University, restored, and then moved to the Nodaway County Historical Society Museum.

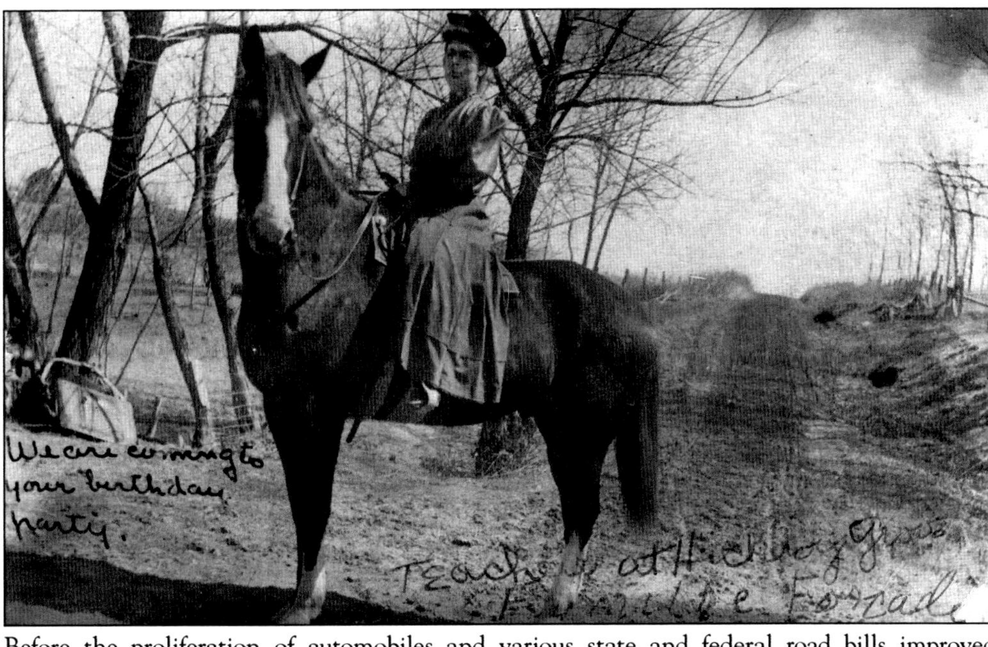

Before the proliferation of automobiles and various state and federal road bills improved transportation in the 1920s, students and teachers of rural schools arrived on foot and horseback. Ermile Forcade arrives at Hickory Grove School near Clearmont unapologetically astride for a day of instruction in early spring of 1908.

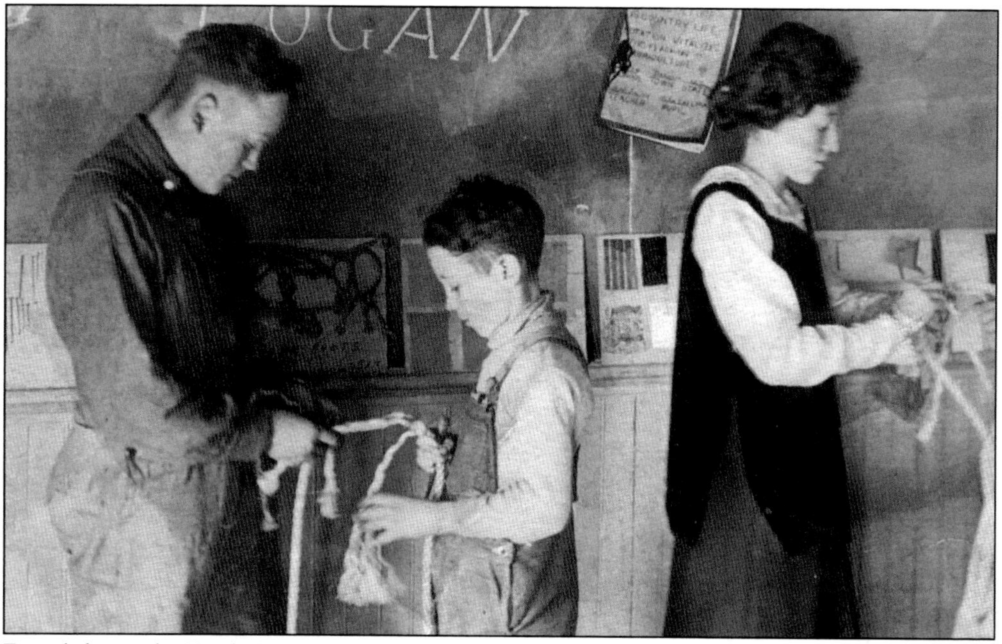

From left to right, Doyle Spoonemore, John Kennedy, and Gertrude Smith study the practical art of tying knots at Logan Country School, located three miles west of Parnell between Orrsburg and Gaynor. The student report pinned to the board proposes in its title that "rotation vitalizes the teaching of agriculture," which was evidence of the growing insistence upon education in agricultural science in rural schools. (Courtesy of Emily McLain.)

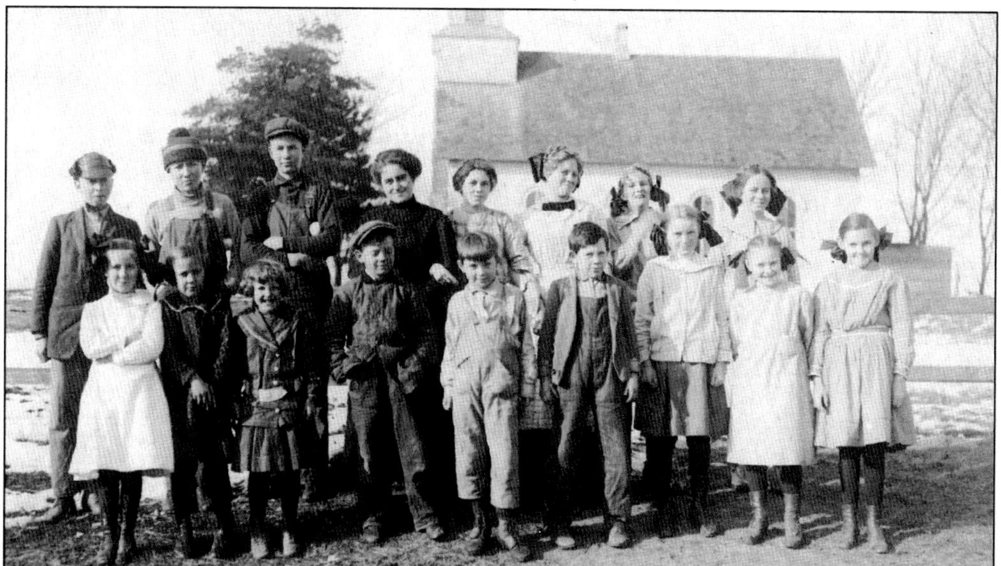

Rural school districts became the center of community activity for farm families. The Rockford School, whose students are posing here in 1914, was in a particularly active neighborhood where the nondenominational church and school sat together. For a half century school picnics, hayrack rides, little parades led by the Rockford Cornet Band, holiday celebrations, quilting bees, and other activities all took place on the property of the school and church where these students stand.

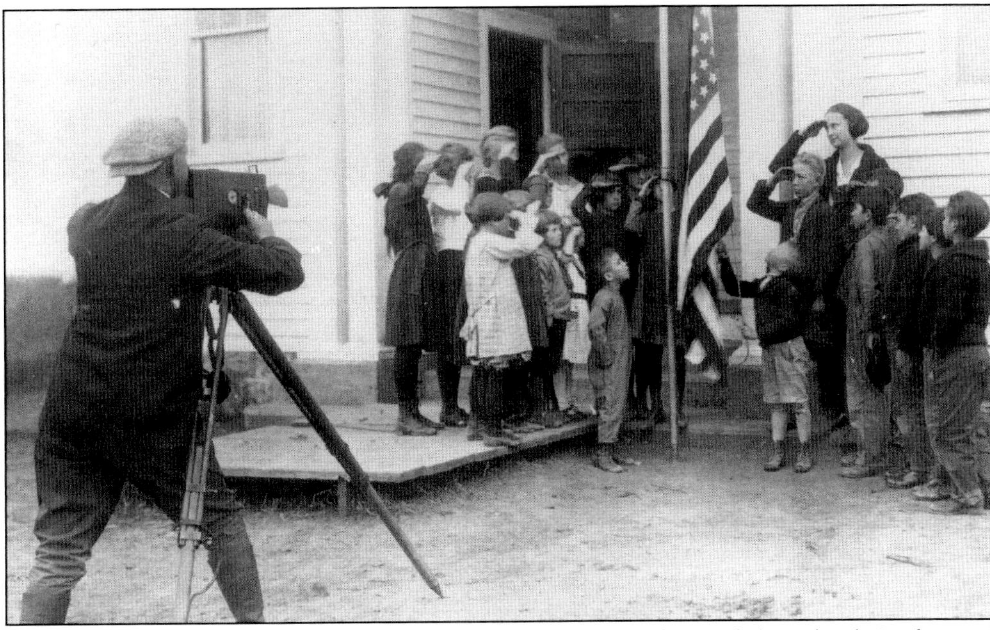

Most of the images of rural education are class pictures in front of the school. Professional photographers operated in every town in Nodaway County prior to 1920 and, much like today, derived steady trade in school photographs. Men like Marcell, Crow, Hopson, Ashbrook, Griffith, Lamonyon, Hickenlooper, Class, Hughs, Kendig, Stroud, and others employed considerable artistry in capturing most of the images that exist of the time period.

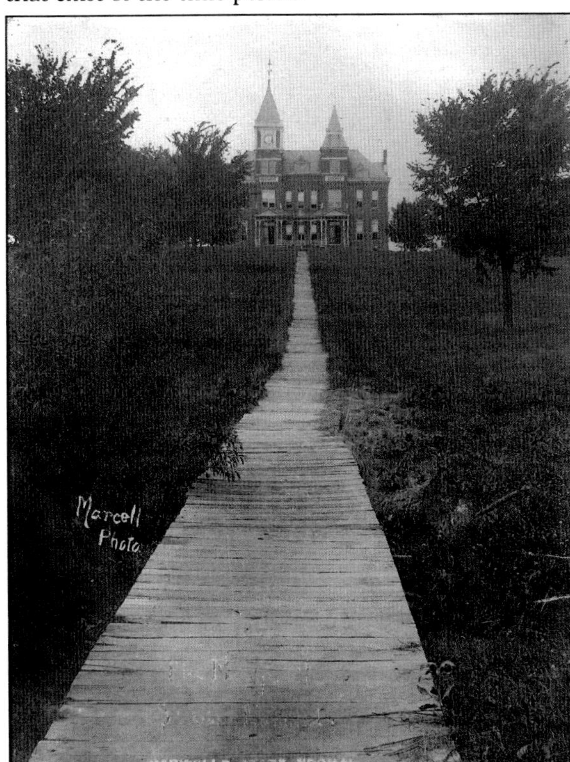

Opening in 1889, the Maryville Seminary operated under the auspices of the Methodist Church and brought teacher training to Northwest Missouri in what came to be known as the old seminary building at the end of West First Street in Maryville. The creation of the state's Fifth District Normal School closed the doors on the faltering seminary. Bricks from the dismantled seminary can still be seen in the walls of the power plant on the campus of Northwest Missouri State University.

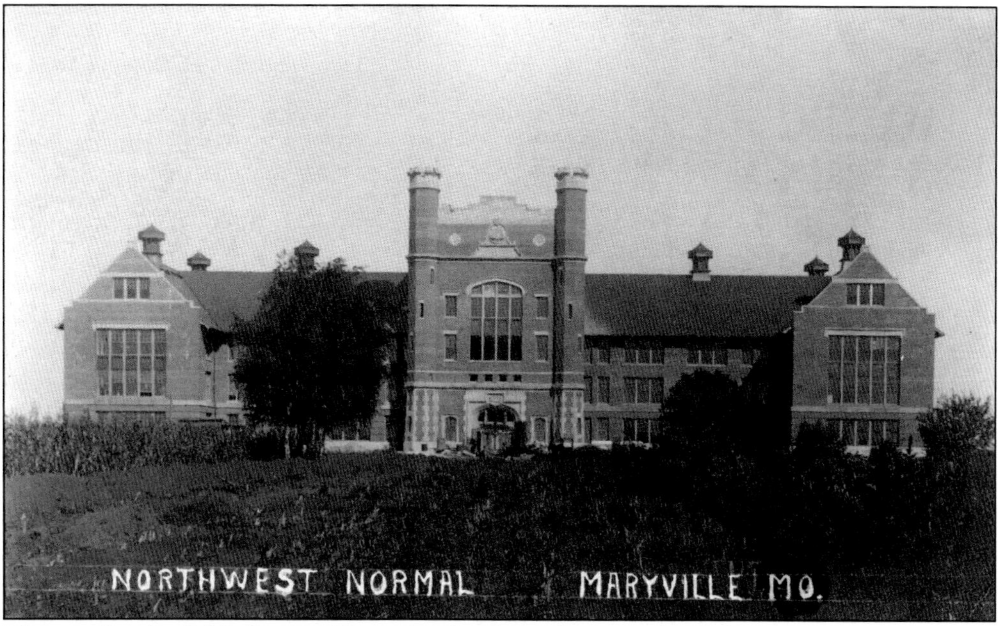

The site for the Fifth District Normal School on the grounds of the abandoned nursery of Thomas Gaunt was heavily criticized. The spot was a mixture of weeds, vines, and a cornfield punctuated by the site's now-famous stand of birches. J. H. Felt designed a Tudor Gothic academic building facing into a quadrangle similar to the style of the University of Cambridge in England, with spectacular results for both the building and grounds. (Courtesy of Coby Lamb.)

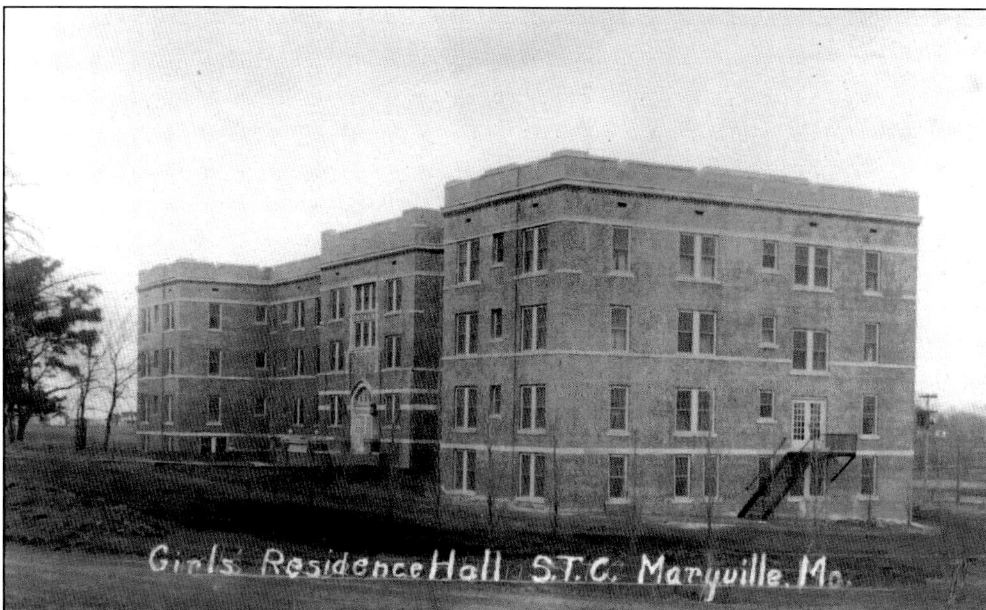

The state teachers college established itself as a residential campus with the construction of the women's residence hall in 1922. The comfortable facility included rooms for 200 women and an elegant parlor for receiving guests. Men added significantly to the local economy by renting rooms around town. An explosion in 1951 caused significant damage to the building and took the life of one resident. It was renamed Roberta Hall in her honor. (Courtesy of Coby Lamb.)

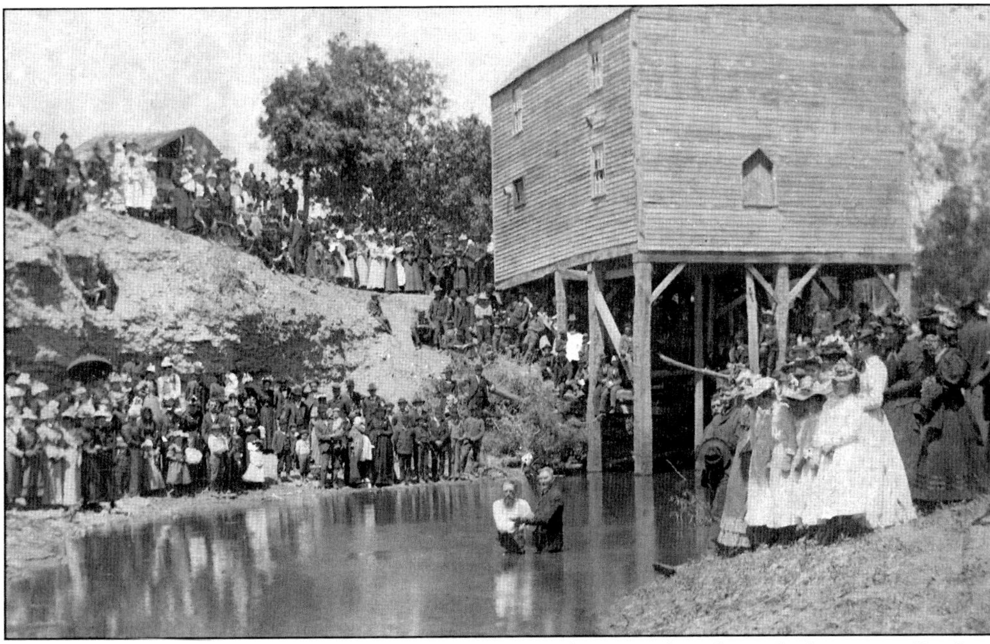

Wilson's Mill on Mill Creek southwest of Elmo served as a preferred site for baptisms. Stephen Lamar recalled being baptized at this site in 1912 by the Reverend Jim Campbell, who was pastor of the North Grove Church northwest of Elmo, while he was holding a revival at the Elmo South Methodist Episcopal Church.

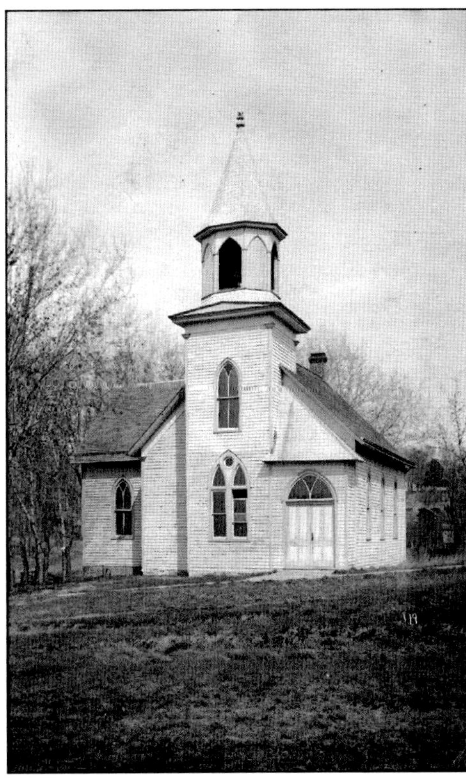

The Methodists brought the first church to Hopkins, followed by the Presbyterians. Next was the United Brethren who built this 24-by-33-foot frame church and sold it for $400 in 1879 to a recently organized congregation of about 40 Baptists. The Hopkins Baptists joined the Northwest Association of the General Association of Missouri Baptists' 1,400 churches. (Courtesy of the Hopkins Historical Society.)

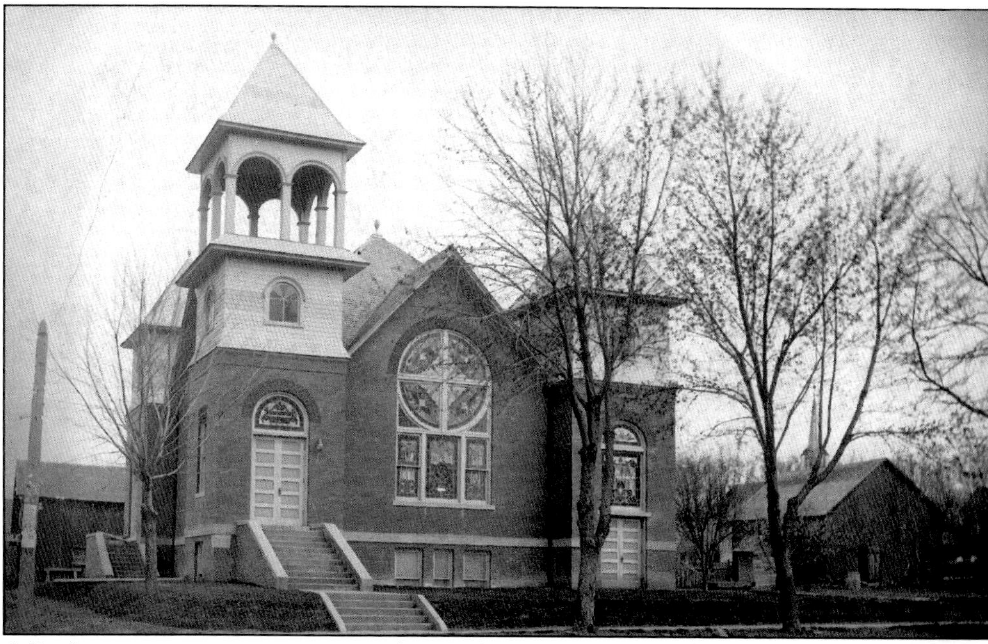

A Presbyterian congregation organized in Hopkins in 1873 and worshipped in a variety of places, including the Methodist church, before completing its own building in 1876. It built a second church on the same location, which was lost to an acetylene light fire. This brick structure replaced it in 1906 at the corner of Fourth and Barnard Streets. (Courtesy of the Hopkins Historical Society.)

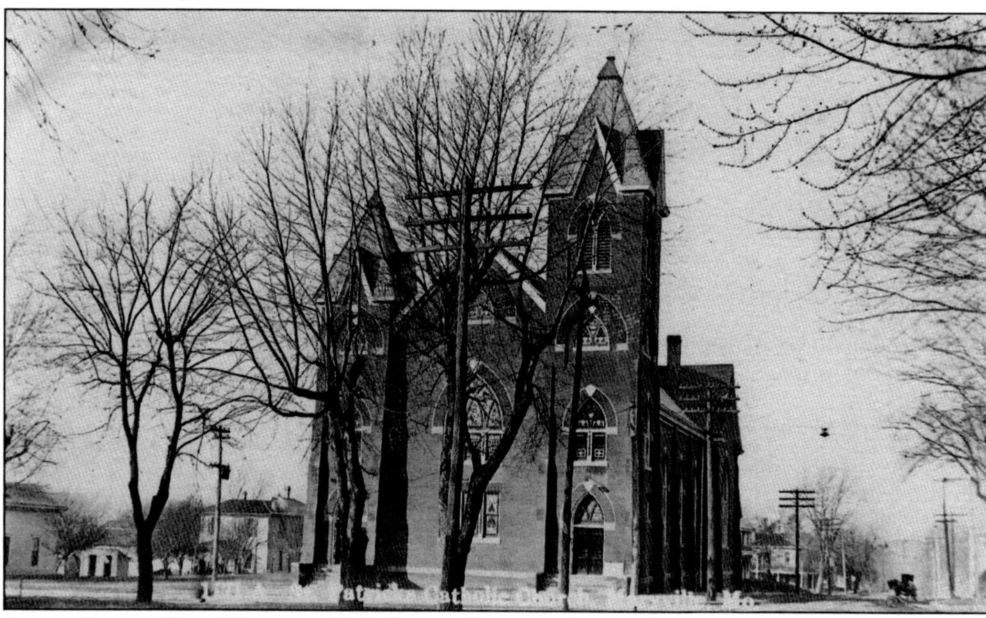

A significant influx of German Catholics in the 1870s shifted the balance of Catholic adherents in St. Mary's Parish from Irish to German, prompting Fr. Anselm Ineichen to begin using his native German in the church and school. The Irish and most English-speaking parishioners left and formed St. Patrick's Parish, erecting a frame structure followed not long after by this substantial brick church with exceptional stained glass.

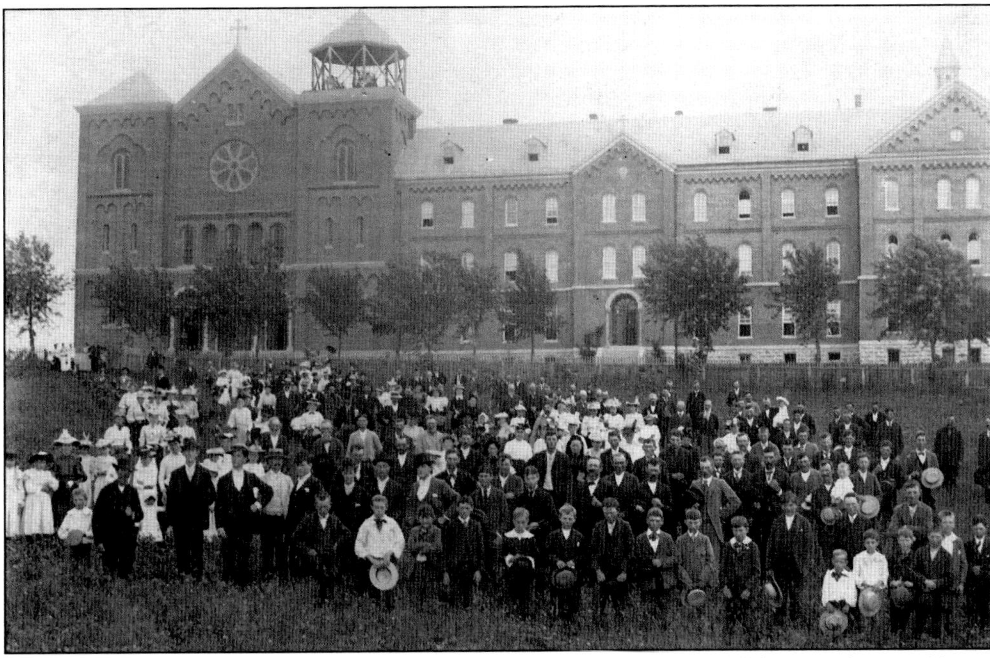

The Catholic community gathered proudly for this photograph in front of the Benedictine abbey at Conception. Only two years after the completion of the church in 1891, the structure was damaged by a tornado. This necessitated repairs and provided opportunity for early improvements to the bell towers and entirely new Beuronese frescos of the lives of Mary and Sts. Benedict and Scholastica.

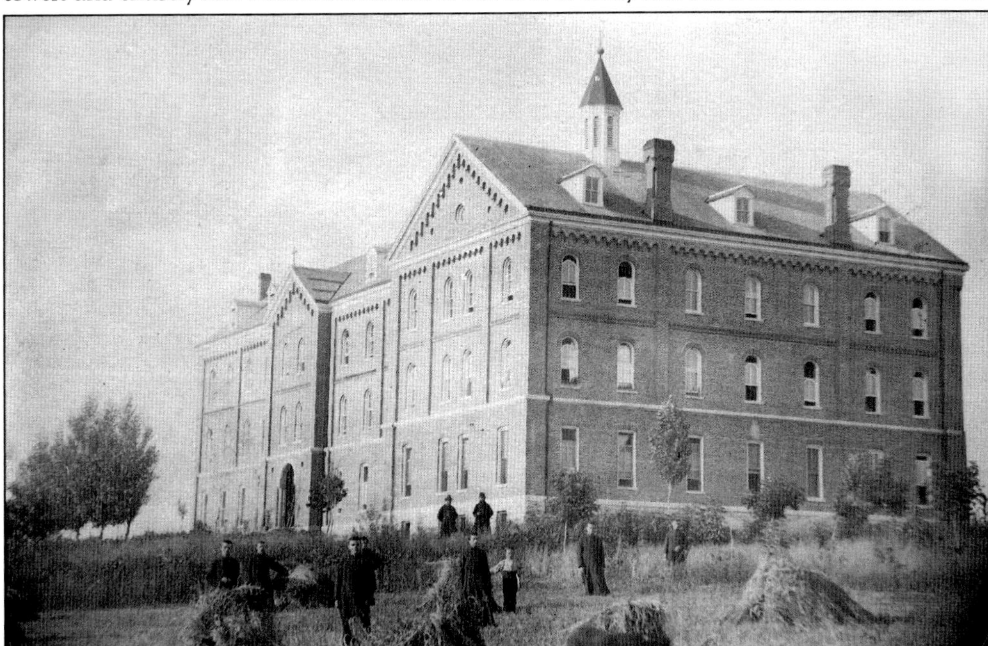

The men of Conception Abbey follow the rule of St. Benedict, which calls for simple lives of prayer and work. Since its inception in 1873, the monks have dedicated themselves primarily to spiritual and scholastic development but have also devoted themselves to the manual labor of agricultural work and to their printery. (Courtesy of Conception Abbey.)

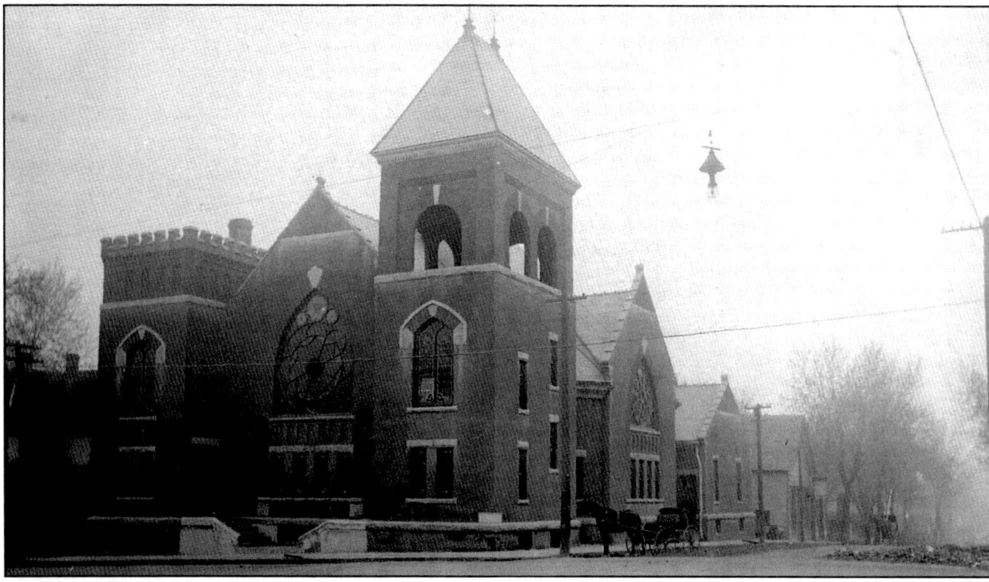

The Christian Church, on the northwest corner of Third and Buchanan Streets in Maryville, housed one of the largest congregations in town at the time of this photograph in 1900. After meeting in a variety of locations for many years, the church completed a frame structure in 1870 and then replaced it with this brick structure in 1893, to which a fine pipe organ was added in 1910.

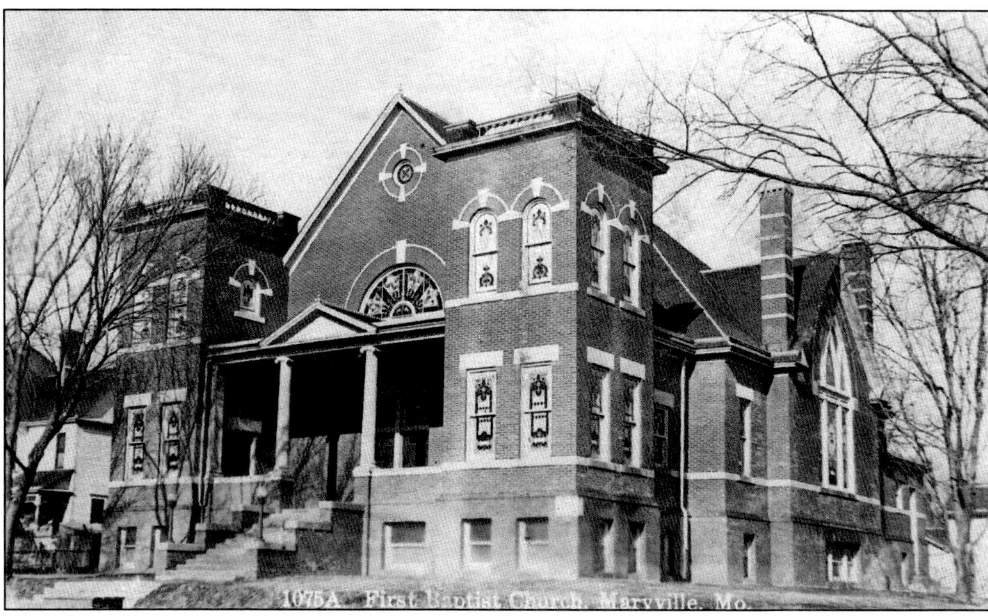

The First Baptist Church in Maryville, located at the corner of Market and Jenkins Streets, began services in its new brick edifice in 1905. The Baptists had been organized in Maryville since the earliest settlement and progressed through several structures before settling their membership of over 500 in this church. Charles Hyslop added the gift of a pipe organ in 1923. (Courtesy of Coby Lamb.)

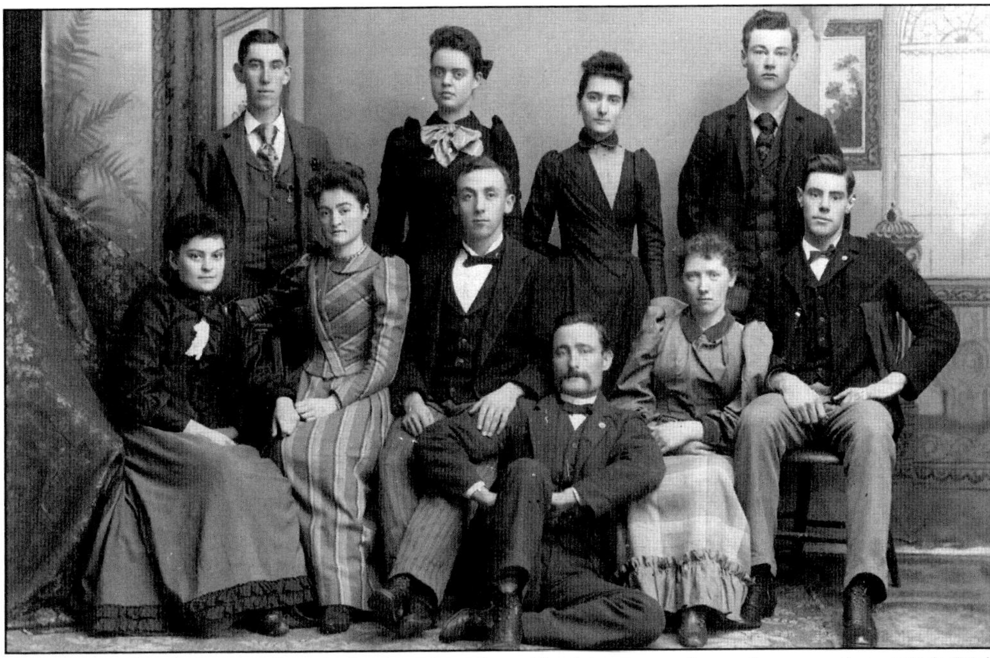

A Sunday school class at the Methodist church in Hopkins poses for a photograph in 1890. Will Crawford is seated in front. From left to right are (seated on chairs) Queite Douglas, Miss Hays, Perry Stewart, Madge McMaster, and Alf Lonsdale; (standing) Ed Wooldridge, Ada Pangburn, Ella Mendenhall, and Logan McCoy. (Courtesy of the Hopkins Historical Society.)

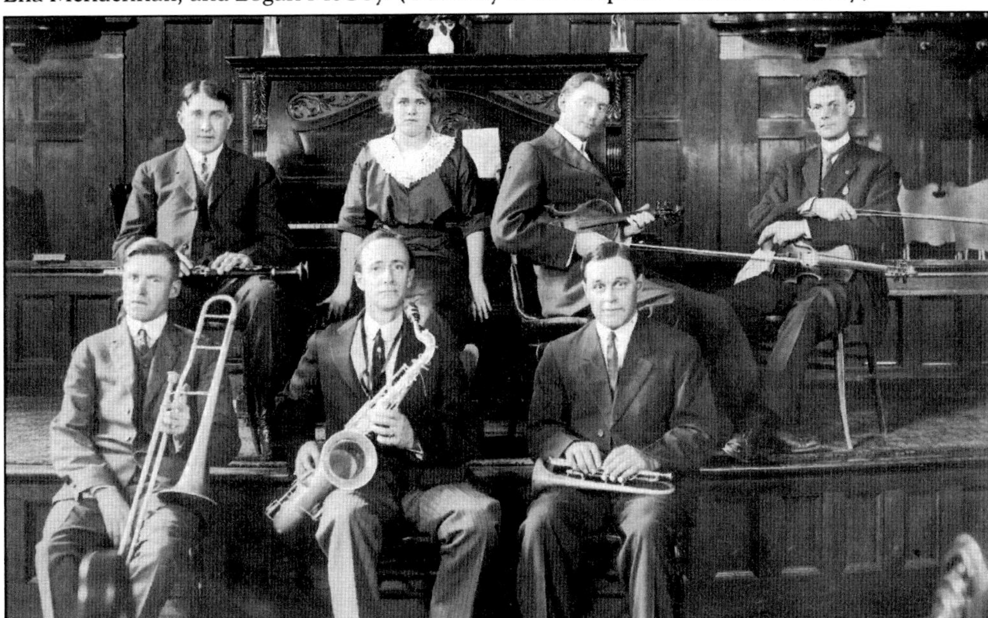

The Christian Church Orchestra in the 1920s included, from left to right, (first row) Paul Basford, Harvey J. Becker, and Lawrence Shanks; (second row) Albert Butherus, Hazel Vandervoort, F. L. Flynt, and W. Lee Griffin. Musicians in the group met the needs of the congregation on Sunday and entertained the community in a variety of concert and dance bands on other occasions. Butherus, in particular, rarely missed an opportunity to entertain in the early 1920s.

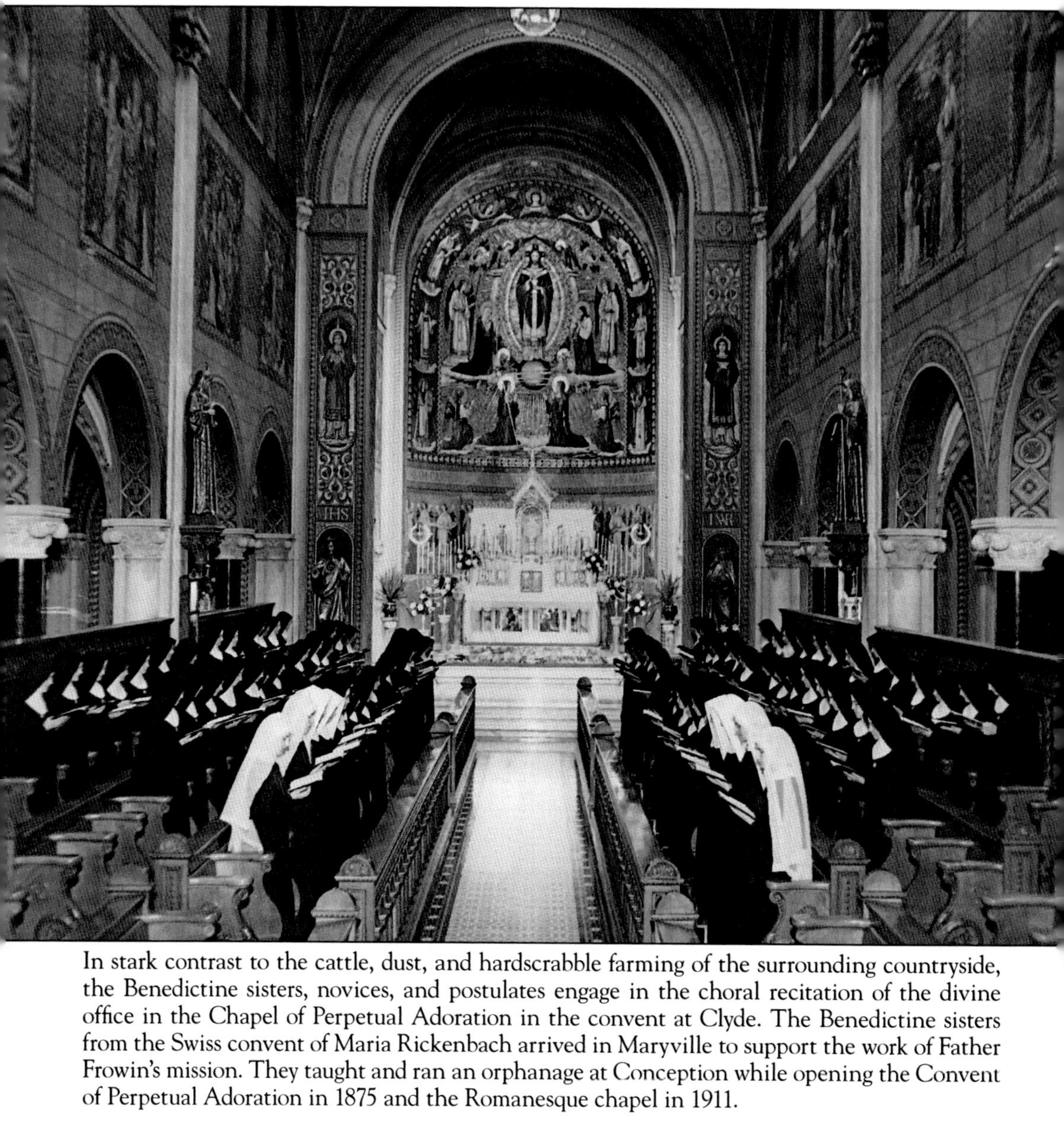

In stark contrast to the cattle, dust, and hardscrabble farming of the surrounding countryside, the Benedictine sisters, novices, and postulates engage in the choral recitation of the divine office in the Chapel of Perpetual Adoration in the convent at Clyde. The Benedictine sisters from the Swiss convent of Maria Rickenbach arrived in Maryville to support the work of Father Frowin's mission. They taught and ran an orphanage at Conception while opening the Convent of Perpetual Adoration in 1875 and the Romanesque chapel in 1911.

Six

DIFFICULTIES

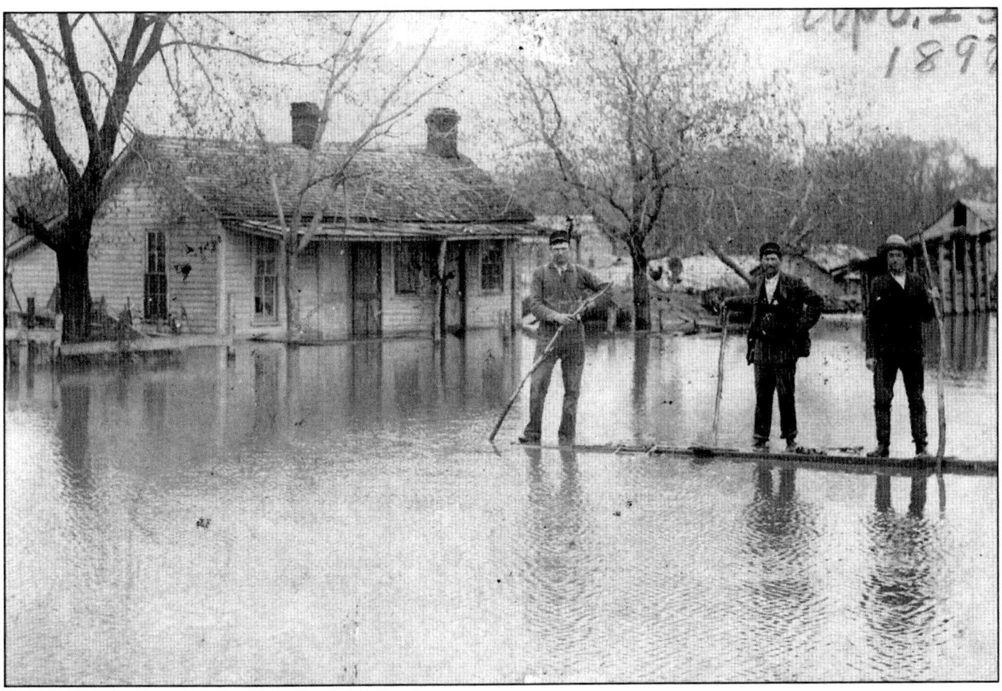

Tom Schoonover, Jim Downers, and Ed Chambers find an adequately high perch near the Schoonover home in the northwest corner of Hopkins during the flood of April 1897. (Courtesy of the Hopkins Historical Society.)

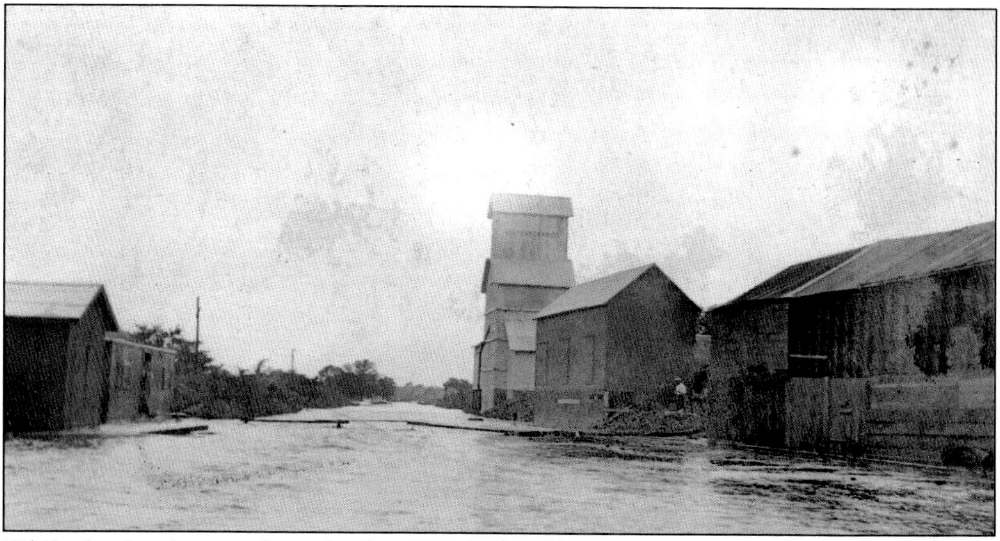

While the river bottom along the One Hundred and Two River provided rich soil for Barnard's ample corn crops, the river regularly flooded the town until substantial channeling of the river provided protection. The view here is of the flood in July 1915, looking northwest from the depot.

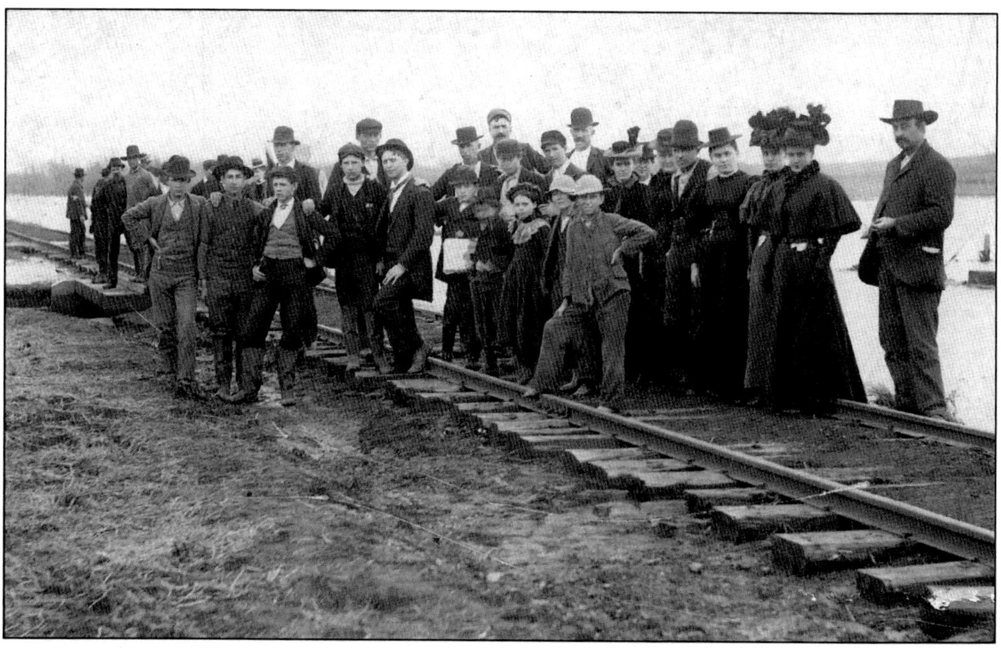

In an age when town boosterism ran high, residents of Hopkins appear to even take pride in their flood. The swollen river made life difficult, however, as the town was shut off from the outside with the railroad tracks north and south of town underwater and telegraph lines collapsed. (Courtesy of the Hopkins Historical Society.)

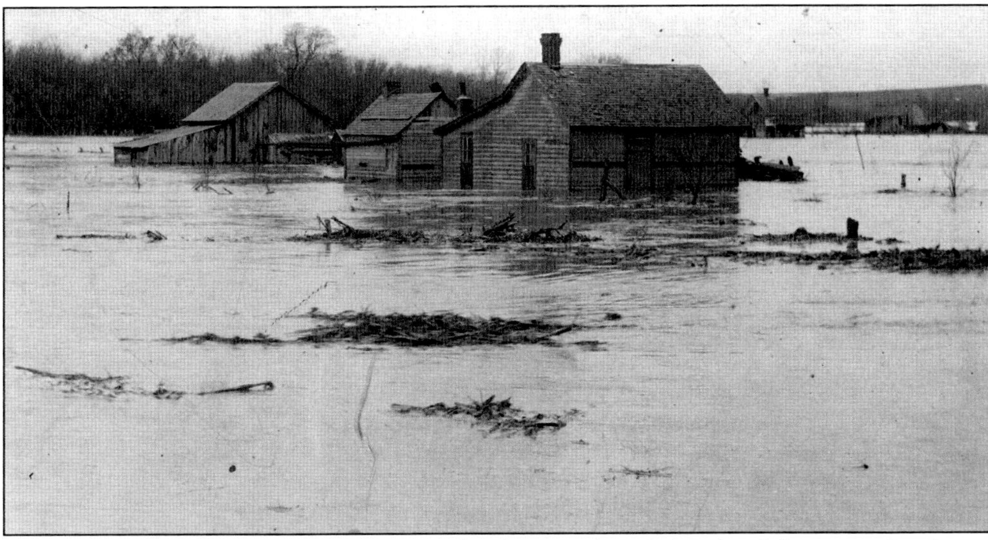

Hopkins experienced its most devastating flood in April 1897. Much of the west side of town found itself several feet underwater. While the damage was severe, residents should have been thankful that in 1871 Edward Wolfers bucked the trend of early settlement west of the railroad tracks and persuaded most new arrivals to join his dry goods store east of the tracks up the hill. (Courtesy of the Hopkins Historical Society.)

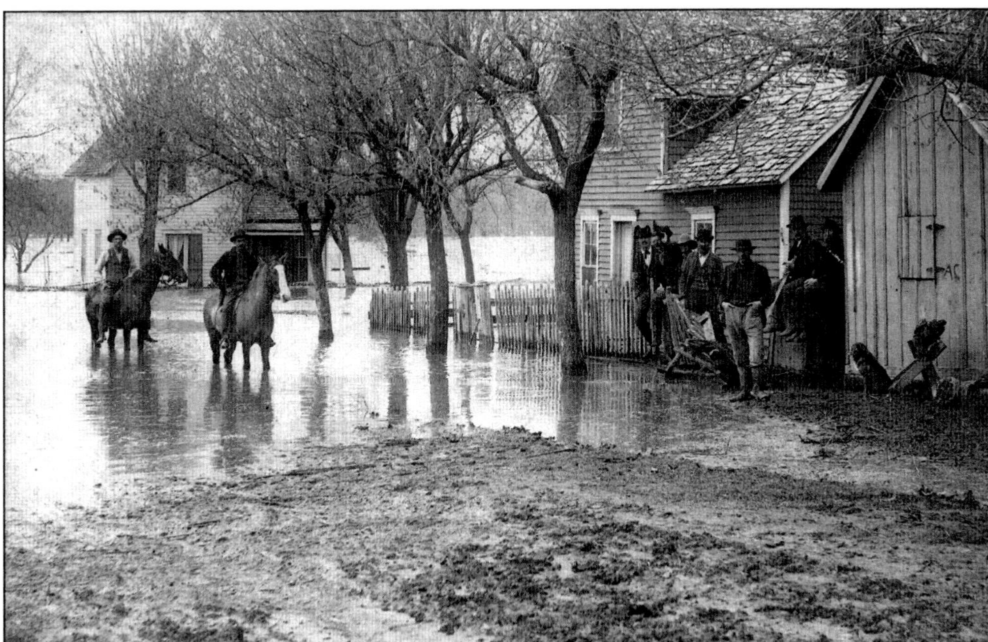

The flood of the One Hundred and Two River in 1900 again left much of northwest Hopkins underwater. Repeated floods plagued Hopkins until significant straightening of the river in the early 1940s reduced the frequency and severity of high water, although heavy rains in 1967 again brought an unwelcome river into town. (Courtesy of the Hopkins Historical Society.)

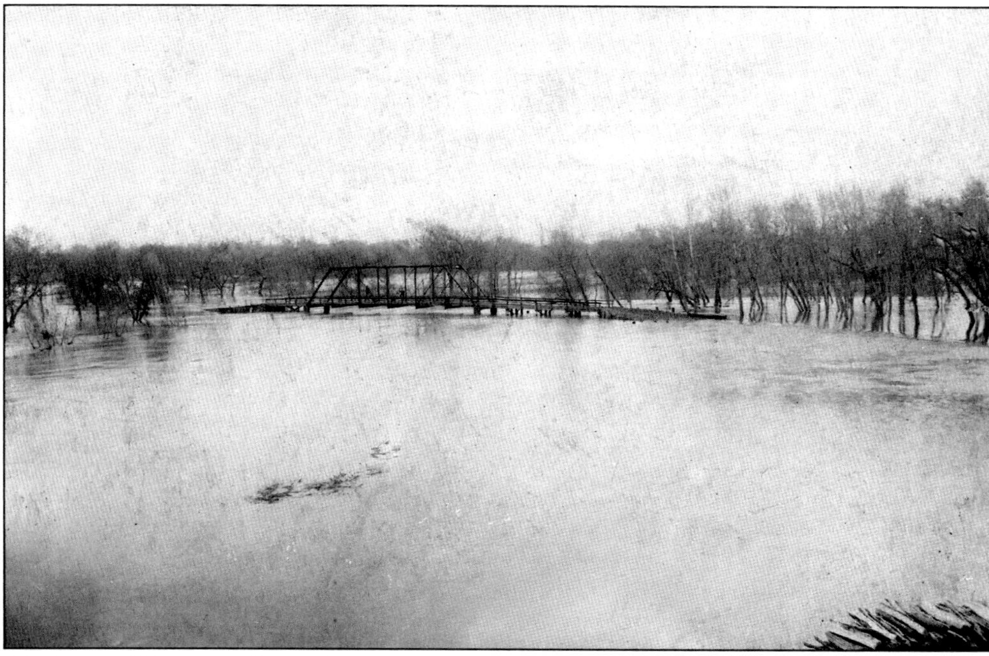

All three of Nodaway County's rivers were prone to flooding despite attempts to dredge and straighten them. A fine iron bridge in Monroe Township stands sturdy against the high waters of the Nodaway River in 1909, but the roads approaching it were unusable for weeks. (Courtesy of the Skidmore Museum.)

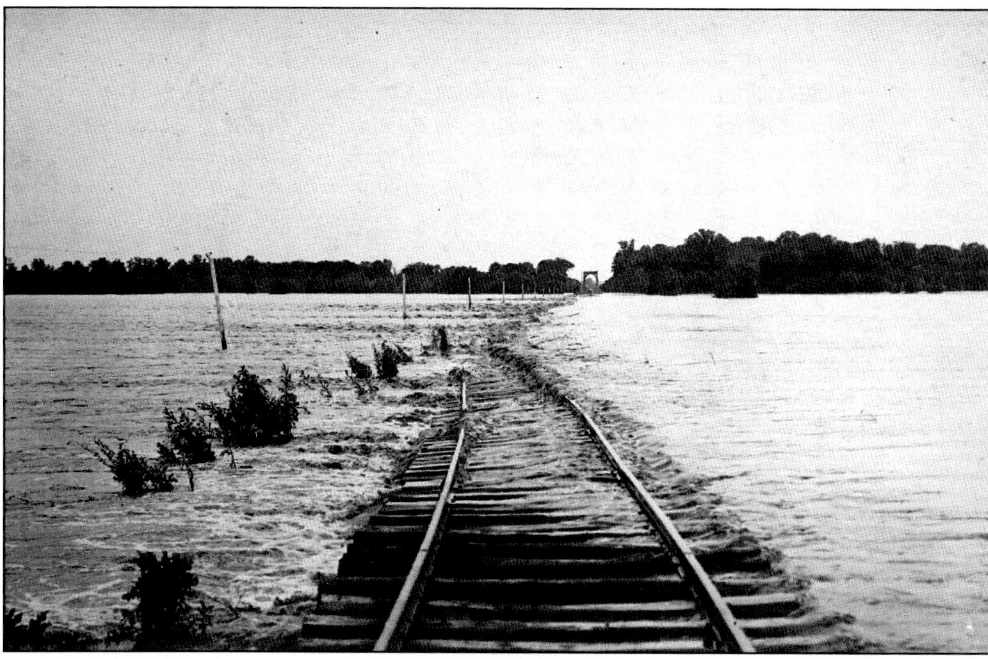

Although valuable as transportation routes to the first settlers, the rivers were more inclined to serve as barriers to useful transportation for the next two generations that were fully dependent upon the railroads. Heavy rains in June 1909 wiped out the Burlington's Nodaway Valley line crossing of the Nodaway River south of Skidmore. (Courtesy of the Skidmore Museum.)

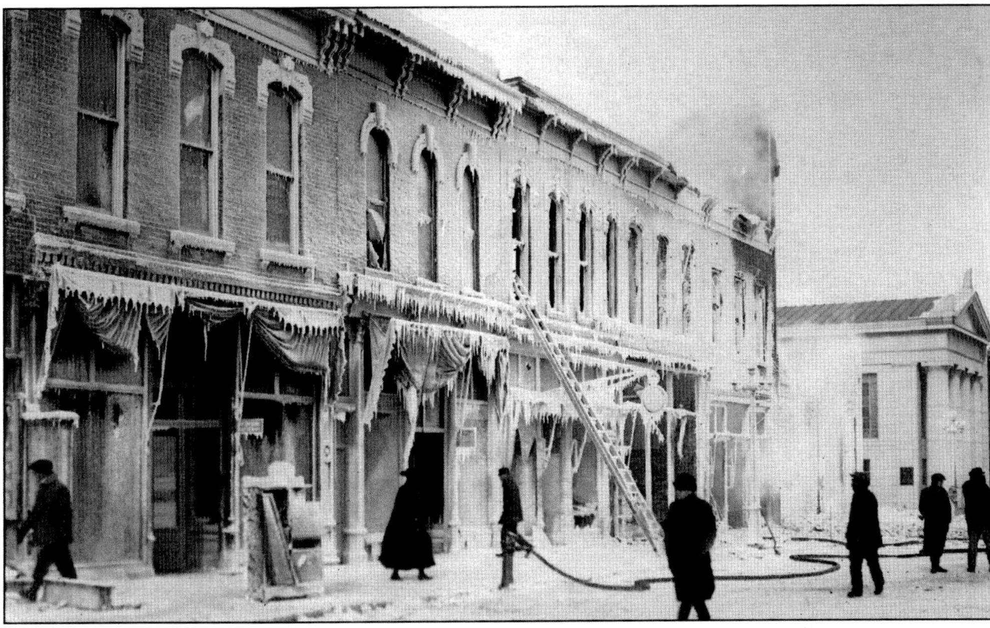

Fires regularly devastated the business districts of Nodaway County communities. Built with an assortment of heating and lighting systems and wired dangerously when electricity arrived, commercial blocks were often fires waiting to happen. Five businesses were destroyed on the west side of the square in Maryville by this fire in 1918. The Townsend family of grocers had a long history of devastating fires in Maryville. Their first loss came in 1890 when the grocery of R. K. Townsend burned at the corner of Second and Main Streets during a night when the temperature was reportedly 30 degrees below zero. E. L. Townsend moved his father's business to the southwest corner of Fourth and Main Streets, which burned in the fire of 1918 on a night that was 20 degrees below zero. The family eventually relocated their wholesale grocery to Fourth and Buchanan Streets, but it burned to the ground again in 1960. The temperature that night, by Townsend fire standards, was a balmy 27 degrees. (Courtesy of Coby Lamb.)

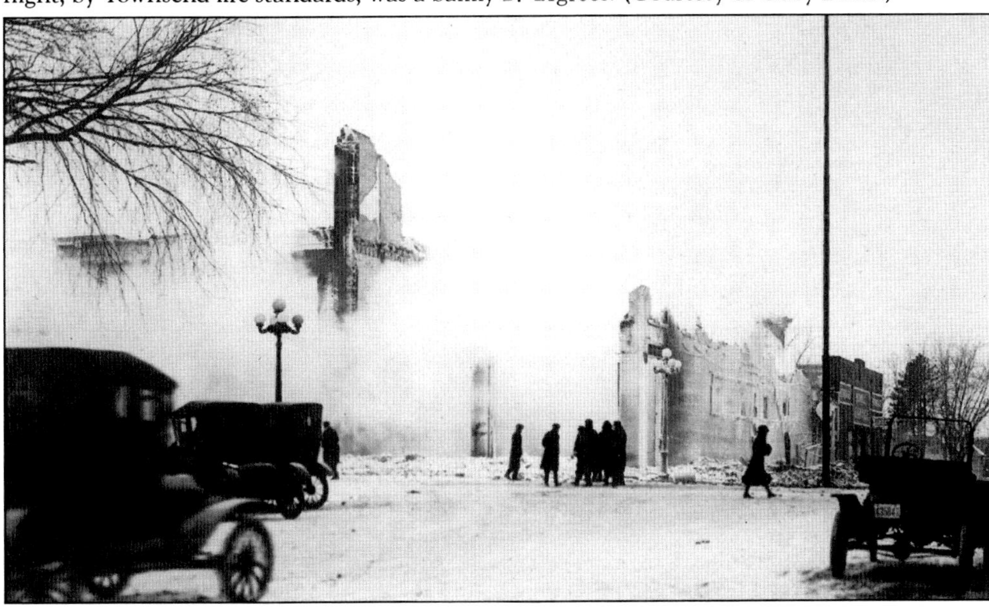

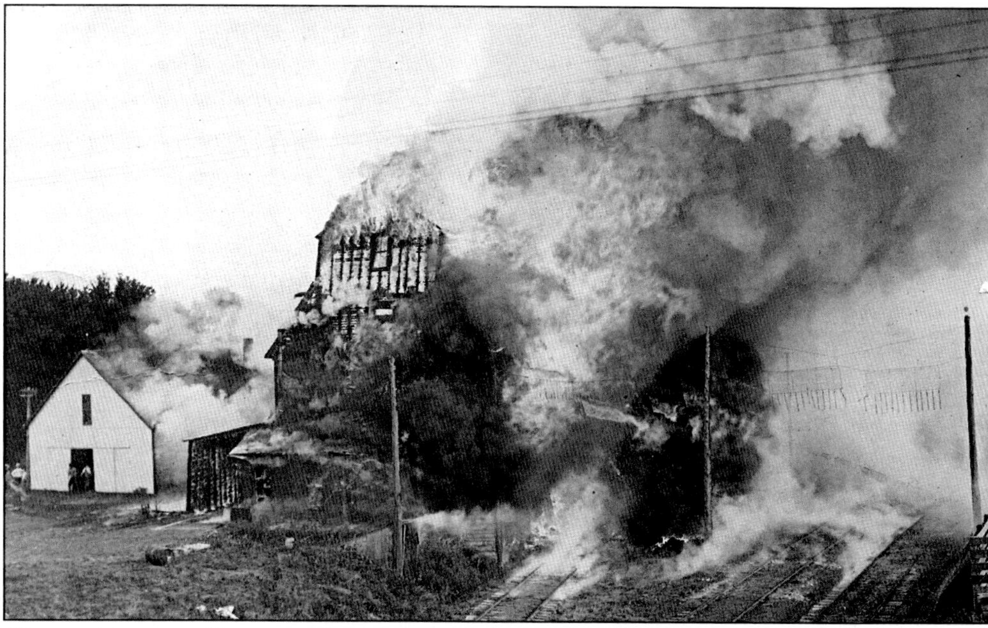

The combination of large wooden structures, grain, and railroad yards were a necessary though dangerous combination. The elevator north of the depot in Skidmore burned not long after 1900. In a separate incident, the Burlington depot in Skidmore also burned and was replaced by another depot of similar design that still stands in Skidmore today. (Courtesy of the Skidmore Museum.)

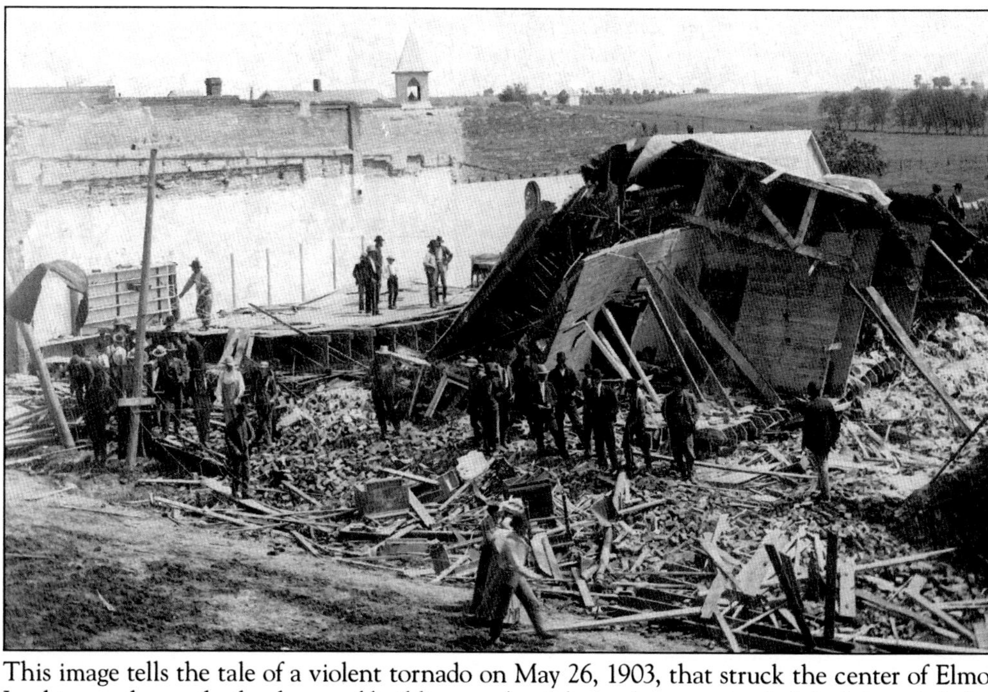

This image tells the tale of a violent tornado on May 26, 1903, that struck the center of Elmo. Looking to the south, the shattered building on the right is what remained of the Masonic lodge building where eight men lost their lives. To the left are the remains of Bush's furniture store and farther to the left is the Kidder building where several fortunate survivors had taken refuge.

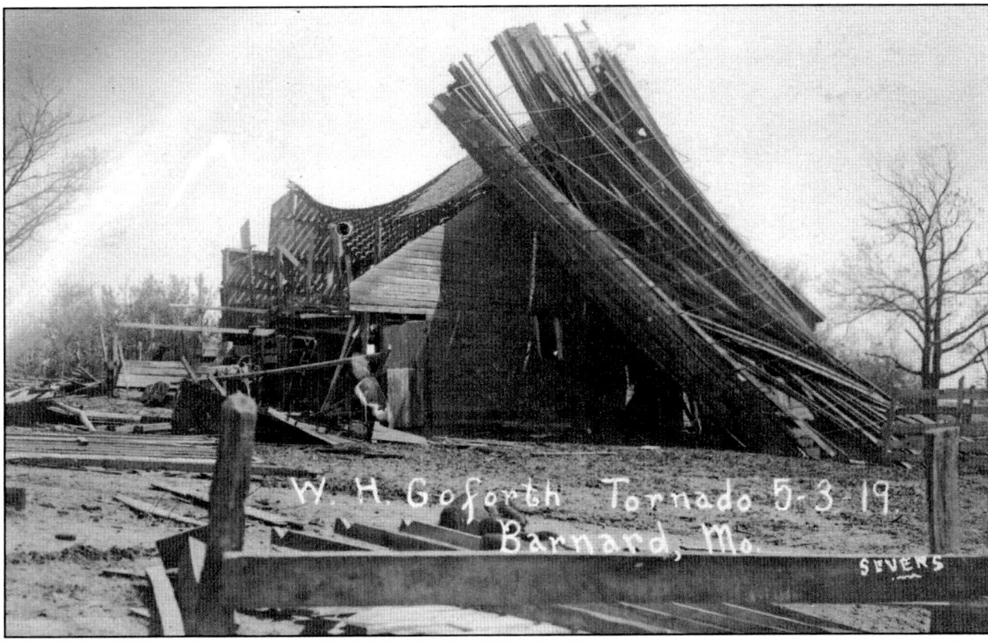

On May 3, 1919, the farms north of Barnard in White Cloud and Grant Townships were struck by a powerful tornado. While no one was seriously injured, the property damage was considerable. Among the sites destroyed were the McKee, Mendenhall, Hilsabeck, Rasco, and Campbell farms. Dark humor among children surely followed the flattening of Fairview Country School. Members of the community rallied to help W. H. Goforth rebuild his mangled barn. When speaking of the Campbell place near Barnard after the 1919 tornado, Bertha Snyder recalled that "this house was turned clear off the foundation and the floors run up through the bed." Although local insurance agencies offered tornado insurance, it was a hard sell to cash-strapped farmers despite the risk. (Courtesy of the Barnard Community Historical Society.)

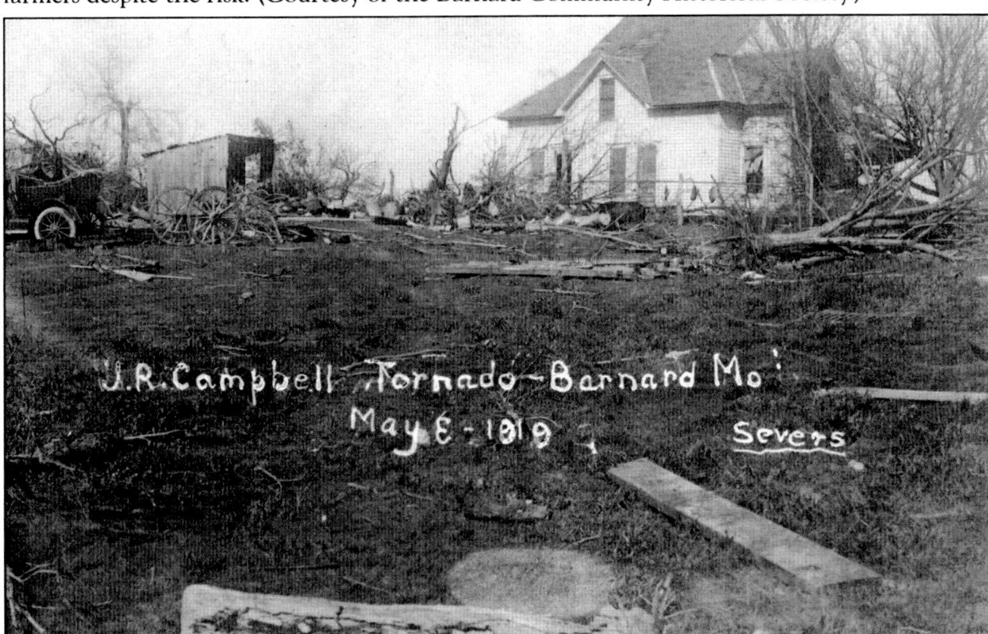

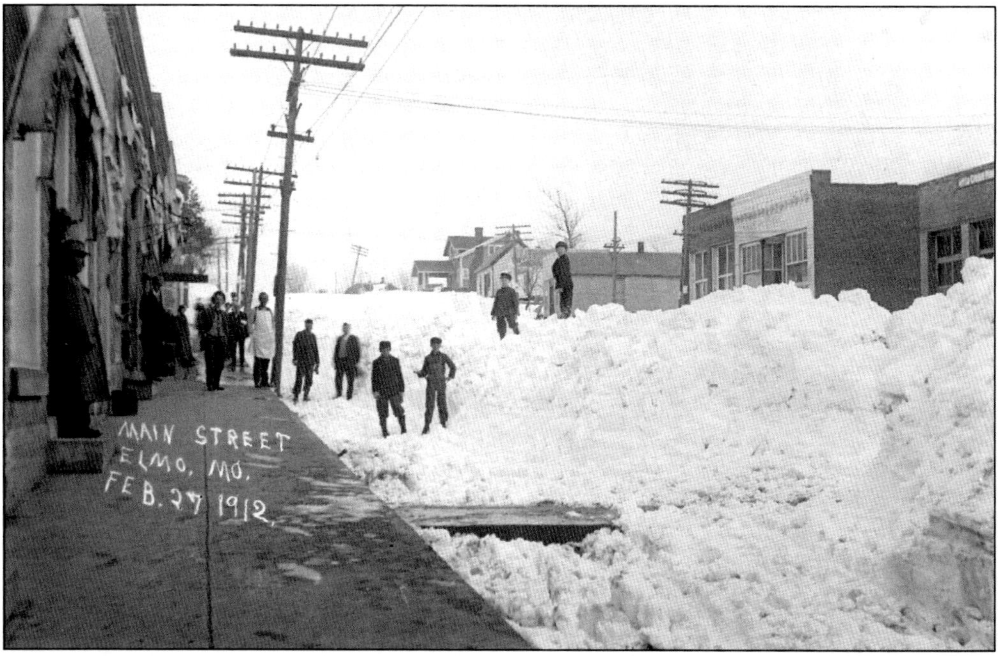

The snow of February 1912 fell heavy on the town of Elmo and the rest of Nodaway County. Twenty-four inches fell on February 23 with snowfall amounts for February totaling over 35 inches. By mid-March, it totaled over five feet for the winter. Some country roads had snowdrifts that were 18 feet deep during a winter that was also was unusually cold.

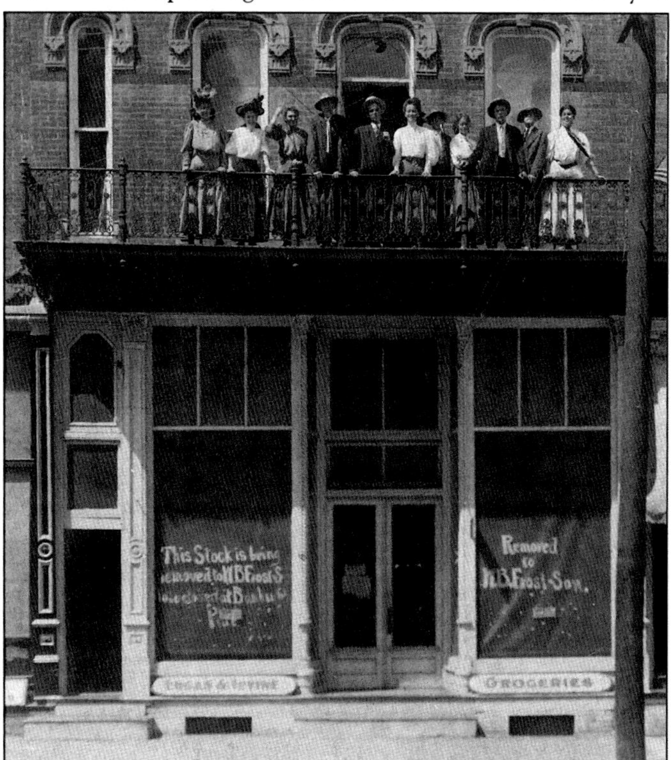

While business for most was booming in Maryville in the early 1900s, the Lucas and Irvine grocery fell on hard times, having declared foreclosure on its windows and the removal of its stock to the W. B. Frost grocery.

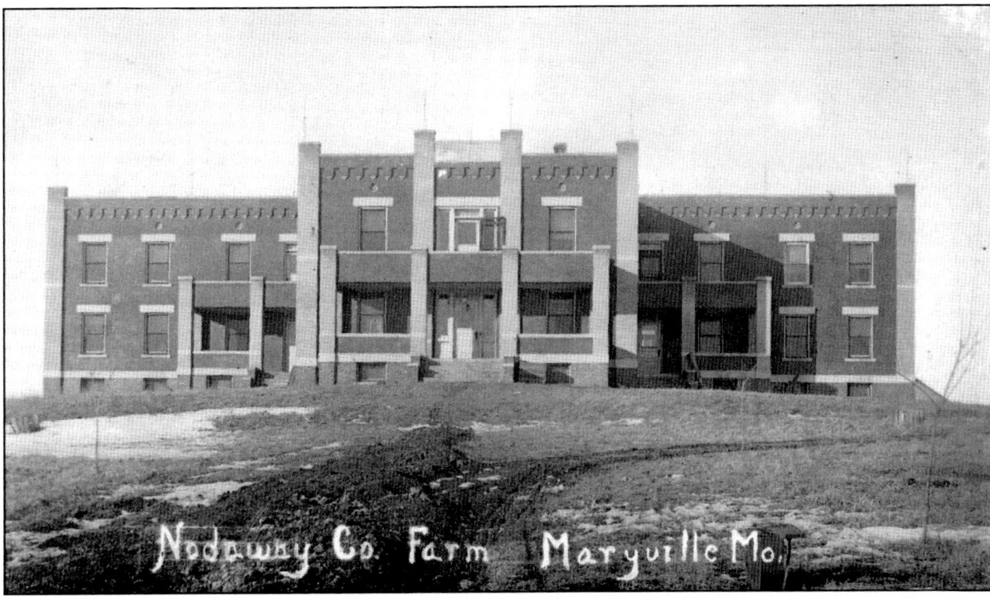

The county court appointed a commission in 1871 that acquired land west of Maryville where it maintained a poor farm. Conditions at the home apparently deteriorated badly by century's end, and a stinging article in the *Kansas City Star* in 1906 proclaimed, "the people of Nodaway County can never escape the humiliation of permitting their negligent cruelty to the helpless poor." Taxpayers responded quickly with the construction of this brick structure, which Nodaway Countians raised proudly as an example of progressive reform.

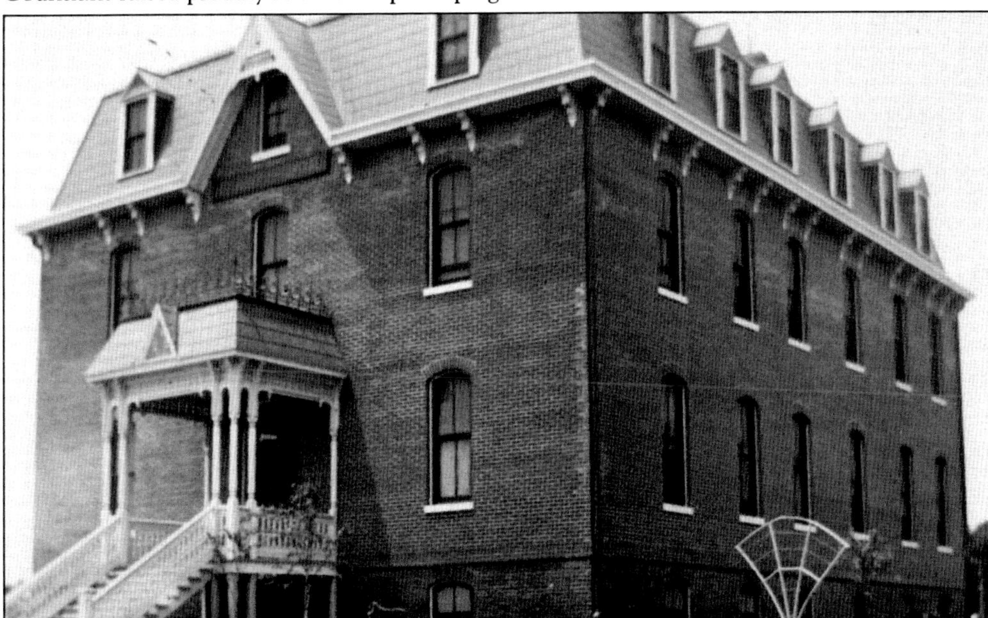

Seven Sisters of St. Francis opened Maryville's first hospital in 1894 and a year later dedicated this newly constructed facility with 30 patient rooms available on East First Street. In its first year, this hospital treated 85 patients, 81 of whom had the good fortune to leave in better condition. Additions were made to the hospital in 1901, 1903, 1920, and 1929, and the structure served the county until 1965, when it was deemed obsolete.

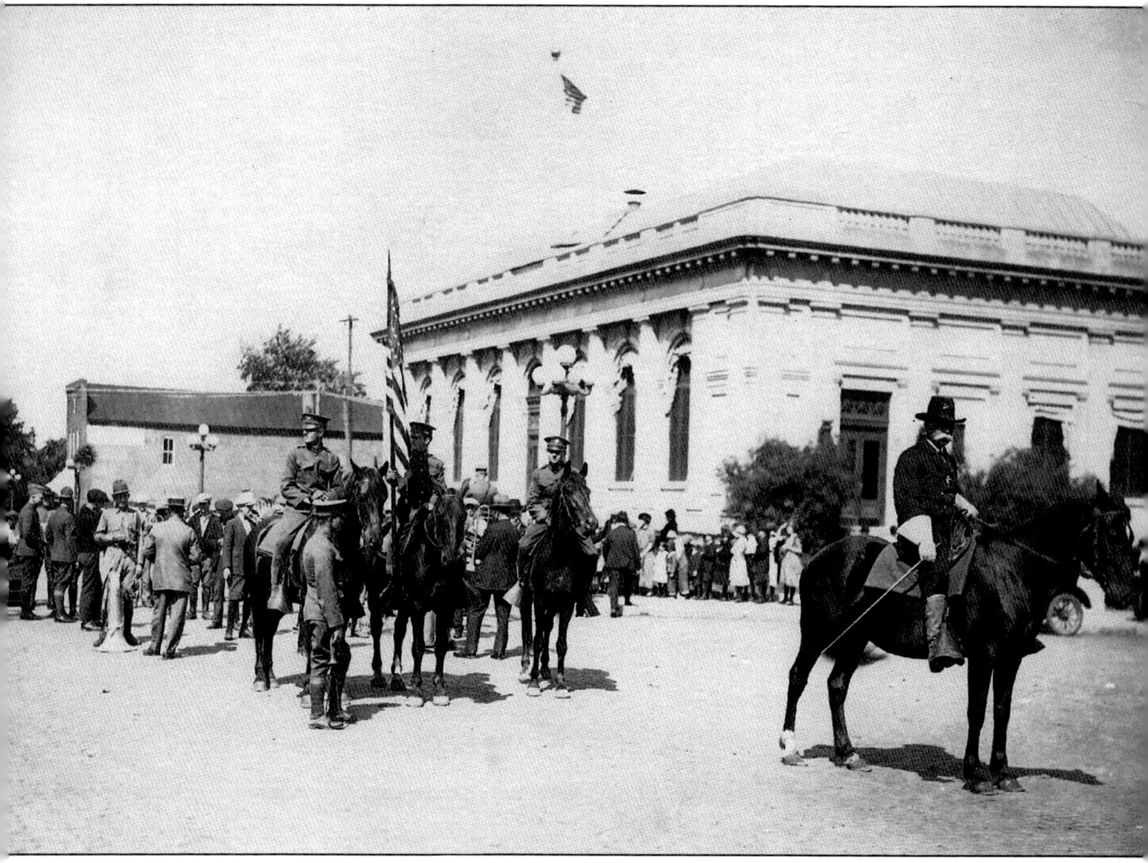

Nat Sisson, former commander of the Maryville post of the Grand Army of the Republic and one of Nodaway County's venerated war heroes, leads a patriotic parade in support of troops serving in World War I. Sisson had volunteered for service in the Civil War at age 17 and served in numerous battles as a brigade bugler, including the capture of Richmond. Significant evidence attests that Sisson sounded the last hostile bugle call in the Civil War while serving under Henry Capehart at Appomattox. At age 20, he set out for the West, making it as far as Maryville, where he spent the rest of his life as a leading citizen. His son Paul served as the first captain of Maryville's 4th Regiment in the National Guard.

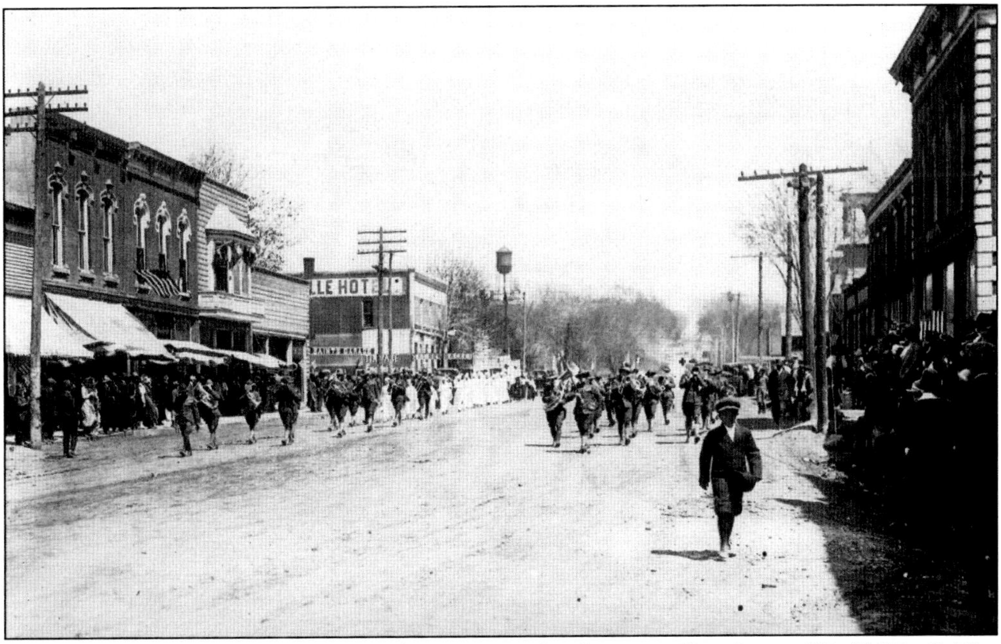

Parades provided an opportunity to show support for the war effort during World War I. The National Guard Army Reserve military band leads the ladies of the American Red Cross in a patriotic parade down Barnard Street in Hopkins toward the depot. Such activities blended entertainment and patriotism and inspired numerous county men to serve.

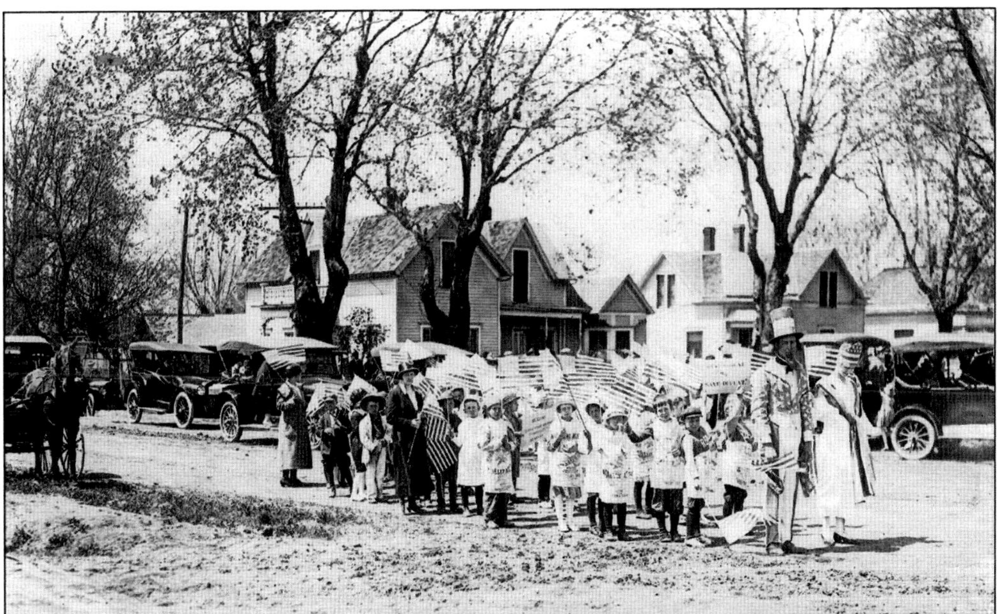

Children were involved in patriotic wartime parades, and the intent of this group of youngsters was to encourage patriotism through conservation. Signs urged citizens to "save wheat and save defeat," and the young ladies conveyed the support of the flour mills by wearing flour sacks from Valley Lily Flour and Skylight Winter Wheat Flour. Another sign reads, "Sugar! Save that extra Spoonful. Sugar!"

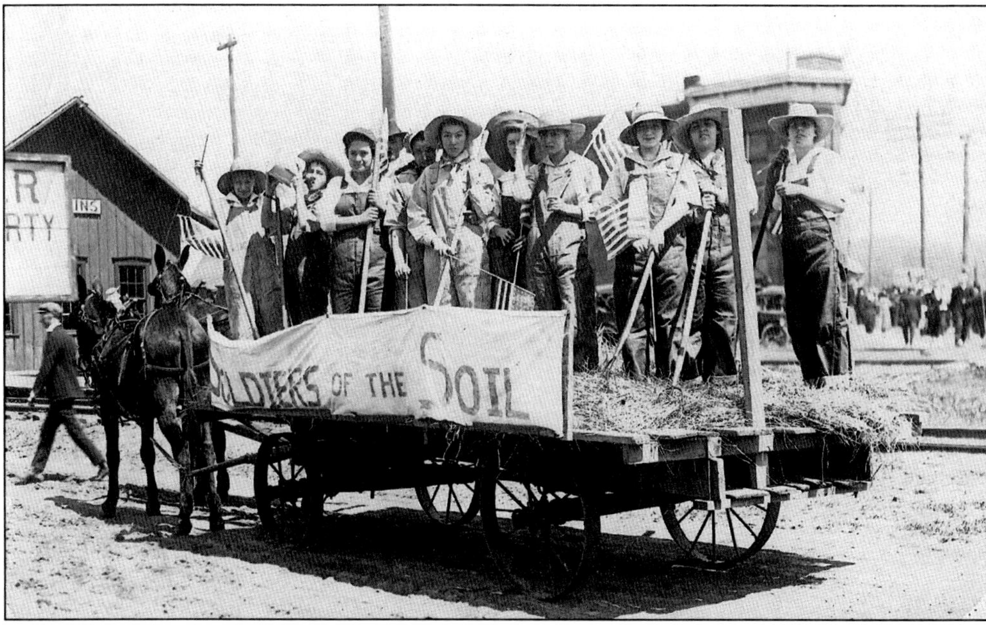

World War I occasioned numerous patriotic parades where citizens were encouraged to offer support in any way possible. Here the young ladies of Hopkins emphasize the critical role of the region's agricultural production to the war effort.

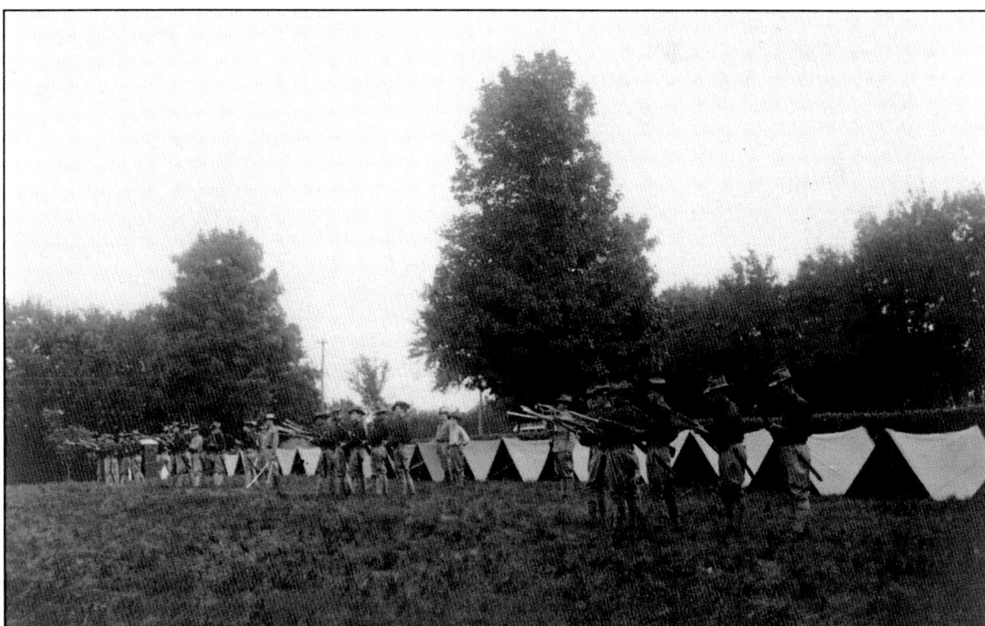

In 1903, the Militia Act created the National Guard out of the numerous state militias. As the primary reserve force for the army, National Guardsmen, like those in the 4th Regiment Infantry of Nodaway County, prepared to be called up for service in Europe, where guardsmen made up 40 percent of combat forces. (Courtesy of Coby Lamb.)

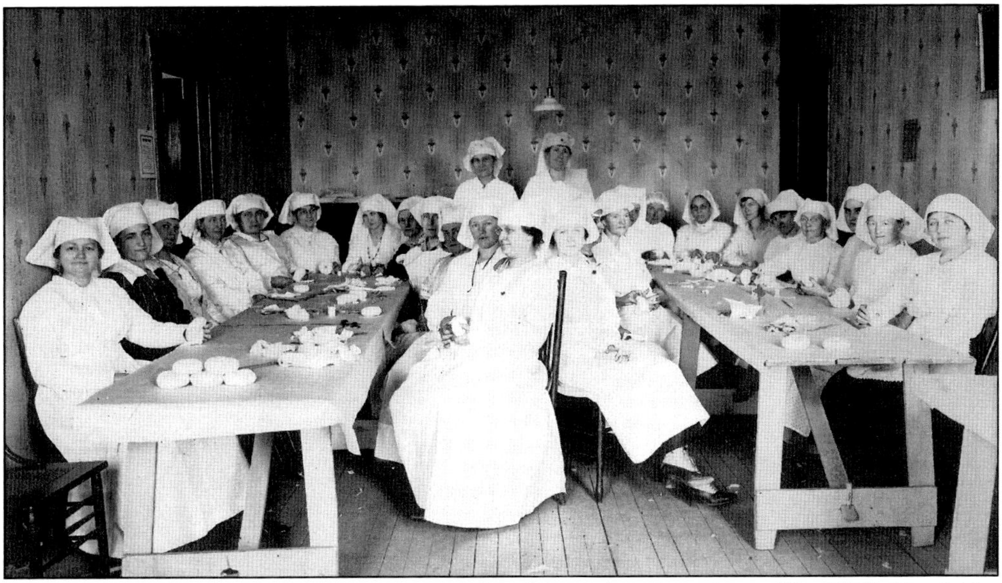

The ladies of Skidmore comprised a substantial Red Cross Auxiliary during World War I and, like similar groups across the county, made bandages to be shipped to Europe. Red Cross workshops across the nation produced hundreds of millions of surgical dressings and garments. Photographs similar to this can be found in collections in several Nodaway County towns. (Courtesy of the Skidmore Museum.)

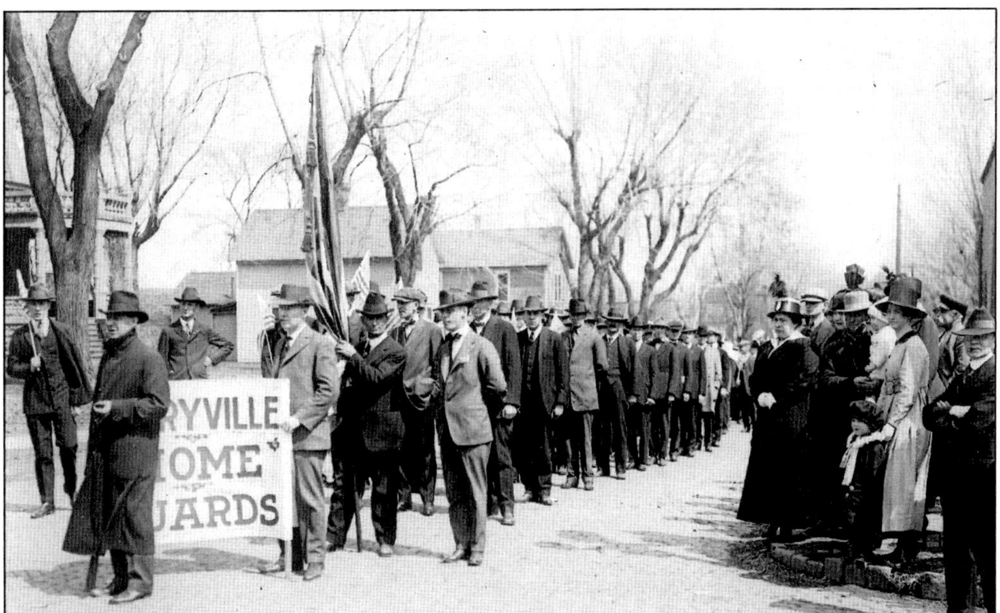

During World War I, the state government authorized communities to organize home guards to substitute for National Guardsmen sent to Europe to serve. Led by Paul Sisson, Harry Snyder, and normal school athletic coach George Palfreyman, 72 men of Maryville signed up for home guard service at a meeting held in the courthouse in March 1918. A parade followed to encourage other men of the community to enlist.

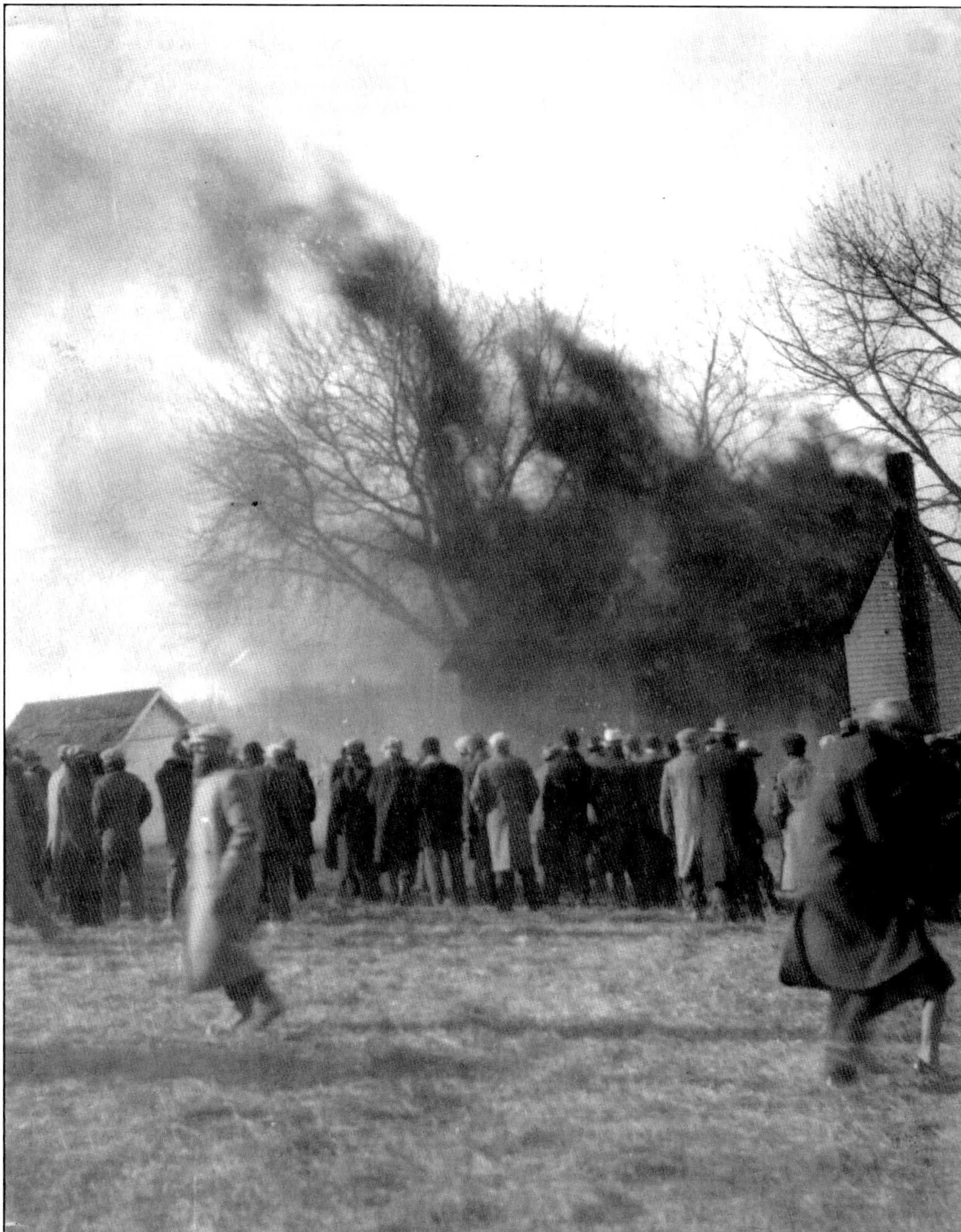

As many photographs attest, African Americans formed a vibrant and active community in Maryville until the early 1930s. Among the darkest days in the history of the county, however, was January 11, 1931, when a mob lashed Raymond Gunn on the roof of a schoolhouse and set it on fire. Gunn was accused of murdering a schoolteacher when the mob grabbed him from the courthouse in Maryville and murdered him in a crime that demonstrated the long reach of racism and dangerous impatience with formal justice. An exodus of African Americans from the county followed, leaving the community bereft of their contributions for many years.

Seven

JOLLIFICATION

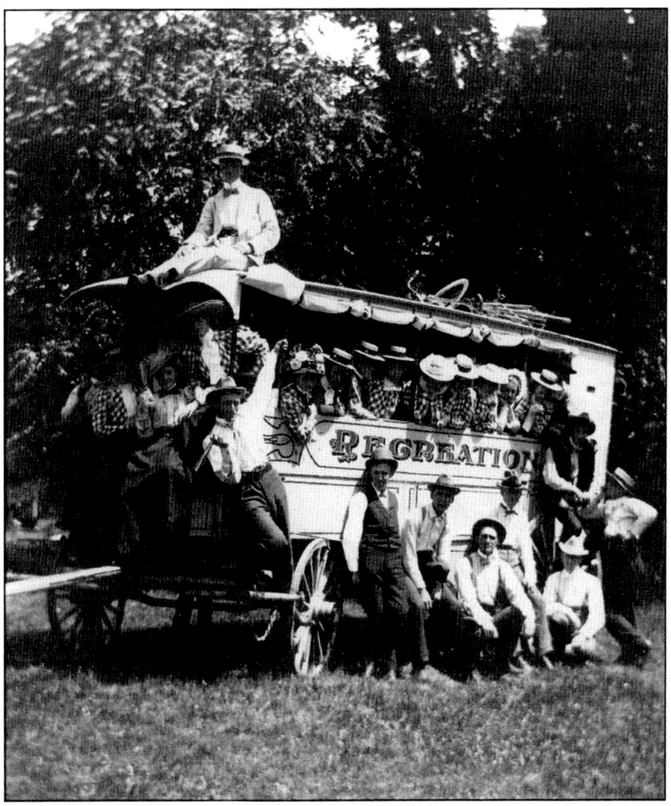

While it is not known exactly what kind of entertainment this wagon transported around Nodaway County, it illustrates for modern viewers that a good time was as valued at the dawn of the 20th century as it is now, and taking it on the road made it even better.

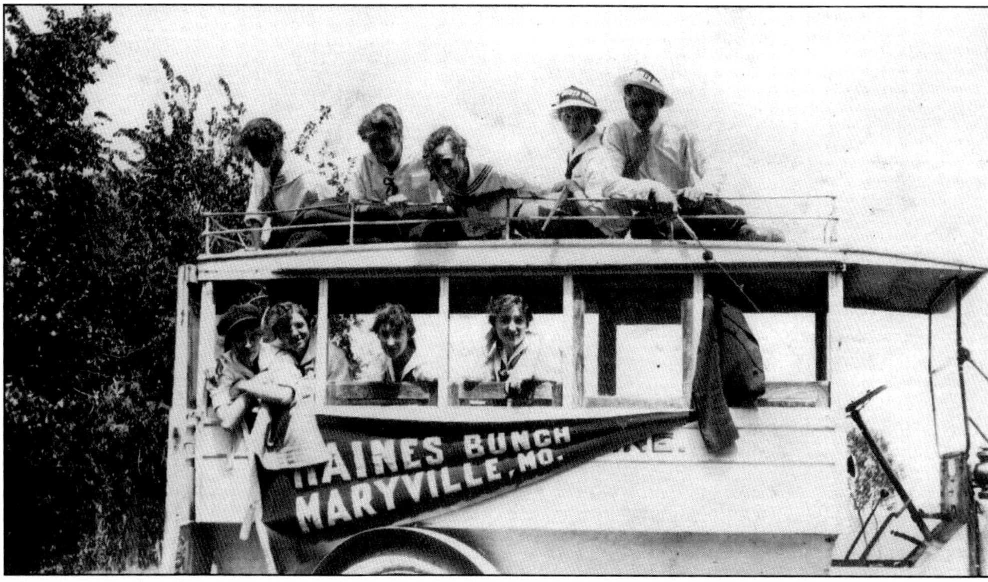

The Haines family, purveyors of goods and clothing for women, set out for a family reunion in Sabetha, Kansas. They crossed the Missouri River at Rulo on a rope-drawn barge that held two cars at a time.

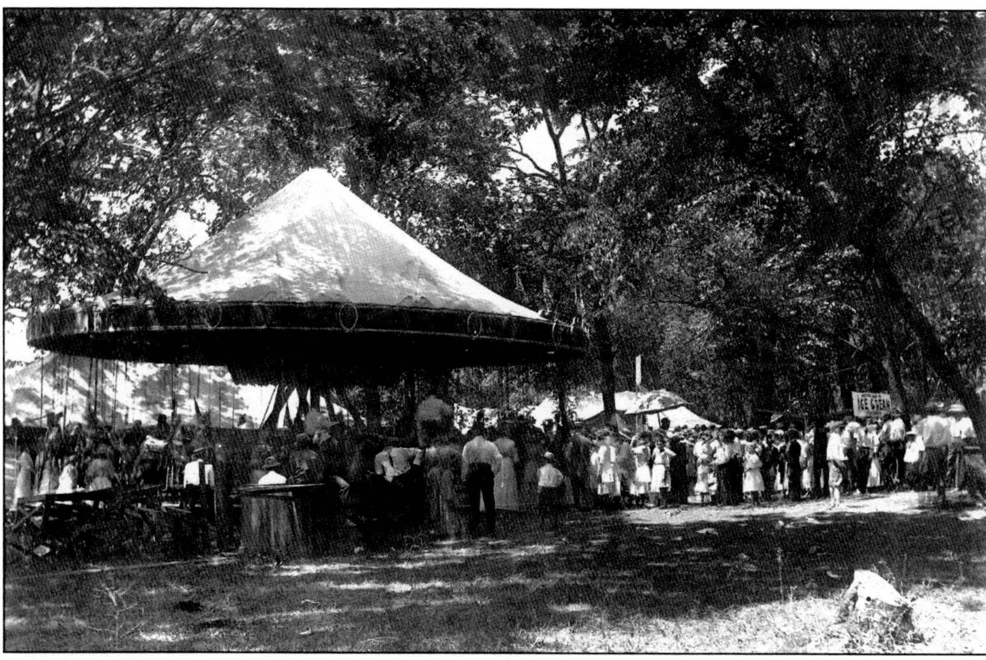

The Barnard picnic is an affair emblazoned in the memories of many childhoods. Starting in 1893, the early years of the event consisted primarily of food, conversation, and band music. As it progressed, Ferris wheels, magicians, circus acts, tap dancers, and the ever-popular merry-go-round delighted attendees from the surrounding countryside.

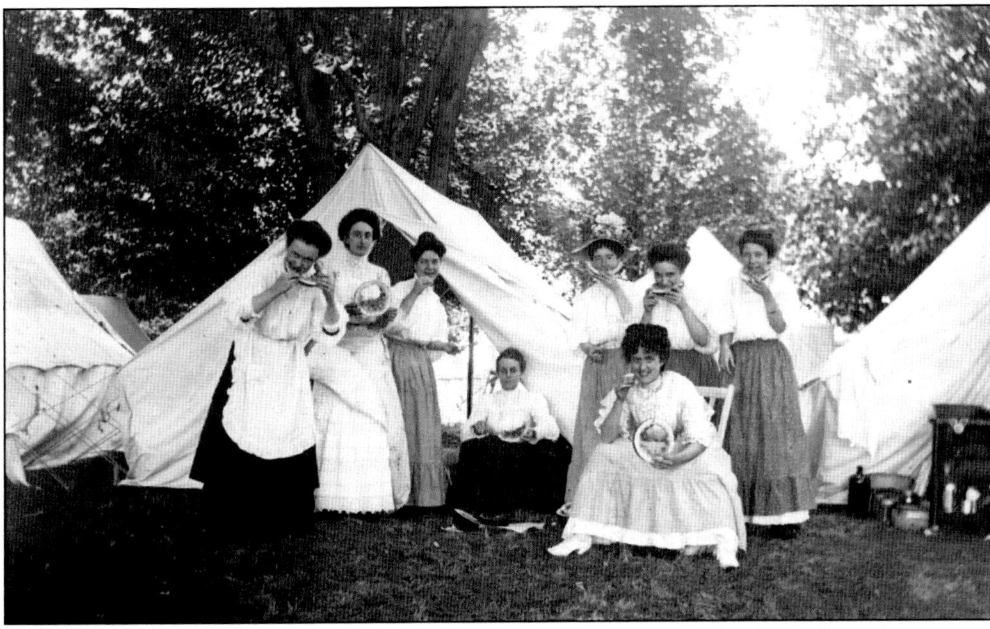

Chautauquas kept Americans entertained during the summer months throughout the country. Beginning in 1904, circuit chautauquas regularly visited the campus of the state normal school in what came to be known as Chautauqua Park through the peak of their popularity in the mid-1920s. Summers were kept entertaining as the week of the chautauqua in Maryville was often followed immediately by another full week of the county fair. (Courtesy of Coby Lamb.)

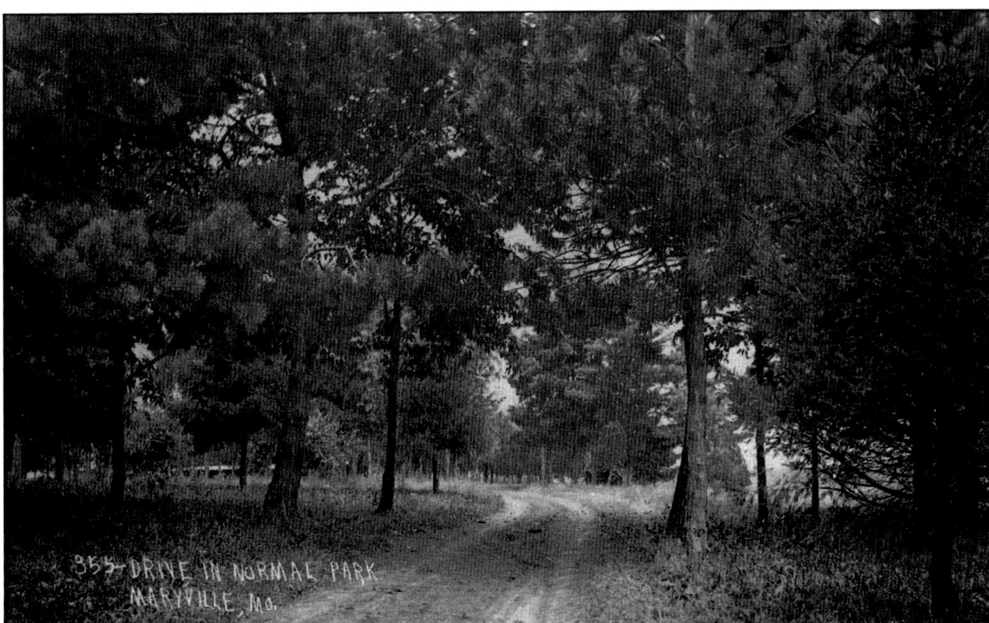

From its inception, the grounds of the normal school, now a state arboretum at Northwest Missouri State University, offered a sylvan setting for walking, riding, and occasionally studying. Normal Park Drive wove its way between the location of the Horace Mann building, now Brown Hall, and the area of the men's dormitories known as the quad.

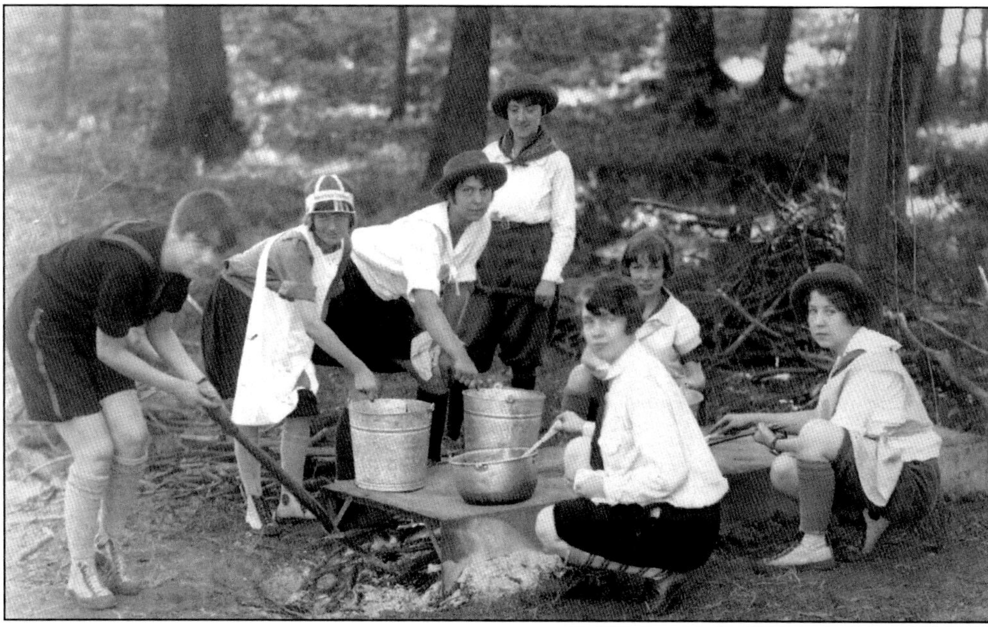

In June 1927, 33 Girl Scouts and two troop leaders from Maryville set up camp on Wrays' farm east of town and engaged in the usual round of cooking, hiking, singing songs, and sleeping under the stars. Apparently disenchanted with their outdoor "sleepers," the Maryville troop built a cabin on White Cloud Creek the following year and furnished it with aluminum cooking utensils, chairs, curtains, rug, and a Victrola.

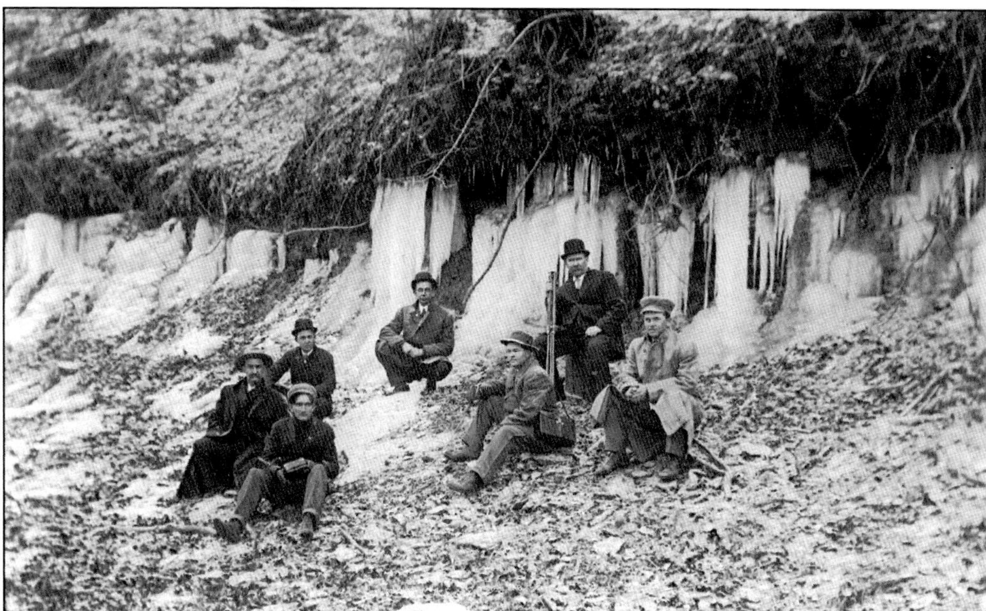

G. C. Ashbrook (holding the tripod), who maintained a photography studio in Skidmore, is joined by several Skidmore men on a photographic outing along the icy banks of the Nodaway River. Pictured from left to right are Ed Stricker, Merve Gray, Frank Manchester, J. O. Miller (lumber dealer), Frank Barrett (grocer), Ashbrook, and Mark Loucks. (Courtesy of the Skidmore Museum.)

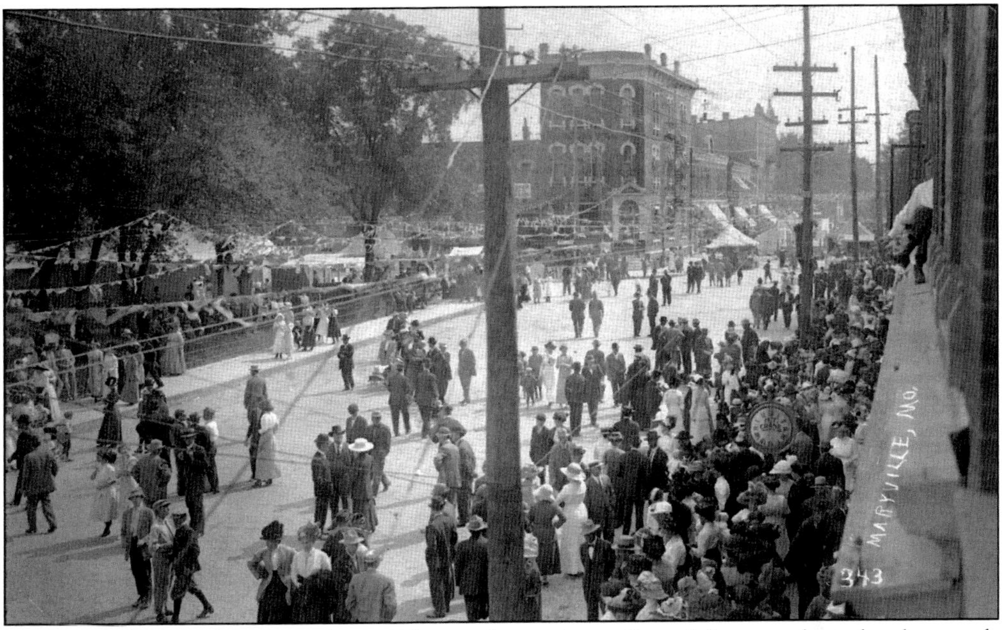

The annual street fair, festivals, parades, and a variety of special events brought thousands of residents to the downtown square in Maryville for the festivities. Such occasions in 1916 demanded a jacket and a tie for men, proper dresses for women, and hats for seemingly everyone. The multistoried brick blocks provided numerous perches for onlookers to get a bird's-eye view through the tangle of utility wires. (Courtesy of Coby Lamb.)

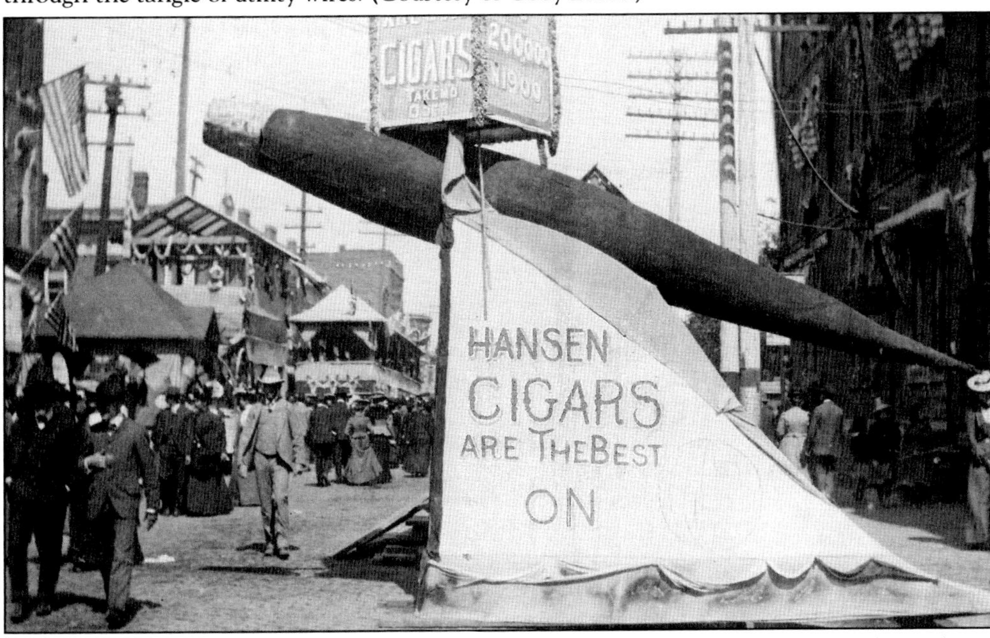

Advertising in epic proportions was the hallmark of Maryville's street fair. Local merchants took out full-page advertisements in the newspapers to announce "special premiums" on many goods. The real competition, however, came in the street with elaborate booths, barkers, and refreshments. For consumers it offered an opportunity to relish in the quantity and diversity of local economic activity, including tobacco.

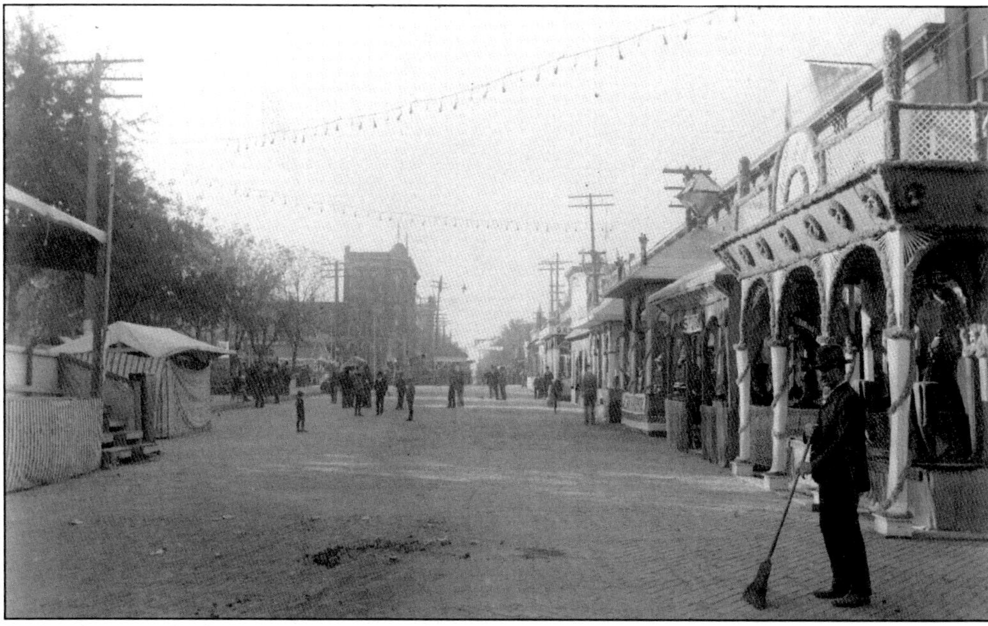

E. Arralt mans the broom, sweeping sand onto the horse's "contributions" during the fair, which the *Maryville Republican* dubbed "a solid week of beauty and jollification." In addition to the contest among businesses in booth construction, the fair of 1900 included the Cameron Military Band; Ella Ewing, "the Missouri Giantess;" trapeze artists; and the annual flower parade that featured elaborately decorated floats driven by "Maryville's fairest ladies and lassies."

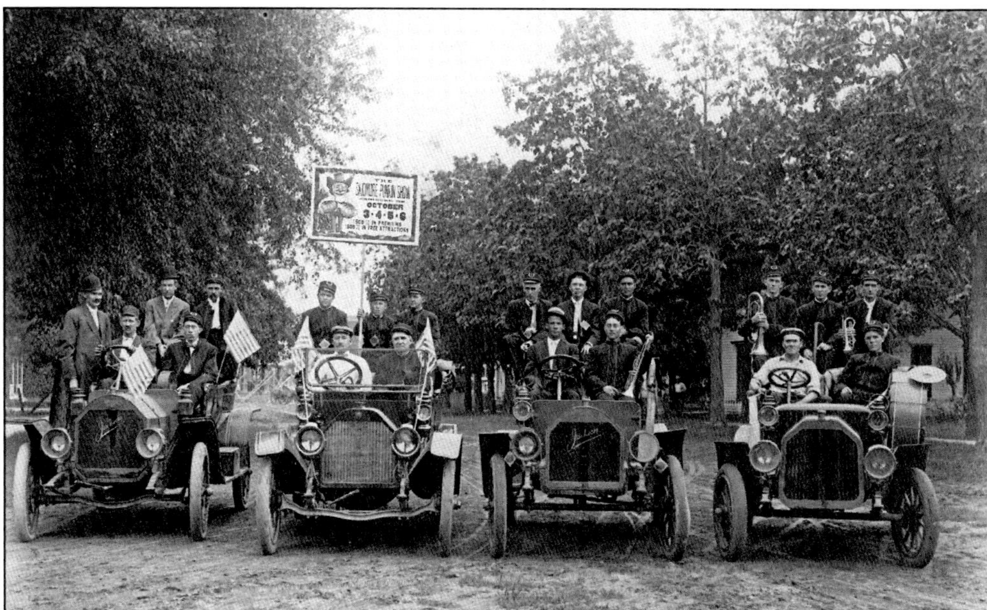

Skidmore decided in 1899 to show its appreciation to area farmers with a day of entertainment, dubbed the Punkin Show, which expanded into a three-to-five-day festival of activity with a wide variety of entertainment and produce displays. William R. Linville (in white) leads a promotional motorcade for the festival, promising a good time and $500 in prizes. (Courtesy of the Skidmore Museum.)

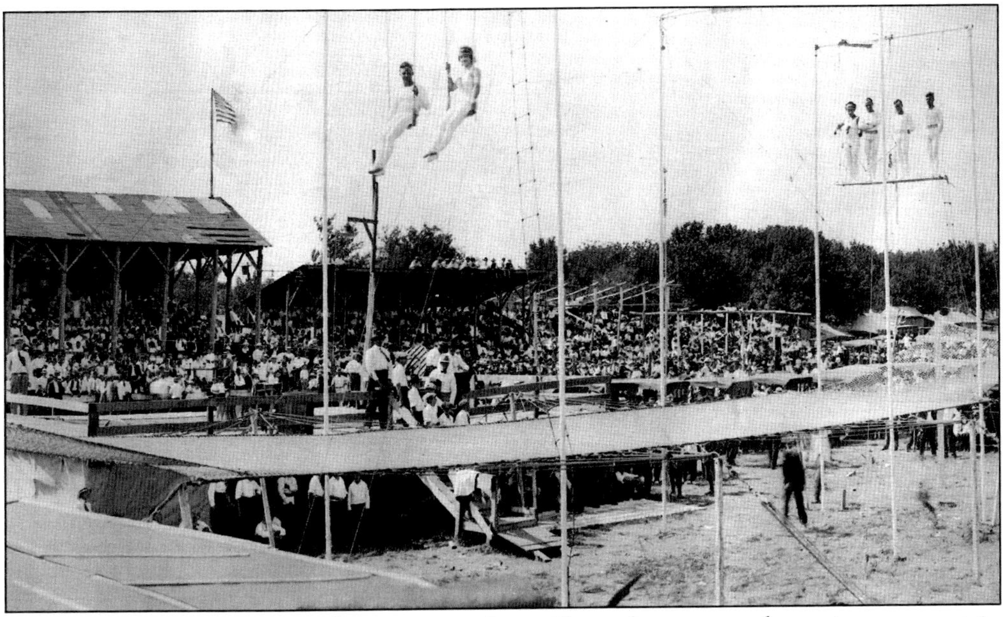

The county fair was an annual opportunity for residents from across the region to entertain themselves in myriad ways. Crowds were large for the six days of activity in August at the fairgrounds in Maryville. Aside from the perennial agricultural exhibits, the 1919 fair featured Margaret Hill's circus dogs and ponies; the "Herculanian Venus," Grom Bailey; Donald McGregor's great Scottish giant; an army aerobatics show; and the Original Flying Wards on trapeze. The horse races, however, garnered the most attention by far. The fairgrounds, located on East First Street on the flat land of the One Hundred and Two River bottom, provided an excellent site for a horse-racing track. Judge Hanecy traveled the Midwest securing high-quality thoroughbreds, trotting horses, and pacing horses for the 1919 races, including Carlos Patch, son of world champion Dan Patch. Among the strongest thoroughbreds were those brought by Ben Jones from Parnell.

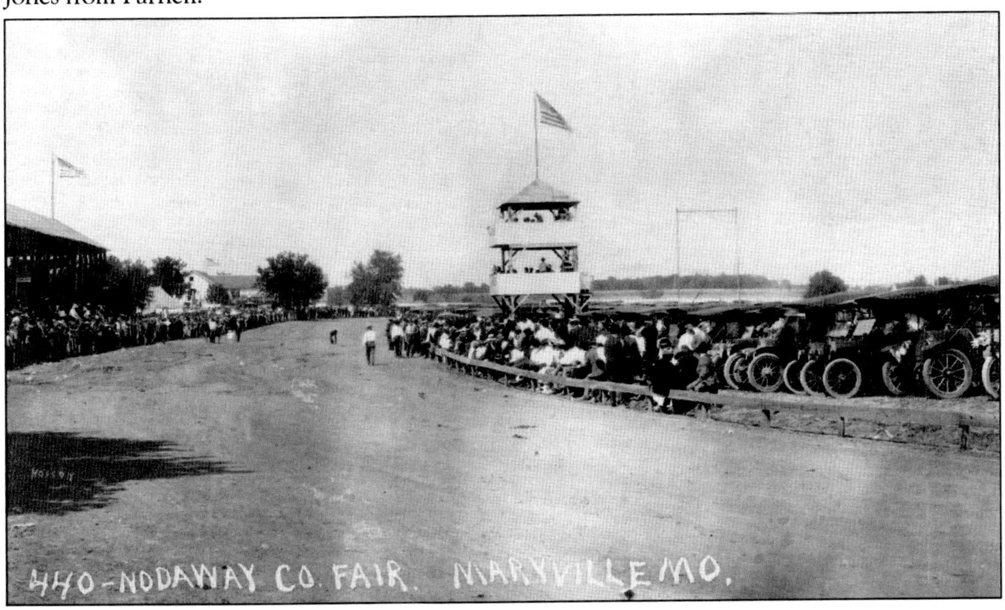

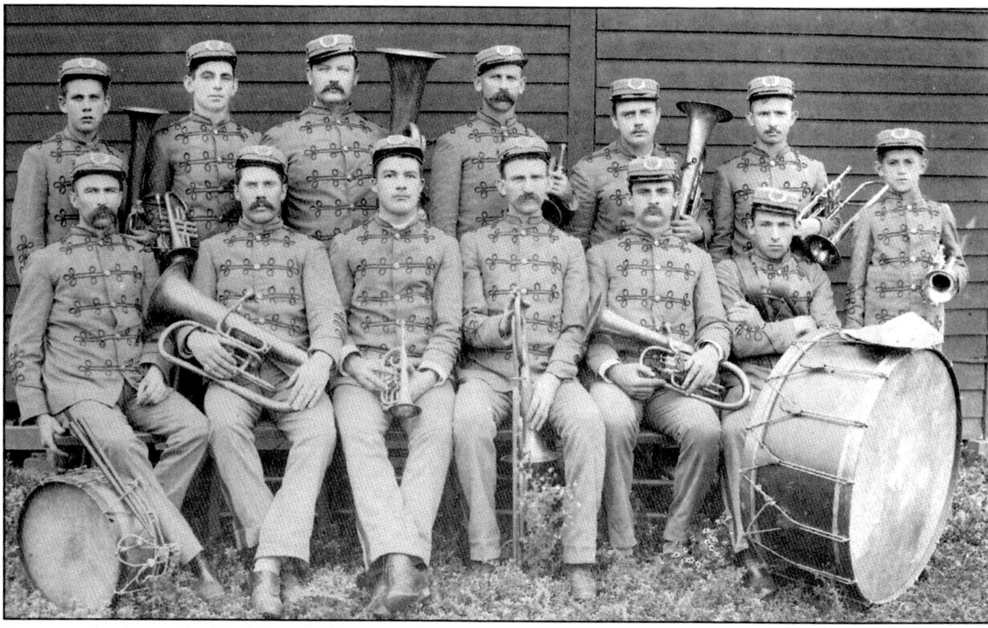

During the latter half of the 19th century, most amateur bands were cornet bands that employed a variety of horns, including Eb cornets, Bb cornets, Eb alto cornets, Bb tenor horns, Bb baritones, Bb or Eb bass, and occasional old slide trumpets. The tuning of these horns varied widely, as there was not a standard pitch for instrument makers until at least 1899. Even then, most horns that had seen hard use were patched and welded back together by local tinners. The Barnard band (above) was a fixture at the Barnard picnic starting in 1890 and continued to play frequently until school bands with reed instruments began to eclipse it in the 1930s. Burlington Junction, like any up-and-coming town, also boasted a brass band for the entertainment of locals and the dignifying of all public affairs.

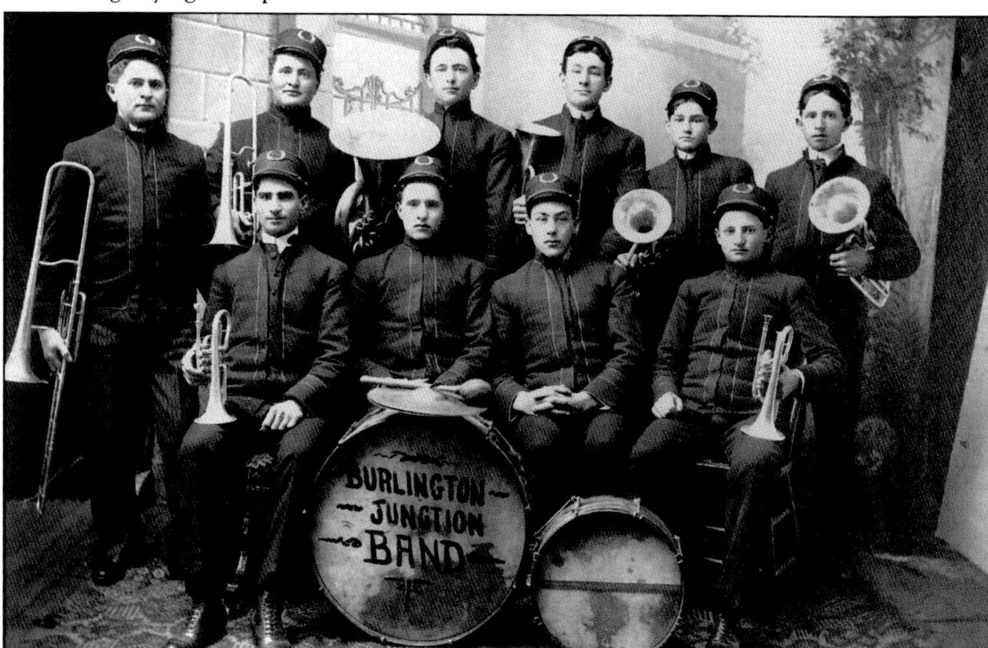

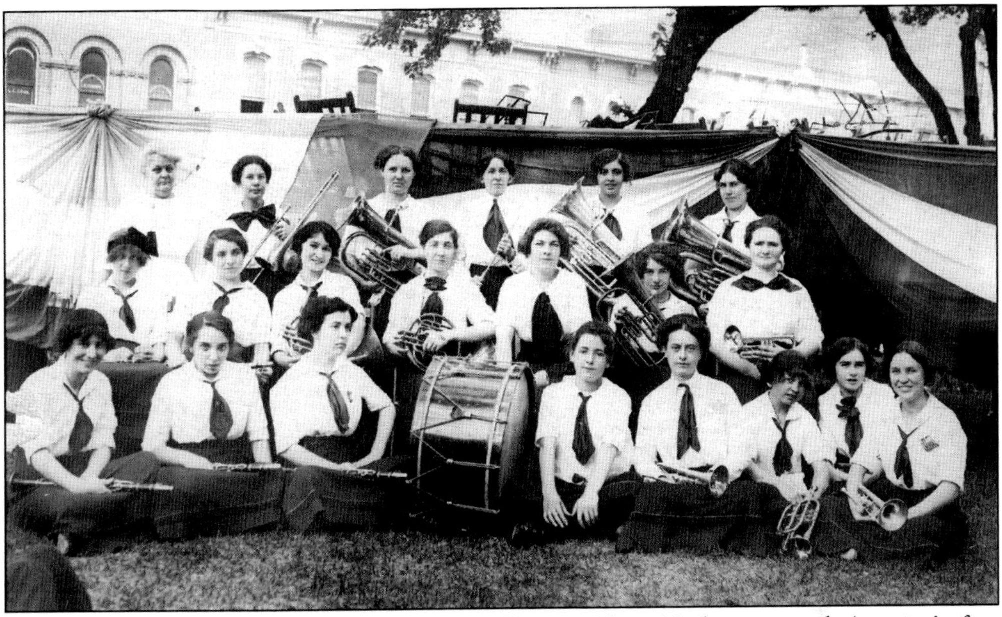

Maryville music teacher and enthusiastic suffragist Alma Nash organized America's first all-women's marching band in 1913 for a parade in Washington, D.C., which was planned by a number of women's rights organizations. The Maryville Ladies Military Band reportedly quieted angry male protesters with music while the parade organizers waited for the cavalry to come clear a path through the mob.

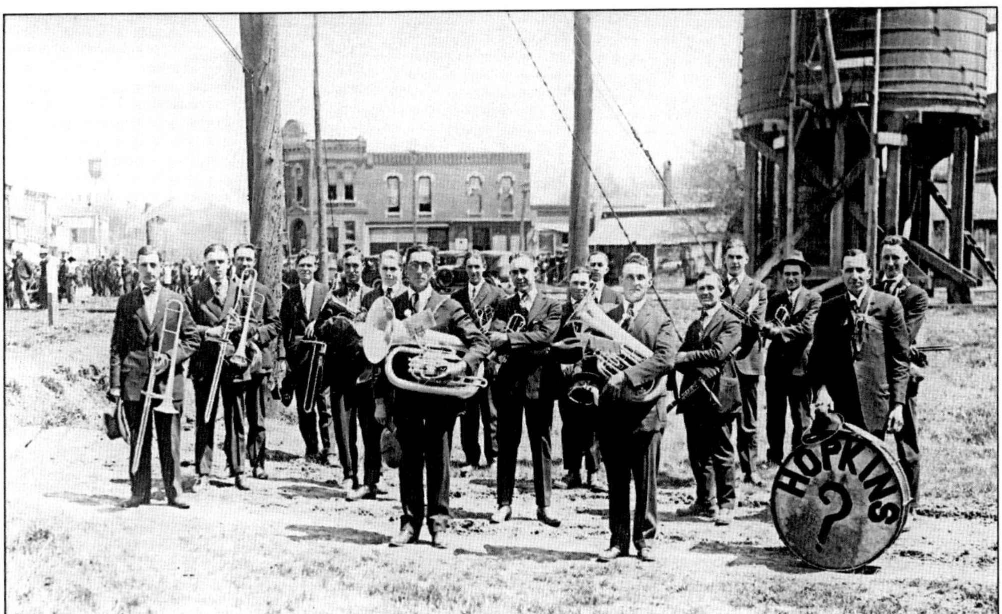

The Hopkins band had been making locals proud since its first cornet band organized in 1874. The band played at a variety of functions and was essential to the annual Fourth of July celebrations. Municipal marching bands lasted well into the 1920s when high school bands began to claim their space in street parades. Adult bands, however, despite suit and tie uniforms, maintained the luxury of a tinge of vaudeville.

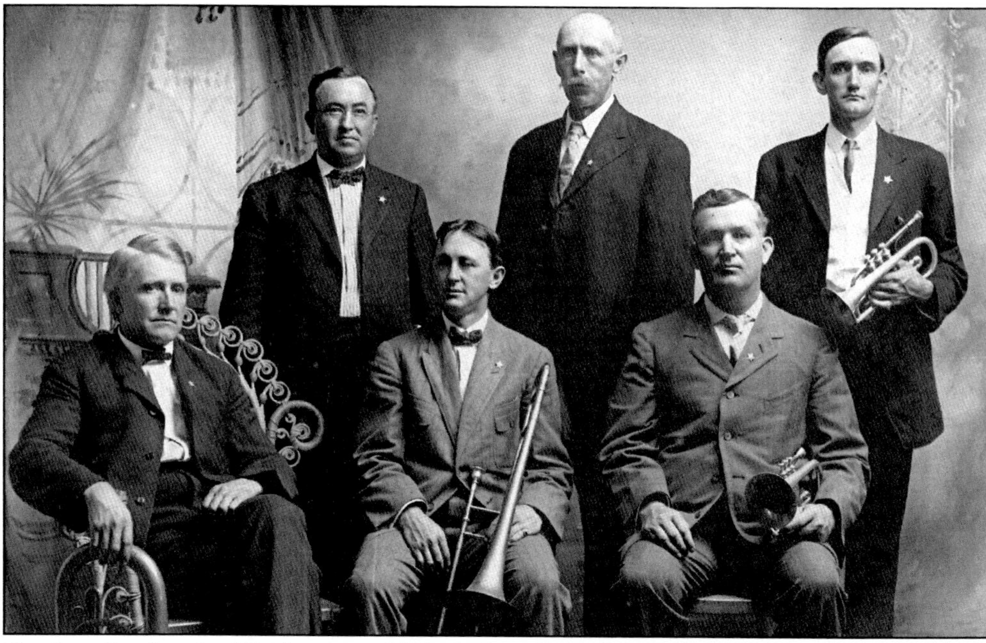

The founding bands of Skidmore established a long line of musical performance groups from the small community. From left to right, this venerable brass group consisted of (first row) Clarence Thomas, unidentified, and George Manchester (hardware and furniture store owner); (second row) Frank Manchester (barber), J. D. Kellog (general store owner), and G. L. Owens (depot agent). (Courtesy of the Skidmore Museum.)

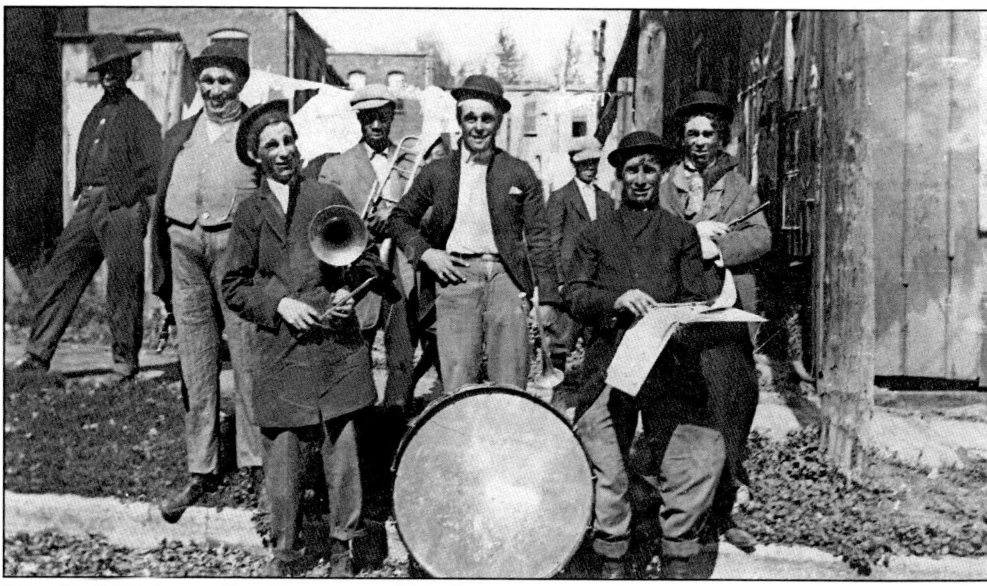

The Catfish Martin Band entertained Nodaway County in the first two decades of the 20th century. They are pictured here posing in their show dress. Omnipresent entertainer Albert "Slim" Butherus, Lou Denny, Lawrence Shanks, and Will Price, who often dressed for shows in drag, added character to a band that was working the overlapping frontiers of band music, jazz, and vaudeville. The band included the Martin brothers, African American musicians who made this an unusual mixed-race band in a community that practiced segregation.

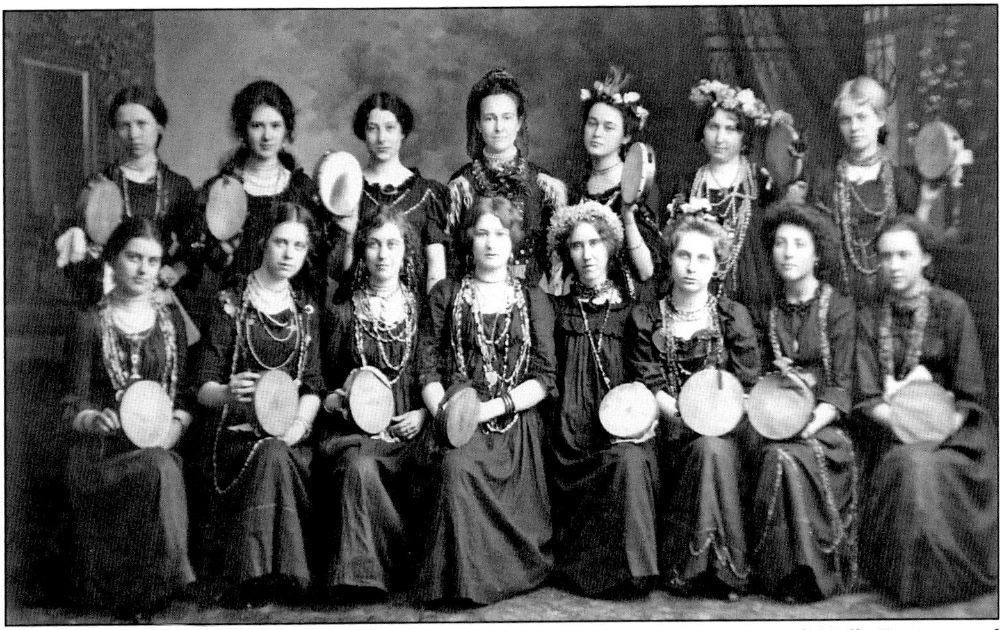

In June 1900, the Tambourine Drill Team presented its latest comic opera, *The Jolly Farmers and the Merry Milkmaids,* at the opera house in Maryville. From left to right are (first row) Gertrude Condon, Alma Storm, Georgia Condon, Lula Seafers, Anna Dooley, Nora Partridge, Lizzie Sturm, and Jene Kemp; (second row) Mildred Morrison, Bessie Crane, Beulah Taylor, Marcia Messenger, Hazel Ford, Retta Searcy, and Lillie Jensen.

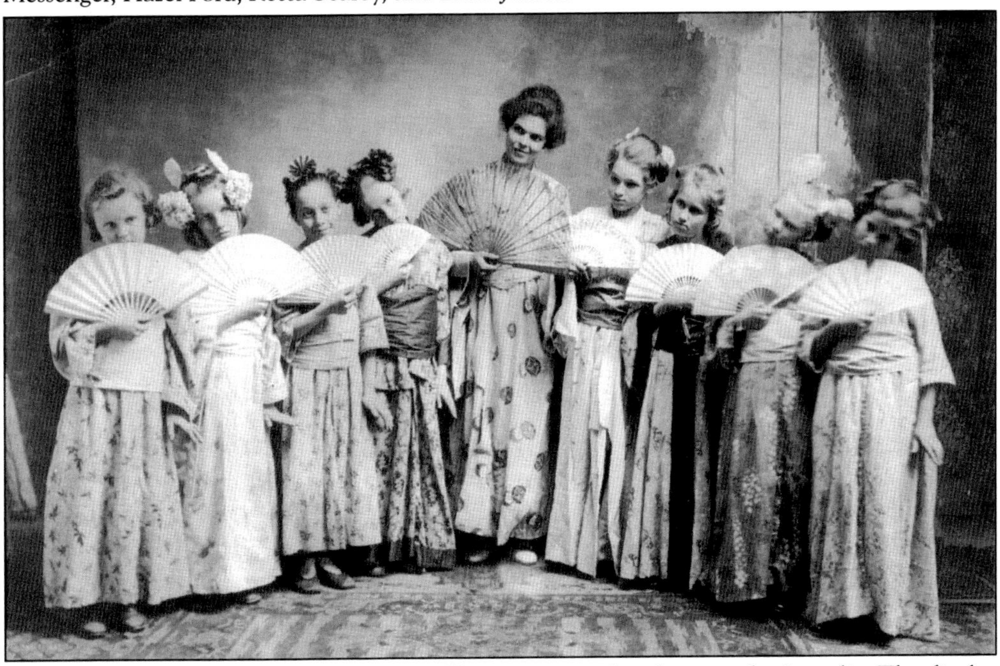

The young ladies of Skidmore present a *tableau vivant* in the photographer's studio. The display likely culminated a project in sewing enhanced by some cultural study. While behavior patterns for young women changed rapidly in the lifetime of these girls, in 1910 they were typically restrained to entertainment in practical household skills and the fine arts.

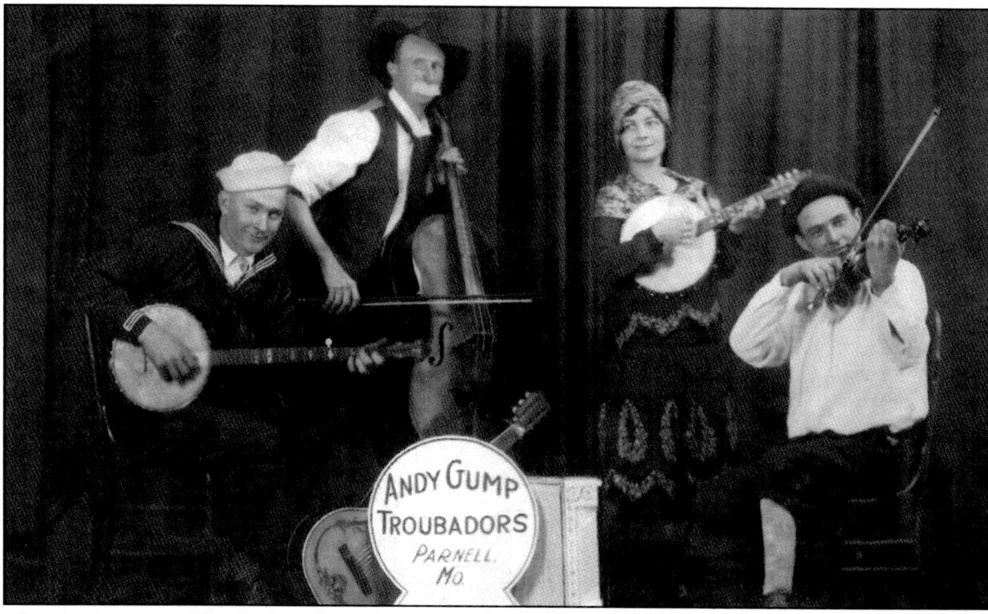

The Andy Gump Troubadors from Parnell took their name from Sydney Smith's popular comic strip starting in 1917, which, for 42 years, lampooned the lives of ordinary Americans. Accordion and bass fiddle player Charlie Harmon played the Andy Gump role with Harley Stutesman and Gertrude Auer on banjo and Frank Auer on violin. The Troubadors entertained audiences throughout northwest Missouri during the 1920s, including a run on Henry Field's radio station in Shenandoah, Iowa.

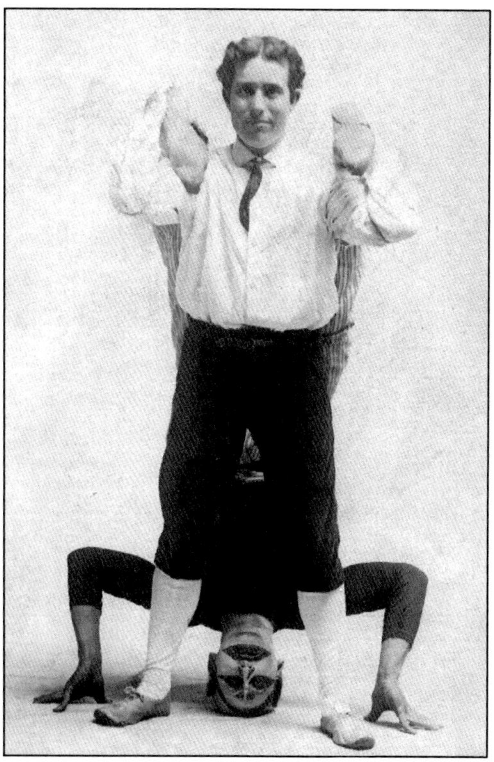

Nodaway County has never been short of local and largely amateur entertainment. Residents were frequently called upon to amuse one another at chautauquas, picnics, parades, fairs, and an assortment of celebrations. Here a couple of unidentified entertainers clown for the camera in Maryville.

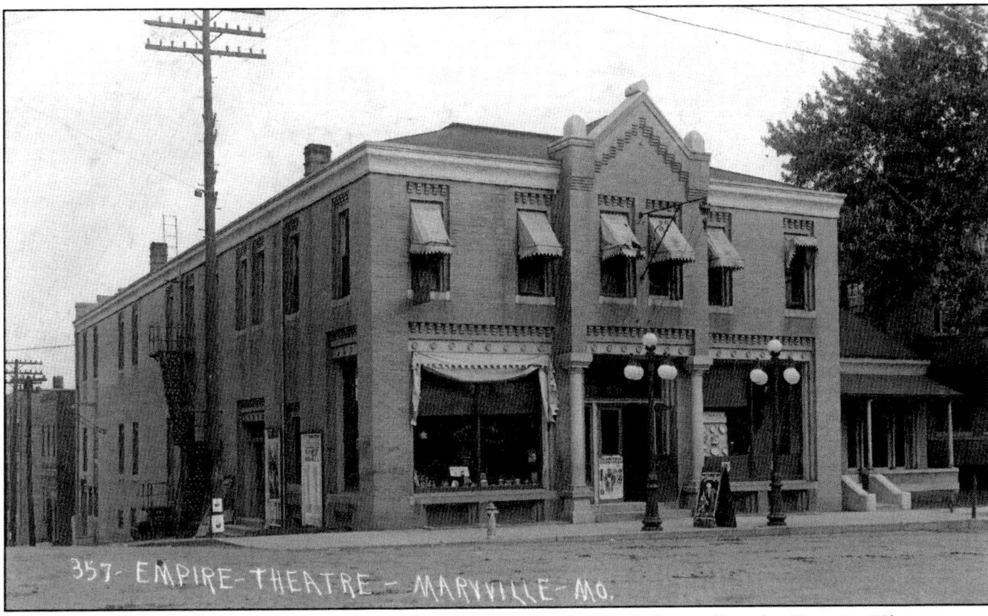

Erected in 1903 at the corner of Second and Main Streets in Maryville, the Empire Theater was owned by Richard Kuchs, who also managed the electric light and power company out of offices in the front rooms of the theater. Residents could also find entertainment in the downtown square at the Crystal Theater, where folks with a little less change in their pockets could catch a vaudeville act or a moving picture.

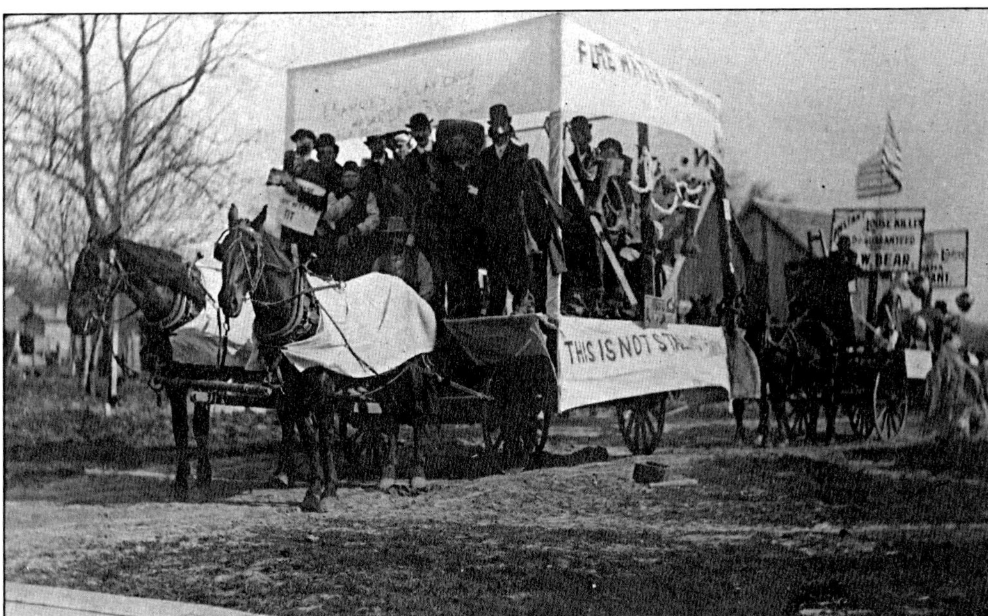

This "calathumpian parade" in Barnard brings the town out for a raucous march in the early 1890s through means that allowed respectable citizens to violate an assortment of social norms. Aside from a bit of advertising for Instant Louse Killer (guaranteed by H. W. Bear), and patriotic flag waving, the point of the parade was nothing other than having a good time with friends and neighbors. (Courtesy of the Barnard Community Historical Society.)

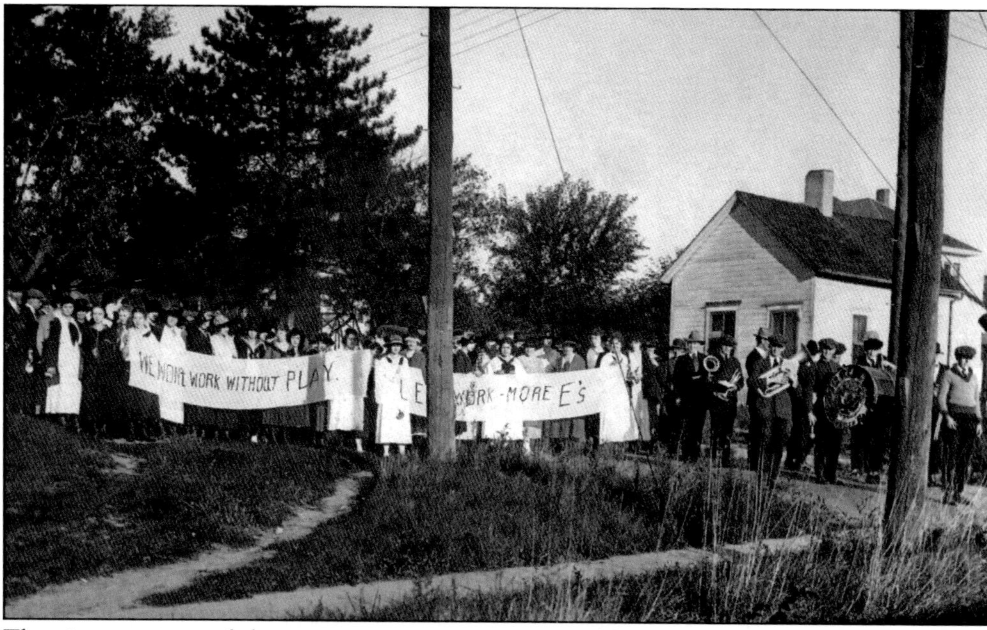

The circumstances of this protest remain mysterious, although it is clear that some citizens of Nodaway County believed they were still not benefitting from enough leisure. The banner reads, "We won't work without play. Less work—more E's." Presumably local authorities were not too concerned, since the marching band included elements of the 4th Regimental Band of the National Guard.

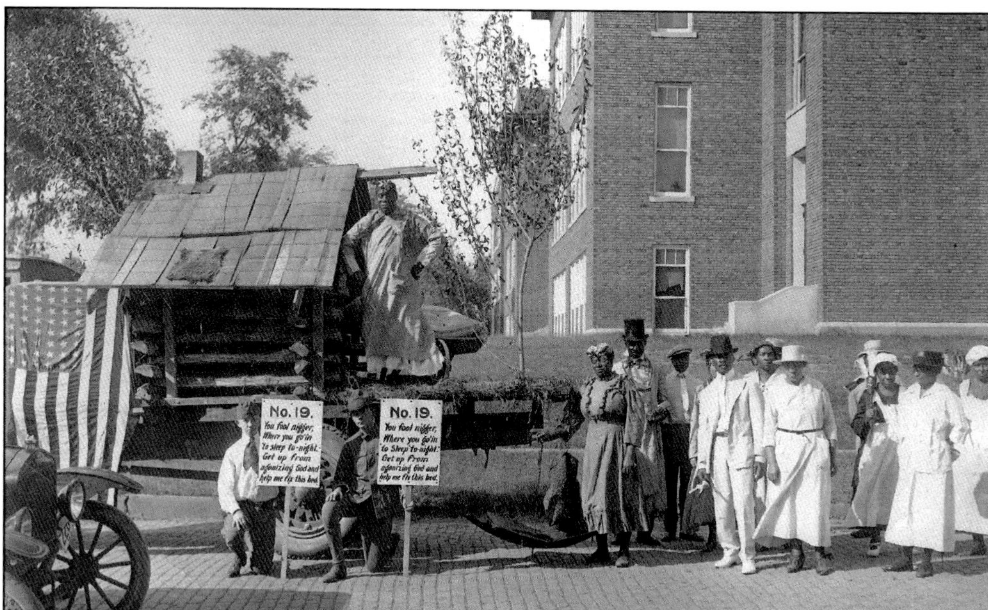

The celebration of the centennial of the state of Missouri provided an occasion for local parades across the state. The parade in Maryville included a float that displayed the heritage of African Americans in Missouri. The display no doubt had varied meanings for white residents watching the parade and blacks who still attended separate schools and churches in Maryville.

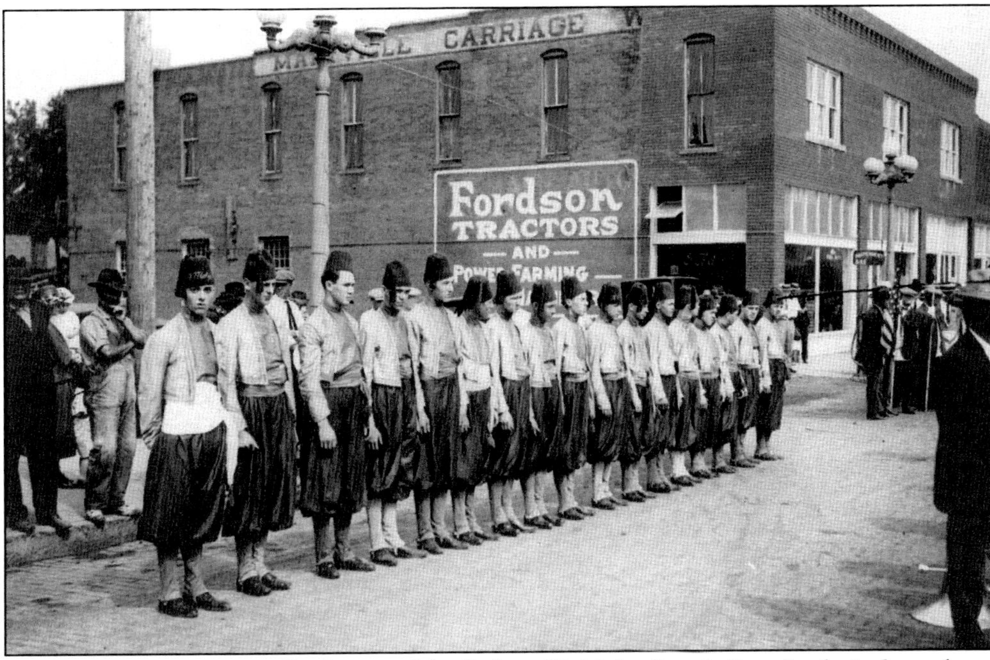

On July 4, 1922, the Maryville chapter of the Order of DeMolay Patrol aligns for the Independence Day parade. Businessman Frank Land founded this Masonic-based organization in Kansas City only three years earlier for young men aged 12 to 21, and it joined the litany of organizations that appeared in every community to provide a variety of civic services.

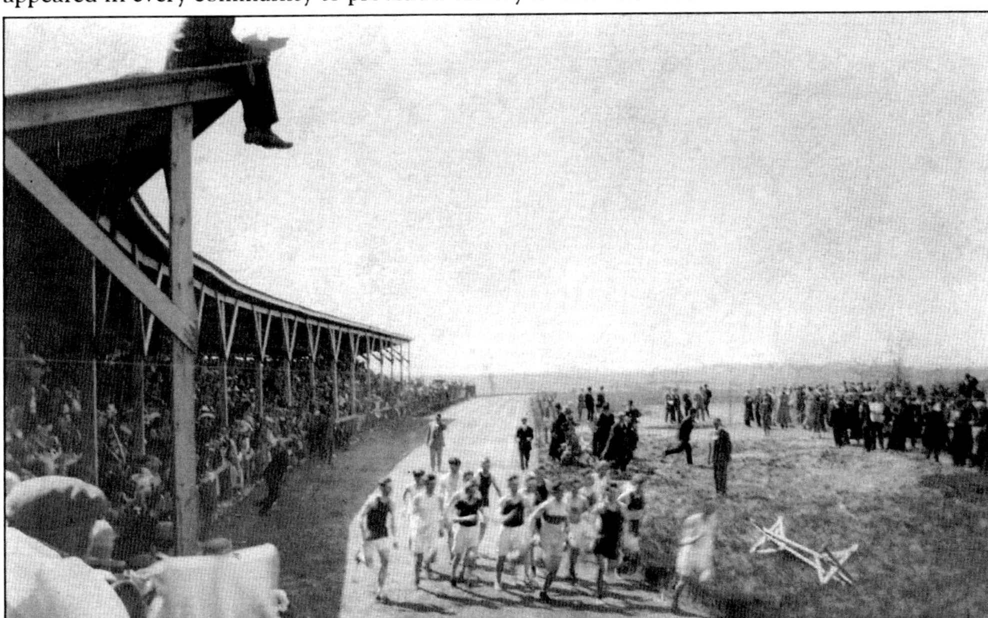

Normal school president Henry K. Taylor proposed the creation of an athletic field north of the administration building at the school to host this invitational meet for high schools in 1910. The stands were packed with excited fans, including a contingent of about a dozen sitting on the roof. By 1912, the normal school fielded a track team for intercollegiate competition. (Courtesy of Coby Lamb.)

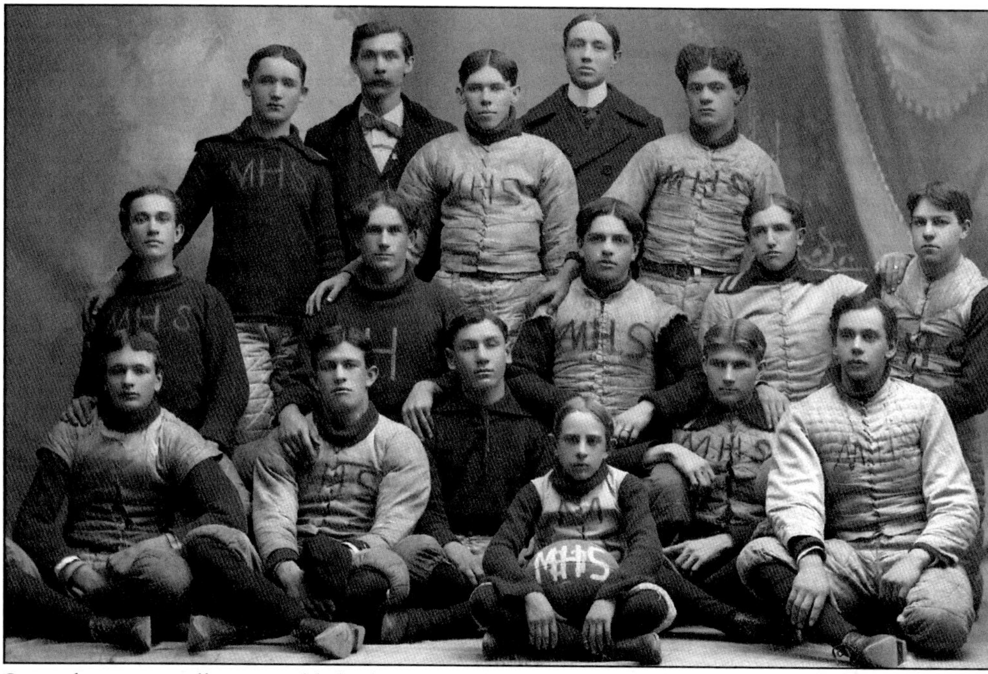

Several eastern colleges established in 1873 the rules for college football. Significant revision in the following years was made by Yale College coach Walter Camp, who established most of the fundamentals of the modern game. The sport spread rapidly across the country in colleges and occasionally high schools, although its brutality and frequent injuries, even deaths, led to significant controversy and a ban at many schools. It was during this period of intense controversy that the Maryville High School team posed for a photograph.

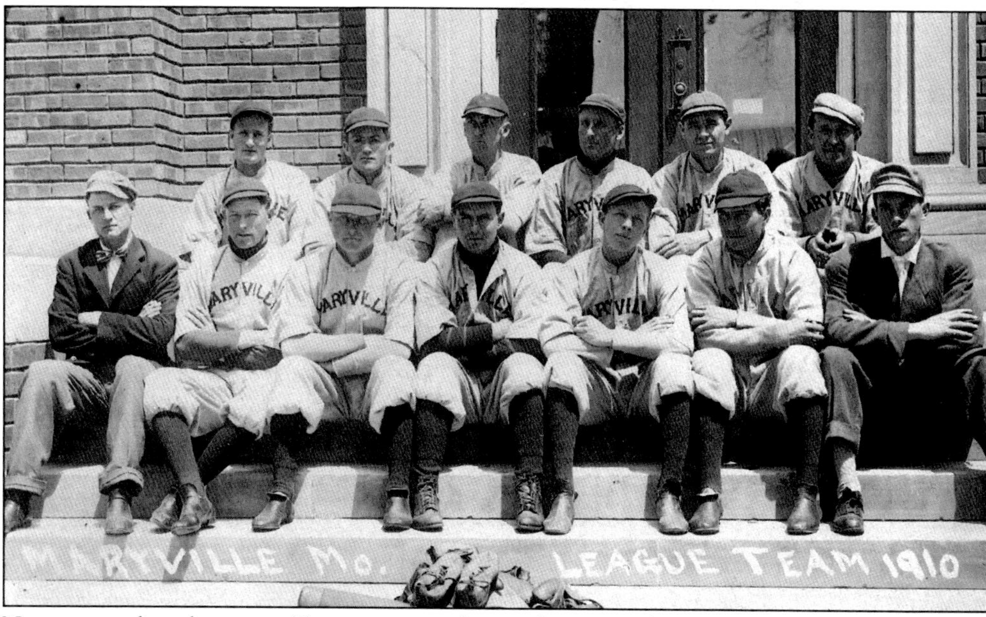

No sport gathered more public interest and stirred civic pride more than baseball. Here the Maryville League team of 1910 poses on the front steps of the county courthouse as if to lay sovereign claim. (Courtesy of Coby Lamb.)

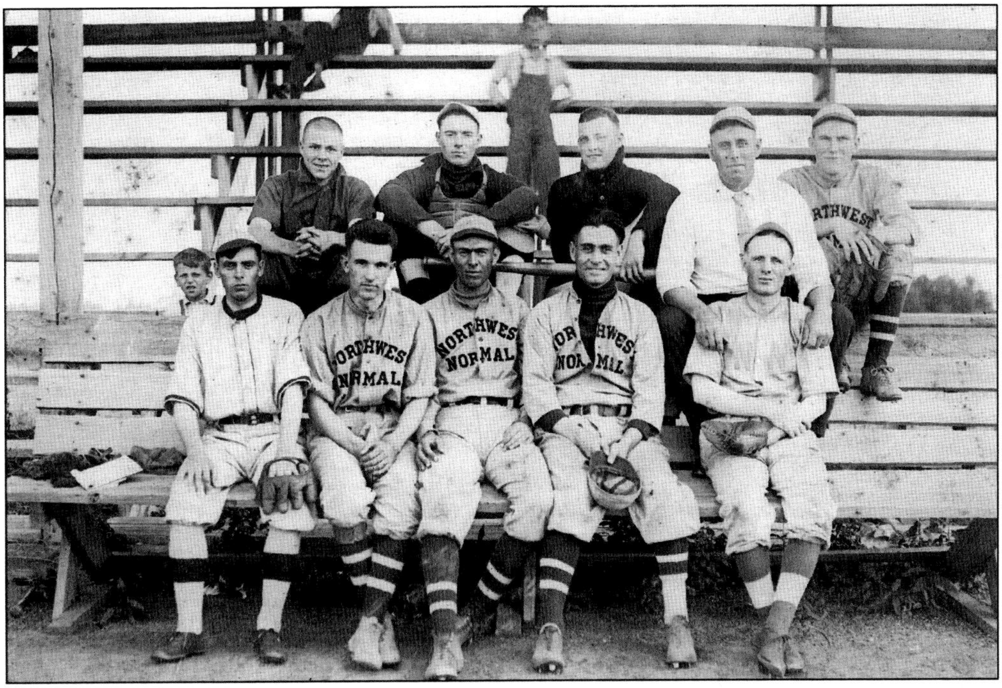

The Northwest Normal School baseball team pauses for a team photograph with a couple of their devoted fans sneaking into the picture. The school fielded its first team in the summer of 1906 to take on the Maryville town team, but two years later it began competing against the football team for status as the most popular sport.

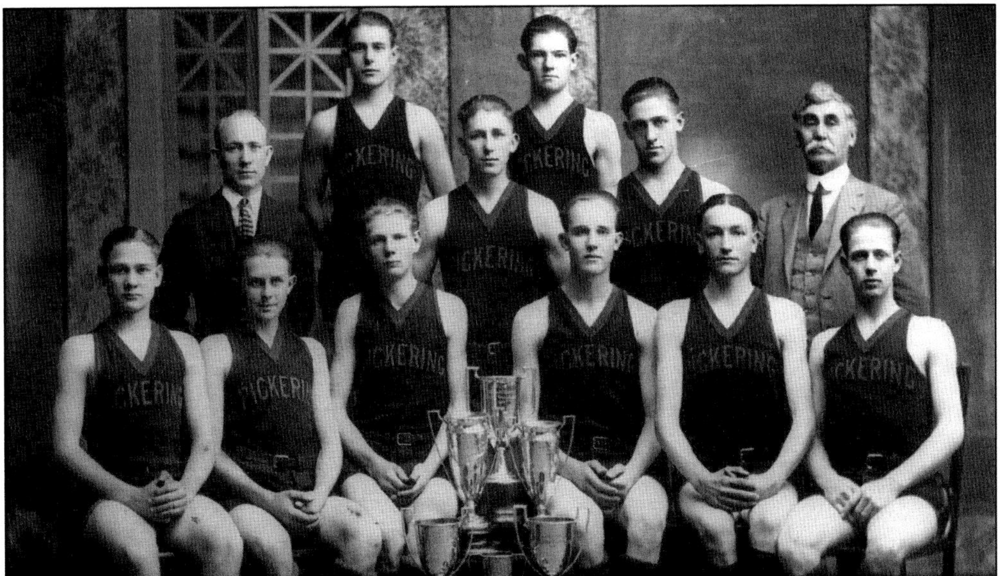

The Pickering High School team poses proudly as third-place winners in the Missouri State High School Tournament in 1925. Trophies from previous seasons attest to the school's strength in the sport. From left to right are (first row) Dennis Hood, Roy Harrington, Romaine Garten, Paul Burks, Raymond McKee, and Virgil Zook; (second row) coach Howard "Hickory" Leech, Earl Locke, Donald McGinnis, and superintendent E. N. Geyer; (third row) Kenneth Swinford and Lorace Gray.

Consistent with our mission to preserve history on a local level, this book was printed in South Carolina on American-made paper and manufactured entirely in the United States. Products carrying the accredited Forest Stewardship Council (FSC) label are printed on 100 percent FSC-certified paper.

MADE IN THE USA